# TREATING THE UNMANAGEABLE ADOLESCENT

## A Guide to Oppositional Defiant and Conduct Disorders

NEIL I. BERNSTEIN, PH.D.

JASON ARONSON INC.
NORTHVALE, NEW JERSEY
LONDON

Production Editor: M'lou Pinkham

This book was set in 11 pt. New Aster by Alabama Book Composition of Deatsville, Alabama, and printed and bound by Book-mart Press of North Bergen, New Jersey.

**Library of Congress Cataloging-in-Publication Data**

Bernstein, Neil I.
   Treating the unmanageable adolescent : a guide to oppositional defiant and conduct disorders / Neil I. Bernstein.
      p.  cm.
   Includes bibliographical references and index.
   ISBN 1-56821-630-0 (hardcover : alk. paper)
   1. Conduct disorders in adolescence—Treatment.  2. Oppositional defiant disorder in adolescence—Treatment.    I.  Title.
RJ506.C65B47   1997
616.89′022—dc20                                                96-15620

Manufactured in the United States of America. Jason Aronson Inc. offers books and cassettes. For information and catalog write to Jason Aronson Inc., 230 Livingston Street, Northvale, New Jersey 07647.

To my mother, who gave me roots
and gave me wings.

To my children, Daniel and Julie,
who give me pride.

# Contents

# Acknowledgments

Without question, the catalysts for this book were the many adolescents and families who have shared their ordeals with me over the years. As my professional identity evolved, I was influenced by the ongoing feedback from both patients and colleagues. Raising my own children has convinced me that good parenting allows for a large margin of error.

I am grateful to Darlene Atkins, Ph.D., for her professional input and editorial assistance. Numerous colleagues have shared their own experiences with me and encouraged me to proceed when the task seemed interminable. Finally, my mentor, E. James Lieberman, M.D., deserves thanks for his influence early in my career, helping me to express complex ideas simply and put thought to paper.

# Introduction

Ralph Rooks ruled the streets of my neighborhood. By age 14 his reputation was firmly established as a bully par excellence. His fighting skills, provocative behavior, rejection of rules, and cruelty to animals were legendary. While most of my friends avoided him when possible, some of us attempted to get on his good side. I vividly remember one occasion when I invited him over to play. Ralph arrived while we were still eating dinner so my parents suggested that he wait in my room until we finished. He said he would just look at my baseball cards for a while. After we played together for several hours, Ralph abruptly announced that he had to leave.

A few days later I was looking through my cards and noticed that my precious Mickey Mantle and Willie Mays were missing. Immediately suspecting Ralph, I phoned him to ask if he knew anything about this tragic event. He vehemently denied any malfeasance, of course. I was a victim without evidence.

Ralph was known simply as the troubled kid on our block. His father drank often and disciplined him violently and sporadically. His mother was childlike and often behaved inappropriately. According to Ralph, he was never quite sure what mood his parents would be in when he came home. Their pet cat was the target of Ralph's frustrations. At times he would pick her up by the neck, squeezing her to demonstrate how he could paralyze her. It seemed as though he was always angry and determined to display his dominance over others. In retrospect, I imagine he felt very lonely and scared.

On one occasion we gleefully watched an older kid pushing Ralph around. To our amazement, Ralph picked up a Coke bottle, broke it on the curb, and proceeded to cut his adversary without batting an eyelash. The other kid ran like hell. I have many memories of his exploits, punctuated with fear, amusement, and perplexity. What stands out most, though, was a time when Ralph had me pinned to the ground and was harassing me in his usual way. I asked him why he was doing this to me. He answered: "I just have to!" It has taken me many years to understand and truly appreciate that comment.

Needless to say, my interest in the oppositional and conduct disorders is of longstanding origin. Many years later I am still struggling to understand what fuels such behavior and trying to develop ways to alter the destructive patterns. My clinical work with adolescents over the past twenty-five years has led me down some interesting paths. I have worked with inner city youth, schools, outpatient clinics, hospitalized adolescents, courts, and private patients.

To date I have not come across an integrated treatment approach that encompasses the diverse thought and research on the disruptive behavior disorders. Each school of thought seems to have its own way of doing things. For years I have sought to answer the basic questions: Why are these adolescents so resistant to help and difficult to work with? What is needed to promote change? On the whole, we have been less successful in effecting durable change in this clinical subgroup than in any other.

Early in my career I was a therapist in search of concrete answers to complex questions. I was hungry to learn exactly what to do with this population. Surely there were specific approaches that would help me to engage these youngsters successfully. My desire for increased knowledge and skills led me to attend many workshops. My clinical training had left me unprepared for the challenges I was facing on a daily basis.

During one particular workshop I found myself feeling increasingly frustrated as a prominent adolescent psychotherapist presented his theories of psychopathology, case studies, and dynamic insights. It was hard for me to tell exactly what he was doing to treat the conduct disorders. I held my breath, raised my hand, and posed the following question: How do you work with adolescents who are often in trouble, defiant, and contemptuous of the therapy process? He thought a moment, smiled wisely, and reminded me that these were not patients he would work with. In fact, he accepted only one out of three youngsters applying to his treatment program— those who wanted to change! That clinched it for me. As a psychologist working with the other two out of three youngsters who were unsuitable candidates, I was determined to find a way to enlist their cooperation.

Over the years I have employed a variety of techniques to engage and treat the adolescent disruptive behavior disorders. Some have served me well, others have failed miserably. About eight years ago I developed a seminar to address the practical aspects of treatment that seemed to fall outside the theoretical and case study formats often presented. To date I have conducted several hundred workshops reaching thousands of mental health professionals, special educators, guidance counselors, psychiatric aides, and others dealing with this difficult population. The great majority have been quite receptive to my ideas and have expressed a continued need for information and techniques focused on the practical application of the useful current treatment approaches.

The thoughtful questions posed along with the personal experiences shared have been instrumental in the development of this book. My intent is to address the daily dilemmas of treatment and provide a useful hands-on approach. I hope the material to follow will fill an existing void and be beneficial to helping professionals of all theoretical persuasions. The focus is on what I consider to be the universal elements in the process of treating adolescents with oppositional defiant and conduct disorders. What follows is a sequential presentation of these components with an emphasis on communicating with recalcitrant youth, challenging resistance, developing the wish to change, and systematically applying techniques that have proved useful.

# 1

# Understanding the Disruptive Behavior Disorders

Disturbances of conduct in adolescents pose a serious challenge to parents, educators, and mental health professionals. They are costly to society and ultimately lead to major social problems (Robins 1981).

According to *DSM-IV* (1994), the disruptive behavior disorders include both oppositional defiant and conduct disorders. While there is considerable overlap between the two diagnostic categories, conduct disorder is by far the more serious. Antisocial behaviors such as aggression, lying, stealing, and destruction of property are more often associated with conduct disorder. They occur in isolation in the "normal" adolescent population; however, an extended pattern that interferes with daily functioning becomes diagnostically significant. A diagnosis of antisocial personality is not employed until an adolescent turns 18.

The prevalence of oppositional defiant disorder is estimated to be between 2 and 16 percent of the child and adolescent population. Estimates for conduct disorder range from 6 to 16 percent for males and 2 to 9 percent for females (*DSM-IV* 1994). The symptoms of both disorders may appear in tandem with other diagnostic categories. Consequently, the extent of the problems posed may be underestimated.

Despite the attention they have received, interventions with antisocial adolescents have met with only limited success (Kazdin 1995). The multiplicity of variables contributing to conduct-disordered behavior make treatment difficult. Patterson and colleagues (1989) point out that interventions often produce short-term treatment effects that are lost within a year or two of termination. The literature suggests that broader-based and comprehensive strategies are needed to accomplish more global and durable change.

## DEVELOPMENTAL CONSIDERATIONS

Adolescent patients present with unique developmental issues. They must effectively balance their urgent impulses and wishes for autonomy with an acceptance of authority and societal expectations. While young people are likely to flex their muscles periodically on their path to separation and individuation, excessive noncompliance will impair the growth process. If serious behavioral disturbances have persisted since childhood, there is an increased risk of developing a lifelong pattern of antisocial behavior (*DSM-IV* 1994). This is of great concern to our nation as violent and criminal behavior is often preceded by a history of conduct disorder in childhood and adolescence.

The emergence of adolescence exacerbates preexisting behavior problems. When thwarted, a heightened need for affiliation and identity can lead to a rejection of society's expectations. The adolescent's feelings of invulnerability further increase their risk taking and malfeasance without regard for consequences.

Peer groups with a propensity for trouble usually require no ticket of admission. Thus, angry and isolated youngsters in search of belongingness need look no further. They can gain acceptance to the group by simply violating rules on a regular basis.

In summary, a comprehensive formulation of antisocial behavior should address the interaction between specific environmental risk factors and the adolescent's vulnerability to stress. Further, deficits in sociomoral development leave them ill equipped to sustain effort and withstand negative peer influence. In effect, there is little incentive to conform to societal expectations.

## TREATMENT STUDIES

Behavioral and cognitive-behavioral outcome studies are the most frequently cited, and typically are specific and well controlled. The usual focus is on discrete symptoms (e.g., aggression or disruptive behavior) and the application of specific techniques. While results have been encouraging, there is evidence to suggest that the generalization of treatment effects to other deviant behaviors and character structure is limited (Kazdin 1985). Further, the oppositional and conduct disorders are more broadly based than the identified target behaviors. Those dealing with this population will attest to the complexities of the disturbance and the associated frustrations.

Traditional psychodynamic approaches have been extensively employed over the years and have met with mixed results. Evidence to justify the exclusive use of insight-oriented psychotherapies is scarce (Kazdin 1995). It is difficult to determine if any specifics of this treatment are uniquely suited to a conduct-disordered population. Even treatment successes are hard to replicate since they may be due to therapist variables rather than to the approach itself. To date little attention has been devoted to developing an integrated, cohesive, and readily applicable format for treatment.

This is not to suggest a lack of progress in the area. Several well-documented cognitive-behavioral and family-oriented techniques have been effective in altering maladaptive behavior patterns (Kazdin 1995). It is noteworthy that considerably more attention has been devoted to child than to adolescent remediation. Children are often more amenable to treatment and receptive to behavioral contingencies (Patterson et al. 1989). Their parents have more leverage and less competition from negative peer influence to contend with. In contrast, adolescents are more likely to resist help and to see themselves as not having significant problems.

Although cognitive-behavioral approaches have received considerable attention, there remains a shortage of information on the specific process of diffusing resistance and facilitating change in this population. Treatment failures are not always related to the techniques employed and may reflect an inability to enlist cooperation. Therapists of all disciplines must develop the skills to open these shutdown youth to the possibility of change.

A good tool is no more useful than the practitioner's ability to apply it judiciously. The competent behavior therapist offers the psychodynamically oriented practitioner a way to systematically apply concrete, demonstrably useful techniques. Likewise, those focused on a psychodynamic understanding must translate their understanding of resistance and defenses into functional insights. This need for integration is paramount when one considers the depth of the resistance.

## THE ROLE OF MEDICATION

Questions are often raised about the feasibility of medicating adolescents for behavior problems. Unfortunately, there are no documented studies to justify the use of pharmacological agents alone in treating the conduct-disordered population (O'Donnell 1985). Stewart and colleagues (1990) and Zovodnick (1995) suggest that medication is most useful as an adjunct to treatment. When a conduct disorder co-occurs with attention deficit hyperactivity disorder (ADHD) or depression, medication should be considered to treat the comorbid disorder.

The psychostimulants are the most commonly prescribed medications in child psychiatry. When properly utilized for ADHD symptoms, for example, they often reduce hyperactivity, impulsivity, and distractibility (Rosenberg et al. 1994). Antidepressants have been helpful in situations in which depression accompanies aggressive behavior. In a recent review of the psychopharmacology of aggression in children and adolescents, Stewart and

colleagues (1990) report that lithium was useful in helping to manage aggressive behavior. Both Schiff and
colleagues (1982) and Campbell and colleagues (1984)
found lithium to be effective in decreasing explosive
behavior in an antisocial population. Zovodnick (1995)
points out that while lithium holds promise for treating
conduct-disordered behavior, the long-term consequences
are unknown.

When medication is indicated, several caveats are in
order. Behavior-disordered youth may be reluctant to try
medication because of their fear of having a pill "control"
them. This ongoing suspicion can hinder their compliance
with a treatment regimen. Consequently, it is important
that the parents monitor the patient's use of medication.
In reality, the parents themselves may have reservations
about the use of medication. They often express concerns
about addiction, side effects, and possible adverse reactions. These issues must be addressed prior to any
pharmacological intervention. Generally speaking, behavioral, family, and other related interventions should
be employed before any trial on medication.


## DESCRIPTIVE CHARACTERISTICS

Oppositional defiant adolescents routinely display negative, disobedient, and hostile behavior. They are typically
noncompliant, stubborn, and unwilling to negotiate
(*DSM-IV* 1994). These youngsters feel that others make
unreasonable demands on them and they take little responsibility for their own behavior. They violate rules and
often clash with authority. Living with them can be a
painful ordeal. They are inclined to split hairs, to be

sarcastic, irritable, and provocative. One gets the feeling that they were born to argue.

## Case Example

Stephen was a 15-year-old boy residing at home and attending the local junior high school. His parents reported that everything with him was a hassle. Minor requests to clean up his room, do his homework, or help with chores were consistently met with protest. He could not tolerate having anyone tell him what to do. Often, when his demands were not met, he would storm off to his room, slamming the door and occasionally punching holes in the wall. He displayed some remorse afterwards, but remained stubborn and convinced about the legitimacy of his demands. This pattern of negative and noncompliant behavior had existed since he was 8 years old, but worsened in the seventh grade.

As is sometimes the case, the school reports were a bit more charitable. Stephen was viewed as a spunky young man with a good sense of humor. Teacher comments reflected that he usually did his work and was a B or C student. His behavior was occasionally disruptive, but he responded well when limits were set. Stephen appeared to do better in the structured school setting. He was liked by his peers and regarded as a good athlete who would get carried away at times. Family friends and neighbors felt that he was manageable as long as no one "crossed him."

Stephen's view was interesting. He believed that

his parents were too demanding and critical. "I'm just not going to let them boss me around all the time," he declared. "I'm almost 16 now and can take care of myself." When challenged on his behavior at home, he acknowledged that he lost his temper too easily, but quickly added that it wouldn't happen if his parents "stayed off my case." With prodding, Stephen confessed that he was easily annoyed, moody, and suspicious of others. He added that he might be better off if he did not get angry so often.

In the absence of appropriate intervention, oppositional defiant disorder often develops into a more serious conduct disorder. This picture is characterized by more flagrant and global disregard for the rules of society. These youngsters are aggressive, intimidating, and contemptuous of authority. Lying, stealing, vandalism, and fire setting occur in this subgroup (*DSM-IV* 1994). They lack compassion for others and seem to take great pride in their exploits. Those around them often report that they are mean, volatile, and unfeeling.

Samenow (1989) has described antisocial youth as self-centered and insensitive to the feelings of others. They are concerned with immediate gratification and often seek shortcuts to beat the system. Even when caught in the act, these youngsters do not admit they are wrong. They argue until their opponent either wears down or explodes and they then complain vehemently about their mistreatment. Parents report that lying seems to come naturally to them. One gets the feeling that these youngsters are determined to be uncooperative. They demand a reason for anything asked of them and attempt to put others on the defensive. Dealing with them on a daily basis can be draining. It seems that they never let up. Attempts to regulate their behavior are often futile. When consequences are imposed, they insist that they don't care. Often they wind up isolated from their family, school, and larger peer group.

Conduct-disordered adolescents gravitate toward one another. They mutually reinforce antisocial behavior and readily justify their actions as necessitated by the situation. Frustration tolerance is typically low in this group— its members anger easily and see aggression and revenge as logical solutions to conflict. Conduct problems with a childhood onset are more serious and likely to persist (*DSM-IV* 1994).

## SOME USEFUL FORMULATIONS

Patterson (1982) suggests that coercive family process is the key element in understanding the development of aggression and the related behavior disorders. Frustrated parents escalate the amount of control and punishment in an attempt to get their children to behave appropriately. The youngsters react by rebelling against the increased demands for compliance. They are unable to tolerate the criticism and authoritarian style of their parents.

As the cycle intensifies, the parents become increasingly inconsistent and intermittently acquiesce to the intolerable behavior, thus rewarding the child for being difficult. They report that they have tried everything and the situation is getting worse. The teenagers describe these parents as rigid, out of touch, and "control freaks."

The conduct-disordered behaviors are fueled by

school failure and peer rejection. This in turn increases the risk for depressed moods and gravitation toward an aberrant peer group. The assumption is made that those following this sequence are at great risk for the development of more severe antisocial behavior (Patterson et al. 1989).

Social learning theory explains conduct disturbance as the result of modeling the parents' deviant behavior (Bandura 1977). In short, aggression is acquired through learning in a social context. Youth who are raised in violent homes where abuse exists are at great risk for delinquency (Lewis et al. 1987). Other variables, including marital discord, economic pressure, and the parents' lack of availability, also contribute to the emerging conduct problems. Despite these adverse circumstances, many adolescents are able to avoid trouble. Neither coercive family process nor social learning theory account satisfactorily for the emotional resilience and seeming immunity of certain youth.

Conduct-disordered behavior can also result from comorbidity. The clinical picture is often clouded by the coexistence of several disorders. A study of psychiatric disturbances in serious delinquents identified multiple diagnoses in all subjects. Substance abuse, borderline personality disorders, and affective disorders were most common (McManus et al. 1984). Academic failure often accompanies the behavior disorders. Each diagnosis must be addressed for a treatment regimen to be effective.

Since school is where the adolescent spends most of his or her time, it makes sense to begin with a thorough assessment of the situation. I prefer to contact the school guidance counselor, who has access to information from the teachers regarding the child's achievement, attitude, and class participation. What can we learn to help us understand the basis for the failure? Is there any suggestion of a learning disability?

Ask youth about their speech, handwriting, spelling, and short-term memory. Some readily acknowledge their difficulty with language retrieval. One young man recalled his summer vacation but could not think of the name of the place with the sand and ocean. "The beach?" I queried.

"That's it," he replied. "Sometimes I just can't find the word I want."

Clues such as these require further exploration. When there is a cluster of signs that cannot be traced to behavior problems, a psychoeducational evaluation is indicated.

Many of these youngsters report difficulty focusing in the classroom. They are easily distracted and describe their minds as "wandering all over the place." A 14-year-old girl recalled her teacher's demonstrating how to do an algebraic equation. The next thing she knew the class was being dismissed. Another youngster heard people talking clearly in the parking lot below his classroom window but had no idea what transpired in class.

Activity levels vary greatly in adolescents, and the symptoms of hyperactivity may be less conspicuous by this time. We must be alert to the possibility of ADHD to determine the appropriate medical and educational intervention. Estimates of ADHD symptoms accompanying disruptive behavior disorders run as high as 75 percent (Kernberg and Chazan 1991).

The possibility of neurological involvement increases with the severity of the antisocial behavior displayed

(*DSM-IV* 1994). Organic dysfunction is often associated with difficulty in regulating feelings and impulsive behavior (Lewis et al. 1987).

Early identification is essential to effective treatment planning. Observe carefully for soft neurological signs such as coordination problems, accidents, or blackouts. Inquire about early problems learning to ride a bike, jump rope, or catch or throw a ball. If the overall picture is suspicious, a medical referral may be indicated.

A 15-year-old conduct-disordered boy described a "wild" experience he was repeatedly having in class. He would sit there feeling like he was "off floating in space." Sometimes he would see bright spots before his eyes, other times he would just peacefully "zone out." I questioned him further about this and he confessed that he had always related it to his prior drug use. I remained suspicious and suggested there might be another explanation he had not considered.

After some discussion, we agreed that he would see a neurologist for a further look. As it turned out, his electroencephalogram was abnormal and a seizure disorder was diagnosed. Afterwards he expressed relief at learning he was not crazy. Indeed, there was a plausible explanation, which led to successful intervention with medication. Most behavior-disordered youth feel that it is better to be tough or disruptive than crazy. Consequently, they are reluctant to describe their "scary symptoms" and need encouragement in a safe setting to express their concerns.

Substance abuse raises other complications. Alcohol seems to be the drug of choice because it increases the likelihood of aggression. Marijuana is frequently used but does not have the same status as alcohol. We are more likely to hear these teens talking about getting drunk and rowdy. They view smoking pot as an opportunity to "mellow out."

It is difficult to readily assess the extent of a substance abuse problem and its role in the disturbance. Teenagers routinely dismiss the seriousness and rarely see themselves as having a problem. When exploring this issue with them, it is safer to assume use and work from there. Rather than asking if they drink or get high, we would do well to inquire about their favorite alcoholic beverage or the going price for a nickel bag of marijuana in their neighborhood. Youngsters interpret these questions as an opportunity to talk freely about their involvement.

If doubt remains about the youngster's candor, it is helpful to recommend a drug screen. Most are familiar with this and may disclose their use if they feel safe. In either event, any evidence for more than occasional use should lead to treatment. Those habitually involved may need residential programs to eliminate their access to the substance and ensure treatment compliance.

Despite their protests to the contrary, depression often underlies disturbances of conduct. Given the troubled family histories, poor self-esteem, and lack of social adaptation, their negative outlook on life is understandable. The adamant denial of symptoms, however, can make diagnosis more difficult.

It is important to look carefully for the presence of depressive equivalents. Substance abuse is often a thin veil for depression. Adolescents self-medicate with drugs to avoid facing their feelings of rejection, sadness, and loneliness. Other common signs include risk taking, accident-prone behavior, and self-mutilation in which the teen burns him- or herself with cigarettes or makes series of scratches on the arms or legs. They are also prone to sexual promiscuity—boys to prove themselves and girls to feel loved and desired. Sometimes the diagnostic clues are apparent in daily activities. The music they listen to, compositions they write, and clothing they wear can all be reflective of a depressed state.

## Case Example

Michael was obsessed with the Led Zeppelin classic "Stairway to Heaven." He would listen to the tape endlessly, write the words in his notebook, and often practice the song on his guitar. Our work together seemed productive and lasted about six months. By termination his acting out had decreased and school performance had improved.

About a year later I received a gut-wrenching phone call from his mother. Suddenly and unexpectedly he had taken his own life. The funeral was to be held the following day and she hoped that I would attend. Upon entering the service I was taken aback. Blasting over the loudspeakers was the song "Stairway to Heaven." His friends had played it as his last request. A tragic yet important lesson to be learned from the obvious.

The possibility of borderline personality disorder should also be considered. McManus and colleagues (1984) found that affective lability and self-injury were highly correlated with this diagnosis when accompanied by delinquency. Relating quite inappropriately to others, these adolescents grow upset at something seemingly insignificant or laugh heartily at a serious comment. They lack any real sense of identity or purpose and describe feelings of profound emptiness. Often this population will go to great lengths to avoid being alone. The possibility of rejection is threatening and fuels an over-reaction to any negative feedback.

Their peers often describe them as "weird." In the company of others they make macabre comments and seem out of synch with the group. Although their behavior is deviant, it is less focused and goal directed. When exploring their views about things, one is struck by the sudden shifts and lack of self- and interpersonal awareness.

## GETTING TO KNOW THEM

Although the breadth of symptoms is wide, several basic defects underlie these disorders.

Adolescents with poor internal controls consistently lack the ability to modulate their impulses. They often react without thinking and wind up in trouble. When questioned afterwards they are invariably surprised by the outcome of their actions. Some will express remorse, but the more seriously disordered often state that "they couldn't care less." This basic lack of self-control extends to most aspects of their lives. Those around them describe these youngsters as hotheads, troublemakers, and kids with bad attitudes.

Both oppositional defiant and conduct-disordered teens come into frequent conflict with others. Other than anger, they are uncomfortable with the expression of

emotion, preferring action to words. Their peer relationships are superficial and based on shared rebellion rather
than any sense of mutuality. They distrust adults and are
frequently manipulative and deceitful. Despite claims
that their friends really know them, these youngsters are
self-protective and fearful of their own vulnerability.
They share little of their concerns, frustrations, and
sadness with others. In effect, the people in their lives are
either all good or all bad.

It follows that poor self-esteem underlies their facade of indifference. Although they insist otherwise,
these youngsters see themselves in a negative light. Often
the prolonged bombardment of parental criticism, failure to meet school demands, and peer rejection have
eroded their confidence. They maintain an air of bravado, yet do not believe in their ability to alter their own
destiny. This longstanding pessimism has devastating
consequences. These adolescents have abandoned their
efforts to succeed and instead devote their energy to
convincing others that nothing bothers them. Acting out
and noncompliance become their statement of dissatisfaction with themselves and the world around them.

These adolescents display a certain irritability and
sensitivity to the perceived criticism from others. Their
feelings bruise easily and they react without any thought
to the consequences. Their parents report that "they have
always been like this" and were never certain about how
to respond. The youngsters feel that they are tense, on
edge, and unable to delay their reactions. They carry a
reservoir of easily ignited anger. Interestingly, they describe a sense of calm after the storm, yet remain unable
to see their role in a situation. Their short fuse gets them
into frequent conflicts with authority.

## Case Example

Keith was a 14-year-old boy who presented with a lengthy history of aggressive and defiant behavior. He strongly resented being in treatment, insisting that the only problem was his parents "bugging him." Keith found most of the interviewer's questions to be annoying. When asked what might make his life better, his response was, "What a stupid question, everything is just fine." He displayed little insight into his difficulties and complained vehemently about several of his teachers provoking him.

Keith's parents reported that he was often resentful at home. He considered any requests for assistance with chores to be an imposition. Attempts to discipline him were unsuccessful as he would "just lose his temper and run off somewhere." The parents recalled that he had been hypersensitive and easily irritated since he was a small child. He had been evaluated for the possibility of ADHD and received a trial on psychostimulant medication, which was unsuccessful in altering his behavior patterns.

A propensity for risk taking is another trait. These adolescents report great pleasure in taking chances and placing themselves in danger. This high need for stimulation is evident on a daily basis. They might jump from cliffs into rivers, run across four-lane highways, drive recklessly, have unprotected sex, and seek trouble just for the thrill of it. When questioned about earlier experiences, they recall having always liked excitement. Farley (1986), who studied this thrill-seeking personality extensively found it can lead to either creativity or antisocial behavior, depending on the available outlets.

Behaviorally disordered youth are particularly susceptible to boredom. They seem unable to manage their time and often lack interests and self-direction. Unfortunately, boredom can lead to trouble. When lacking something to do they may go to great lengths to seek stimulation. Many fear being by themselves and describe feelings of loneliness, emptiness, and uneasiness at this time. Rather than tolerate these feelings, they take actions to avoid them. These kids are routinely in the wrong place at the wrong time. It is as if they gravitate toward trouble in their search for stimulation.

When asked about their parents, they often describe them as "twenty-four sevens." This translates to a parent's being absorbed with work twenty-four hours a day, seven days a week. Whether the unavailability is due to overwork, travel, or preoccupation with other relationships or vices, the outcome is inevitable: a very resentful child. These feelings of being unloved, deprived, or abandoned run deep. The kids believe they have been treated unfairly and harshly. Usually they see their siblings as favored, and feel that they have had to press for the things that they wanted. The parents may have been critical and unfeeling, reacting in anger and frustration to their behavior, and relying on extremes of discipline despite repeated failure to alter the misbehavior.

The cumulative rage felt by these youngsters is readily apparent. Many report lengthy histories of injustices that they may or may not have been subjected to over the years. They justify their anger and misbehavior by placing blame outside themselves and attributing hostile motives to others. A low tolerance for frustration and criticism makes them particularly volatile. Minor annoyances often lead to major outbursts. This feeling of being wronged fuels much of their acting out.

Considerable bravado is displayed by these adolescents, who go to great lengths to show they are tough and do not care what others think. This couldn't be further from the truth. Many feel vulnerable and fearful of failure. Their identity is invested in masking their real feelings and keeping others at a safe distance. This results in a readiness to argue and defend themselves. A 16-year-old boy once told me that he had to fight because "my pride is all I got." We must understand the significance of this chip on the shoulder and the emptiness that underlies it.

Coupled with this attitude is a seeming immunity to consequences. One gets the feeling that these youngsters no longer care about being punished. They are often placed on restriction at home and detention in school. Unfortunately, it is rarely effective. The disturbing behavior persists because they are already serving an extended sentence and have ceased trying. Worse yet, they violate their restrictions by sneaking out of the house, using the telephone, watching television, or otherwise beating the system. It is necessary to find effective and enforceable punishments to modify these patterns.

Many of these youngsters feel little guilt or shame about their behavior. They either justify their actions as warranted or deny any fault or responsibility. When remorse is expressed it is often short lived.

Generally, a decreased capacity to experience guilt worsens the prognosis (Kernberg and Chazan 1991). An absence of empathy for others often accompanies this lack of remorse. These youngsters have great difficulty seeing things from another's point of view. They readily state that they do not think about how they made the other person feel or consider how they might feel if treated similarly. Developing this capacity is an essential element of the treatment process.

Antisocial adolescents display poor judgment in daily situations. They do not pick up on social cues and interpret events according to their own negative belief systems. Frequent conflict with authority is reflected in their difficulty in accepting rules and limits. Although they can sometimes tell you the difference between right and wrong, they do not choose to apply their knowledge. "I just don't think about that stuff when I get into trouble," lamented one youngster. This inability to connect behavior and its consequences is common.

## FAMILY PATTERNS

The families of conduct-disordered youth display a high frequency of emotional disturbance, often reflected in parental deviance, substance abuse, and child abuse (Reeves et al. 1987). The parents insist that their child was impossible to control and deserving of harsh treatment. These conflicts are frequent and problems never seem to get resolved. Family members do not speak directly to one another and typically feel misunderstood.

Discipline in these homes is either extremely harsh, too permissive, or a confusing mixture of both. The parents are inconsistent and may display the same behavior they find so distasteful in their child. The primary mode of interaction is negative. They rely heavily on criticism and rarely offer compliments.

The onset of adolescence only heightens the struggle. The more the parents attempt to exert control, the more the youngster rebels. This escalation of conflict further alienates the adolescent, who draws closer to the negative peer group that offers acceptance.

These youngsters prefer to spend most of their time outside the home. Some avoid home to elude supervision; others feel unwanted and scapegoated by their families. At times they are caught in the middle of their parents' struggles and resent having to take sides. Feeling overwhelmed and at a loss to know what to do, parents may resort to extremes, such as employing a "cops and robbers" mentality. In this scenario parents closely monitor the suspects' activities, which may include eavesdropping on phone conversations, searching rooms, and following them to local hangouts. The adolescents respond by developing increasingly sophisticated ways to deceive their parents. They concoct elaborate stories to conceal their whereabouts, hide illicit substances in their rooms, and seek creative ways to flirt with trouble. The stage has been set for continued difficulties.

Many roads lead to the development of behavior disorders in youth. As we begin to understand their thoughts, feelings, and actions, it gets easier to relate to them comfortably. By integrating this awareness with an assessment of the cognitive and behavioral deficits, we can develop an individualized treatment program.

## A DAY IN THE LIFE

School is the job of our youth. Unfortunately, many find it cumbersome and unrewarding. Their class attendance is sporadic and participation rather limited. Grades are usually low and teachers' comments include lack of motivation, poor study skills, and a negative attitude toward learning.

The youngsters comment that hanging out with their peers is the only thing they like about school. While their frustrations and negative experiences are multidetermined, there is a common feeling of isolation. Many report that their parents are always pushing them and care only about their grades. Considering the time demands of schoolwork, a turned-off youngster has few places to turn other than to those who are like-minded.

The peer group becomes the haven for the disenchanted. They find ways to pass time while simultaneously avoiding responsibility. Shopping malls, friends' houses, rock concerts, and football games all present opportunities for trouble.

The festering anger, need for stimulation, and avoidance of sadness can lead to experimentation with drugs and sex, violating rules, and seeking conflicts. Some are flagrant about their activities, others secretive. The less experienced get caught; the veterans avoid detection. As the desire to avoid their home strengthens, the propensity for trouble follows. When parental supervision is either limited or excessive, the risk increases greatly.


## INNER-CITY YOUTH

A different set of issues is raised by urban teenagers who grow up in a culture of poverty. Although many are diagnosed as conduct disordered based on the presenting symptoms, the causes may vary greatly from other socioeconomic groups. Economic hardship, poor role models, chaotic homes, and crowded schools provide kids with limited opportunities to transcend their environment. A naturally evolving emphasis is placed on subsistence. Consequently, these youth often grow up with a different value system. Socially acceptable behavior is defined by the norms of their neighborhood.

## Case Example

David was a 14-year-old urban youth whom I worked with in the early 1970s. He was referred to our clinic because of lying, stealing, disruptive behavior, and failing grades.

His teachers complained that he was often the "class clown," and never turned in his homework assignments. They noted that he would sometimes put his head down and go to sleep in the back of the classroom. David was well liked by his peers but maintained rather superficial relationships. The school counselor commented that no one really knew him.

The father had abandoned the family when David was 6 years old. He lived with his mother and five siblings in his grandmother's house. The mother worked long hours and was exhausted when she arrived home. David received little supervision but was expected to care for his younger brother and sister after school.

His mother felt that he was not a behavior problem at home and was surprised by the school's concerns. She was quite angry with him for "causing even more problems for the family." A recent stealing incident had resulted in his suspension and a mandatory school conference. The mother expressed great concern for him but had little time and energy to devote to the family.

My early contacts with David were unproductive. He sat quietly in my office and responded to my inquiries with indifference. We both knew that our meetings were accomplishing very little. One morning I offered to take him to lunch at McDonald's, feeling he might be more comfortable in a neutral neighborhood setting.

How right I was! I told him that he could order as much as he wanted. He was thin and wiry so I figured he was a "cheap date." David proceeded to order three Big Macs, one large fries, and a jumbo drink. He finished everything in short order and seemed content. I commented on how hungry he must have been. He smiled, looked at me sincerely, and said, "I haven't had much to eat this week."

Suddenly I began to understand. "You always look so tired, David, I wonder if—." He cut me off.

"Well, look, Doc, there's not always a place to sleep in our house. There are seven of us and only four beds. Some nights it gets real crowded so I just hang out on the streets."

"So that's when you get in trouble," I commented.

"Yeah, but I only take what I need and never hurt anybody," he replied.

Now I was really determined to help. "Look, David, I can see that you have it tough, but an education would help you later on."

He looked at me knowingly again. "Listen, man,

I can hardly read, I don't know what's going on in class, and I'm bored and tired. What's the point? I've got other things I have to do, you know, helping out any way I can." I replied that it must be hard for him to imagine his life being any different. "You got it," he said.

One luncheon and a lifetime of understanding. Our relationship flowed more smoothly after that. On another occasion I told David of my own embarrassment about growing up and having much less than my friends. I thought I could understand how he felt. His comment has stuck with me through the years. "Any time you want to trade places, Doc, just let me know!" Conduct disorder or neglected child of society?

While lack of opportunity, poor socioeconomic status, and crowded living conditions seem to predispose youth to trouble, they are clearly not a guarantee. Gardner (1988) points out that inner-city youth from intact families are at less risk. Further, many faced with these hardships do not gravitate toward gangs or deviant behavior. Comer (1991) suggests that having adequate role models, opportunities to spend time constructively, and concrete achievable goals seem to greatly reduce the risk.

## WHERE DELINQUENTS FIT

An overlapping but somewhat distinct grouping of adolescents are those who exhibit antisocial and delinquent behavior. Juvenile delinquent is a legal term, not a psychiatric description. To be labeled as such, one must be adjudicated through the court system. This group is prone to join gangs and adapt to a violent subculture with a deviant value system. Remediation is particularly difficult because the behavior is socially acceptable to the peer group. They adamantly justify their behavior by citing influences outside their control. Attempts to alter the pattern with harsh punishment only seem to make matters worse (Hollin 1989).

Gangs have become increasingly prevalent in recent years. Members interact regularly with one another and typically share a common identity (Huff 1993). They are often involved in illegal activities and pride themselves on controlling specific turfs, which might range from an ice skating rink to a particular section of a shopping mall. Stories of intimidation are commonplace and aggressive behavior is mutually reinforced.

The Crips and the Bloods are two of the most familiar gang names, emanating from the Los Angeles area (Huff 1993). They have cropped up in a number of cities throughout the country but are not centrally organized. At their worst these gangs promulgate violence and engage in frequent criminal activity. At best they are loosely affiliated youth who choose to hang out together and play out their interpretation of a "real gang." In either case the allure of belonging to a group whose members stand by one another and fulfill the need for male bonding is powerful. Girls often hang out with gangs but are generally not members. These urban gangs often come from lower socioeconomic groups but attract youngsters from all walks of life.

## FROM EVALUATION TO TREATMENT PLANNING

Oppositional and conduct-disordered adolescents minimize their difficulties, resist intervention, and distort
information. Despite this, we must find a way to assess
their overall functioning before we initiate treatment.
When possible, meet with the parents first to get a
developmental history, perspective on their relationship,
and elaboration of their concerns. Be certain to speak
with school personnel, probation officers, coaches, and
any significant others in their lives. If the youngster
resides in a group home, detention center, or the home of
a family friend or relative, invite the people who live
there in to talk.

Assessment is an ongoing process. As we get to know
the adolescent better and trust increases, we begin to
understand the emotional and environmental hardships
he or she has encountered. Our careful look at individual
and family functioning should lead to heightened awareness of the psychodynamics and the behavioral deficits.

Explore any previous experience with treatment to
determine what barriers might exist. Often we find that
receptivity to therapeutic interventions varies inversely
with the exposure. Those who have experienced multiple
frustrations and failures will either resist openly or
accommodate to the process by learning to say the right
things, but never intend to change. Sometimes their
contempt for the helping process is obvious, at other
times subtle.

## Case Example

I'll never forget my experience with Alan. Prior to
our first visit I had reviewed some of his records.
There was a lengthy history of difficulty with authority and repeated violations of the rights of others. He
sounded mean and intimidating, certainly not someone who could readily accept the treatment process.

Imagine my surprise when I walked out to the
waiting room and saw a preppy-looking teenager in
a three-piece suit. He stood up to greet me, shook
hands, and told me it was a pleasure. Alan went on
to tell me that he had heard many good things about
me and was looking forward to working together.

I recovered from my shock quickly. Within ten
minutes of our first meeting he asked me if I would
be willing to testify as an expert witness on his behalf.
It seemed that he was due to appear in court the
following week and needed assistance. He viewed me,
of course, as simply another person to be manipulated. We must always guard against youngsters
with this smooth facade.

The bottom line is to ask ourselves if we can get the
job done in our particular treatment setting. If the
personality structure is fixed and the youngster has
committed multiple offenses without showing remorse,
the prognosis is poor. Often the net result is a need for
more intensive and longer-term intervention, with no
guarantee of results.

Finally, consider the individual's strengths as well as
the defects. Many of these kids are quite likable, yet
rarely receive compliments or positive feedback of any

sort. In fact, they stand prepared for criticism. As we convey our acceptance and recognize their good points, they become more amenable to treatment.

Interviews remain our major source of information. Self-report inventories are not always useful because antisocial youth do not see themselves realistically or accurately report their feelings and behavior. Information gathered from the parents is helpful but often insufficient. Behavioral observations from other sources can be especially useful. When difficulties are limited to home, school, or the community, the prognosis is better (*DSM-IV* 1994). A consistent pattern of maladaptive behavior across situations is suggestive of more serious difficulties.

A careful look at the disruptive behavior disorders underscores the need for a multifaceted treatment approach. The thorough assessment should lead to a major effort to diffuse the resistance of the adolescent and translate the symptoms into workable foci of treatment. Clearly, family involvement is necessary to simultaneously address any marital conflict, substance abuse, or ineffective parenting skills.

# 2

# Laying the Groundwork for the Therapeutic Alliance

A ngry, defiant, and antisocial adolescents vehemently deny having problems. They come to our attention because of their repeated conflicts with society and unwillingness to change their behavior. Referral sources include the schools, courts, parents, family physicians, and agencies dealing with them. Unless there is a treatment mandate, they will likely refuse to participate. Often the families avoid dealing with the ongoing problems because of their frustration, embarrassment, and pessimism about the possibility of change. This must be addressed from the start.

## ENLISTING FAMILY COOPERATION

When the need for treatment is clear but the parents do not comply with the recommendations, all possible avenues to enlist their cooperation must be explored.

Frequently the school is the starting point for the referral. Guidance counselors and school administrators often call attention to a youngster's problems. They can exert some pressure through the use of detention, suspension, and setting conditions for continued enrollment at the school. Unfortunately, some parents have the same authority problems as their children and cannot tolerate being told what is best for them.

If a school-based referral fails, other possible influences should be sought. Many families have religious affiliations that are meaningful to them. Clergy can play a useful role in encouraging families to participate in treatment. With the family's consent, one can contact their minister, priest, or rabbi to discuss the child's current difficulties. Many are willing to reach out by setting up joint meetings with the family either in their office or the therapist's. This type of pressure is less stigmatized and may foster compliance.

A similar contact may be made with the family physician. Families have often used the same doctor for many years and may rely on him or her for advice on a number of matters. Here too it is possible to exert subtle pressure on the reluctant family.

We must take great pains to help the beleaguered parents to feel understood. This can be accomplished by empathizing with their feelings of frustration, anger, and helplessness. If possible, concrete suggestions should be offered. Perhaps we can help them to manage their youngster's defiant behavior at home more effectively. These parents have come to dread telephone calls requesting them to attend meetings about their child. An offer to visit the home can be made to discuss their child's situation. Many parents consider such an overture less threatening and humiliating than an office visit.

When other options have been exhausted, it may become necessary to involve the legal system. We can contact the juvenile court and speak with the probation officer. Are there ways to hold the parents accountable for the continuing problems? Some judges will consider ordering treatment if the circumstances warrant it. Perhaps the truant officer can be helpful. Has school attendance been sufficiently poor to warrant intervention? If so, additional pressure can be exerted.

On occasion, I have asked uncooperative parents to sign a "release of responsibility" form that I designed. It reads as follows:

> I acknowledge that I have been notified by [name of school, clinic, etc.] that my child is having the following difficulties [specify]. I understand that therapy has been recommended but I decline to follow up on this. Therefore I release the [school, agency, etc.] from any responsibility for further problems that might occur and agree that I am accountable.

While this is not a legal document, it does call attention to the seriousness of the problem. Some parents will accept treatment at this point rather than be held accountable for their child's behavior. There is something convincing about a signed form that is to be kept on file.

Treatment typically begins with the initial phone call from the parents. Many believe that they have tried everything and look to therapy as a last resort. They may state adamantly that they need to be seen as soon as possible. Despite their eagerness to begin, there is often a reluctance to acknowledge their role in their youngster's problems.

From the start the importance of their involvement in the treatment process is stressed. When possible, the parents are seen first so that a realistic perspective on the problem and a plan for intervention can be developed. The boundaries of confidentiality are discussed along with the balance to be struck between individual and family work. The parents must understand that discussions with their child will not be shared. They are assured that we have their best interests in mind, but must simultaneously help the adolescent to feel safe in disclosing his or her feelings and actions. The more we know, the better we are in a position to help. If there is a serious risk, or information that we feel parents must have, it will be disclosed. Otherwise we must ask that they rely on our judgment in the helping process.

Sometimes the parents confess they cannot get their child to attend an initial session. "We've asked her several times and she tells us that she doesn't need or want help." I remind the parents that if their youngster truly knew what was best for her, we wouldn't need to have this conversation.

After our first session, I suggest that they tell their child that they have met with me regarding their concern about her and the family. They should inform her that I work with teenagers and families who are having trouble.

My basic position is that after I hear the parents' side of the story, I need to hear the child's as well, so that I can determine how to best be of help. I ask that they be concerned only with getting the child to the first visit and let me explain the rest once they have met me. Evaluation and treatment must never be presented as a punishment.

Sometimes the family is ambivalent about the necessity of treatment. They may describe their child's schedule as filled with social activities, sports, band, or other commitments that they are heavily invested in. Could the therapist possibly see them on Tuesday nights between 6:30 and 8:00 P.M.? After all, they really "don't want to interrupt his schedule or free time."

The desire to accommodate their youngster only fuels the difficulties. The teenagers, of course, are always too busy to come in. And then there are the hectic schedules of the parents themselves. Here's where the parents must draw the line. What's more important to them? Is it getting help for a serious behavior problem or maintaining the status quo?

These seemingly benign initial encounters have major implications. If the parents are to take treatment seriously, they must take a stand and make a major time commitment. Therapy must not take a back seat to the endless demands of their schedules. This message must be strongly conveyed to the youngster as well. It both challenges the denial and establishes the ground rules for effective treatment.

If the parents call back to say that they still can't get their youngster to come in, it may be necessary to consider more restrictive alternatives. When the behavior problems are serious, the parents must consider what leverage they have. Allowance, driving privileges, and curfews are all possibilities. Should all else fail, they can tell the youngster that important decisions will be made without them present. Youngsters often comply when they see that their parents are serious about this. If not, parents can also enlist help from extended family, family friends, or even some of the adolescent's own friends if they are concerned enough to want to help. Grassroots parents' organizations such as Tough Love (York et al. 1982) can sometimes be helpful with such interventions.

I adamantly discourage any use of deceit to get adolescents to therapy. I have had them come to me thinking that they were to have a physical exam, get help with their homework, or even just to "visit with some guy my parents know." Without fail, this spells trouble. Patients are likely to assume immediately that the therapist is a partner in the deception. The treatment has been sabotaged before it even begins.

There is one notable twist to this principle. Often youngsters will reject treatment because it interferes with the time they spend hanging out with their friends. Since this may be the only activity they find gratifying, coming in after school may feel like a punishment. Under these circumstances one can consider an alternative approach. The youngsters are asked to identify their least favorite school subject. If they pick math, we might say, "How would you feel about coming to therapy during math class?" This might be an offer they can't refuse. Attending a therapy session would probably be less aversive than the dreaded class. Furthermore, they might be cutting or failing that class anyway. Certainly they could make better use of the time, at least for the short run.

## MOVING TOWARD AN ALLIANCE

Assuming that the parents or other referral source succeed in getting the youngster in, the initial focus is on developing a therapeutic alliance. Regardless of the treatment approach employed, it is necessary to enlist cooperation, facilitate dialogue, and begin to build trust. Meeks (1986) provides an excellent description of this engagement process. An established alliance reflects a subtly evolving agreement between a patient and therapist. In effect, they have elected to work together to explore feelings, identify areas of difficulty, and utilize therapeutic techniques. The alliance is a prerequisite to change. The process is gradual, ongoing, and demanding of considerable patience. It may take anywhere from one meeting to several months, depending on the severity of the disturbance, the patient's motivation, and the therapist's skills. In some instances it is not possible to establish the alliance. These adolescents have had long-standing difficulties in the bonding process and the development of trust.

Behaviorally disordered youth feel compelled to work under protest. The moment they enter our office we must decide where to begin. If the patient displays anger, hostility, or feigned indifference, that feeling must be acknowledged. Simply saying "You look pissed off" should initiate some discussion. The patient is encouraged to talk about his or her resentment toward treatment and any feelings about its being unnecessary. When the discomfort is more subtle, we might inquire, "Who has been hassling you lately?" or "How can I be of help?" The other option is to make a nonjudgmental comment on their troubles and invite a response.

## Case Example

Susan's parents brought her to treatment because of escalating rebellious behavior at home. They suspected that she was drinking and smoking marijuana. Susan was angry, hostile, and defiant. She refused to follow her parents' rules and was spending an increasing amount of time outside the home with deviant peers.

Susan arrived with her parents for the first meeting. As they had forewarned the therapist of her anger and resentment about coming, it was decided she would be seen alone, initially.

*Susan*: (After a few moments of silence) This is going to be a waste of time.

*Therapist*: How do you know?

*Susan*: There is no reason for me to be here. My parents make a big deal out of everything.

*Therapist*: So you are angry that they brought you here.

*Susan*: Yeah.

*Therapist*: Well, they did mention that you were failing in school and staying out all night on the weekends.

*Susan*: So? It's my life.

*Therapist*: You're right, it is, but it doesn't sound like a very happy one. I understand that you often cry at home.

*Susan*: I get really upset with them sometimes. They just don't understand anything. Besides, as long as I'm out of the house, I'm fine.

*Therapist*: You really go out of your way to avoid your family.

*Susan*: Damn straight!

*Therapist*: I'll bet that you have some good reasons.

*Susan*: I sure do.

*Therapist*: Well, I'd like to hear about them. Everyone seems to be blaming you for stuff, but I'll bet they also play a part in the problem. I might be able to help if I had more information about your family. What do you think?

*Susan*: I can try, but I don't think that there is any point in doing this.

*Therapist*: I can understand that. Let's just see what happens.

Questions pertaining to how they view their problems should be avoided. These are likely to lead to hostile or sarcastic remarks about those whom they blame for their conflicts. Prolonged silences also increase discomfort. It is helpful to wait a few seconds to see if the adolescent talks first, but anything longer than that courts trouble.

The issue of confidentiality is raised early on by saying something like this. "Look, I figure you've heard a lot of things about therapy before coming here. Probably some people told you that it's helpful, but others, like many of your friends, feel it's a waste of time. Eventually you'll be able to judge for yourself."

Many kids wonder if the things they say will be held against them. Here's how I address that. "Therapy is a very personal sort of thing. When I spoke to your parents, I told them that they must understand we'll be talking about stuff they may not approve of or know about. If I'm going to be of any help, I must be the one to decide what they should or shouldn't know. This means that I will not tell them what you talk about. If something comes up that I feel should be discussed, I'll check with you first, and we'll find a way to talk about it together. If you want it to stay private, I'll respect your wishes.

"There is one exception to my policy that you should know. If I think you are putting yourself or others in danger, I reserve the right to break confidentiality. That includes things like weapons, drug dealing, or any intent to harm innocent people. Can you live with that?" Most kids seem satisfied at that point. On those occasions when disclosure to parents has become necessary, we have been able to deal with it.

## THE THERAPIST'S POSTURE

We must strike a delicate balance between authority and tolerance. The emerging relationship should be different from their other historically negative experiences with adults. This is best accomplished through actions rather than words. We try to accept them as they are and avoid passing judgment. Teenagers may present themselves by acting or dressing outrageously to make an initial state- ment of their independence. An objective comment on their appearance can be useful. You might say, "I can see you're wearing all black today." That invites them to offer some type of explanation, which can be pursued.

Although we don't want to relate to them as a friend, we must convey a genuine interest in their lives. It is best to speak in conversational tones to help them feel like a person rather than a patient. The overall approach is firm, forthright, and yet relaxed. To whatever extent possible, technical jargon should be avoided by speaking briefly and to the point. The therapist should serve as a model for good communication.

A sense of humor is always useful. Most of these adolescents appreciate a lightness of being and welcome the opportunity to exchange laughs. A spontaneous approach toward the early sessions helps to facilitate the alliance. Overall, those who can laugh at themselves or see humor in their predicament are more likely to develop resilience in their daily lives. We must be careful, however, about the use of sarcasm. Their feelings bruise easily and they are likely to withdraw when they feel insulted. On the other hand, developing a climate for sharing embarrassing moments, mistakes, and foibles facilitates the process.

## THE ADOLESCENT CULTURE

This population is likely to have a narrow range of interests. We must be informed about the aspects of adolescent culture likely to be of interest to them. A few minutes a week spent browsing through *People* and *Rolling Stone* magazines should suffice. The focal points are music, sports, clothing, cars, and electronic gadgetry. It is extremely useful to integrate this knowledge into the conversations.

Several years ago I saw a young man who was rather quiet and indifferent during our first meeting. I noted that he was wearing a Guns and Roses tee shirt and recalled something I had recently read about the rock group. "Did you hear what happened at the Guns and

Roses concert in St. Louis last week?" I queried. "No, what?" he quickly responded.

Suddenly I had his undivided attention. "Well, there was a riot there. Axel [the lead singer] got angry at someone in the audience, jumped off the stage, and punched him in the mouth. Everyone got into the action, people were getting hurt, and the police got involved."

My patient was enthralled at this point. He wanted to hear more but also started talking about his views on the importance of defending oneself when provoked by others. What became a productive discussion was launched by my initial observation and the sharing of a newsworthy item. Sometimes that's all it takes.

## TALKING TO TEENAGERS

There is an art to getting teens to talk freely. Simply asking questions that lead to yes or no answers does not facilitate dialogue. While questions do lend considerable structure to a session, they make our patients dependent on us to do the work. Worse yet, if they feel the questions are simplistic or intrusive, they will respond with hostility. Although some information can be gathered by direct questioning, it is best to move beyond this format as soon as possible. One can pick up on subtle cues, comment on topics of interest, or volunteer information about other youngsters that relates to their experiences.

The conduct disordered are forever curious about their peers' problems with school, authority, and family. They are much more likely to disclose information when they feel a sense of universality. When asked to describe their friends' difficulties, they are likely to project their own onto the situations. It feels much safer to talk about someone else's problems. Any attempt to pressure for premature disclosure may lead them to shut down.

Everyone wants to be liked and accepted. While antisocial youth may boast about their wrongdoing, it often stems from an underlying need for recognition. Since they see themselves as problem free, it is useful to encourage them to tell you why they don't need help. This may free up some energy to talk about some of their anger and frustrations.

Try and be aware of the balance between how much you're talking and how much they are talking. As therapy proceeds, the patient should be conversing more comfortably and taking more initiative. A continued imbalance favoring the therapist suggests a difficulty in developing trust, which should be addressed. At this point it may help to encourage the youngster to talk about how he or she has been "burnt" in relationships over the years.


## THE EARLY SESSIONS

Adolescents rarely begin treatment with an in-depth description of their presenting problems. Instead, they deny any significance to their behavior and elaborately rationalize their actions. It is easier to get them to talk about whom they hang out with, their parties and exploits, and the people whom they feel treat them unfairly.

It is important to display an active interest and curiosity about their lives. We need to remember the details of their daily concerns and follow up on previous conversations about them. This is illustrated by a youngster who talks about a girl he has just started going with.

We can inquire about the relationship in the following session. How does she treat him? Can she be trusted? What do his friends think of her? These kinds of questions convey an unwavering interest and offer an opportunity for further discussion.

As the level of trust increases, these adolescents usually begin to share more of their doubts, concerns, and even their unpleasant and frightening experiences. The business of daily life is important to them. We should never interpret their small talk as resistance. Gradually, it is possible to look at the significance of each issue. Most teenagers, and especially these youth, are more focused on the present than on the past.

There is an old saying that a good teacher enters the world of students through their door and takes them out through his or her own. This is precisely what we want to accomplish in the treatment process. The initial alliance is based on an inquisitive, enthusiastic, and empathic approach to their lives. Ultimately, the evolving relationship should lead the patient to explore other behavioral options and develop more gratifying ways to interact with their environment.

Often patients ask about how long they will have to attend sessions. Although it is tempting to appease them by saying "You'll wind things up quickly," this can be a mistake. We must be careful about promising something we can't deliver. It is best either to admit that you don't know how long treatment will last or to offer an estimate based on your previous experience with similar problems. They may not like the answer, but will certainly respect the candor. We can then proceed to explain that the length of time spent in treatment is determined in part by their cooperation, effort, and willingness to change.

Behavior-disordered youth love to bicker. Discussions of current societal issues such as drugs, drinking, sex, violence, and crime usually reveal the intensity of their convictions. Despite a lack of evidence to back up their arguments, we listen carefully without passing judgment. This process of interchange can lead to increased trust and comfort with disclosure.

Throughout the work, the therapist serves as a mirror, helping youngsters to see themselves through others' eyes. Many adolescents are unaware of how they come across and have distorted self-perceptions. It is useful for them to have the benefit of objective feedback. To accomplish this, I sometimes ask them how they would feel about my role-playing their behavior. Their answers usually range from indifference to enthusiasm, so we proceed.

I might portray an image of bravado, take on an attitude, or just look angry. They are often amused by my antics but usually get the point of the illustration.

This provides the opportunity to tell them that they were a good sport and now deserve a chance to imitate me. After all, I am also curious to know how I present to them. Their impressions can be quite enlightening. The youngsters might stroke their chin, say "I hear you," or just sit stiffly in their chair. It usually is amusing and we share a laugh. I thank them for the "supervision," and we have moved one step closer to an alliance.

## AS THE STORY UNFOLDS

Many new patients waste no time telling you about their exploits. Since their identity is so tied up with their misdeeds, they will comfortably talk about them. Often they have been referred as a result of their defiance, aggressive behavior, stealing, or other violations of the rights of others. Although it is tempting to challenge them immediately on their actions, we run the risk of alienating them before they get the message that our wish is to help rather than to judge. We should never condone wrongdoing, but it is important to avoid premature conflicts over right versus wrong.

As they continue to share the details of their lives we display our perplexity and concern. One might say, "You don't seem to care about what happens to you," or "Why do you do this to yourself?" They often have no ready answer but do sense our involvement. The reality is that we are not there to tell them how to live their lives; rather, our goal is to help them to make good choices for themselves.

As we get to know them better, they will continue to reveal their misbehavior. We encourage this disclosure through our curiosity and animated discussions. Wrongdoing rarely occurs in isolation. For example, a youngster who was referred for stealing might be told the following: "You know, when kids get caught doing something, it is usually because their luck has run out. I'll bet you got away with taking lots of things from stores before this happened." If they agree, the history can be explored. One might say, "I can see that you enjoy the thrill that trouble brings. Tell me about some of the other things you've gotten away with recently." Many adolescents accept this invitation and share other situations in which they have violated rules.

This ruse in talking about their lives becomes important as treatment progresses. We want the youngsters to be receptive to feedback and willing to exchange ideas. Frequently, the more they speak, the more willing they are to listen. This should pave the way for further therapeutic intervention.

When the alliance has evolved well, it should be apparent to both the patient and the therapist. These youngsters might comment that sessions do not feel much like therapy anymore. They may acknowledge that they don't mind coming—but quickly remind us that they would rather be someplace else. Minor concessions such as these often represent marked progress. There may be similar indications in their behavior outside the sessions. For example, a patient may call for advice on a day-to-day problem. Perhaps their parents won't allow them to go to a friend's house on a school night. What should they do? Questions such as these reflect developing trust and should be responded to candidly.

Finally, a patient may express concern about the therapist by saying that they don't look well or look like they could use a vacation. Any genuine expression of feeling should be met with appreciation rather than interpretation. One youngster offered me advice on improving my office. She pointed to an empty wall and suggested that I put a Metallica poster on it. (That's about as good as it gets!) I thanked her for calling my attention to the barren spot, agreed it really needed something, and further explored her interest in music.

## TESTS ALONG THE WAY

The road to a good working relationship can get quite bumpy. Adolescents early and inevitably find ways to challenge our resolve. Some ask if we can get them out of the hospital, school, or other unpleasant location. Others may wonder if we'll put them in the hospital or jail if they tell us what they're really doing. I've had kids mention that their last therapist was a "jerk" because he repeated a private conversation to their parents. Each of their inquiries reflects an attempt to see how we operate. Will we bend to accommodate their wishes and gain their approval or do we stand firm about therapeutic protocol? The antisocial adolescent feels rules are made to be broken and constantly tests the water. Clearly defined boundaries at least make it difficult for them to overstep the limits.

Every so often a patient will insist that they just don't have anything to talk about. They point out that therapy is a waste of time since they have no problems and no need to be there. If that's the case, ask how you'll know that they're so well functioning if they don't talk to you. Perhaps they don't need to be in treatment, but they'll need to do some convincing.

The tests may be much more subtle. For instance, during an initial session a youngster asks to go to the bathroom shortly after the meeting has begun. Or perhaps they need to leave a few minutes early to get to their next activity on time. Although the requests may appear polite and benign, their intent is transparent. How far can I push the rules? Again, the need for clear, consistent policies is demonstrated. As the therapist passes these early tests, a pattern of adherence to a defined structure is established. This theme remains important throughout the course of treatment.

## BASIC THERAPEUTIC PROCESS

The transition from a focus on the alliance to the need for change is rather subtle. Our initial curiosity about their difficulties is accompanied by reflection and acceptance of their feelings. As we encourage the expression of even negative affect, they begin to see us as allies.

Interpretive work is difficult with this population. They are not motivated to learn about themselves, resent being "analyzed," and maintain a defensive posture. On occasion they make sweeping generalizations that might benefit from deeper probing. A youngster talking about his entire school being filled with "jerks" might be told, "It's really lonely when you feel like you don't belong." Complaints about parents being unavailable can evolve into discussions of whether they have ever felt loved. Patients' reactions to any interpretation should be carefully observed. If they indicate some acknowledgment and openness, we can continue with the line of thought. Otherwise we may need to back off.

The use of dreams can be a less threatening entree to the unconscious. Many kids wonder about these "weird" nighttime occurrences and respond favorably to an offer to decipher them. Many do not view their dreams as a personal disclosure and are willing to explore them.

One common theme in their dreams involves the youngsters' feeling stuck to a spot and unable to move. Someone might be pursuing them with a knife and they can't get away. They wake up with a scream and feel relieved that it's only a dream. The significance of this often relates to conflicts over opposing impulses or wishes. This can be discussed and related to current events in their lives.

Another often repeated dream involves a youngster's falling off a cliff or a building and free-falling through the air. This can easily be related to the fear of losing control. Ongoing difficulty with managing anger and impulses should be discussed. On one hand they pride themselves on their reactivity, yet on the other they may be fearful of some consequences. Themes such as these should be sought and explored at every opportunity. Youngsters with behavior problems are constantly dealing with issues of self-protection and hyperreactivity to perceived threats.

When kids either can't or don't wish to recall dreams, we can encourage them to talk about their fantasies or daydreams. After all, everyone tunes out sometimes and escapes into their favorite thoughts. This is yet another way to get to underlying issues. A daydream may represent the flip side of an insecurity that is readily accessible. Consider the adolescent who feels very vulnerable, yet fantasizes about being the toughest one in his grade. These recurring thoughts are excellent springboards for discussion.

The sequence of change is attended to throughout the therapeutic work. Oppositional and conduct-disordered youth rarely experience the type of pain that would motivate them to seek relief. Rather, their energy goes into the denial and avoidance of their conflicts. Their lack of self-awareness in part explains their limited motivation to change.

Once the therapeutic alliance has been established, a basis for developing alternative behavior patterns exists. The ongoing relationship leads to an acknowledgment of difficulties followed by gradual openness to change, and culminates in increased efforts to develop new coping skills.

# 3

# Creating a Climate
# for Change:
# Diffusing Resistance

A substantial proportion of deviant adolescents resist help from the start, thereby making it difficult to employ conventional therapy techniques. Their lack of cooperation, reluctance to reveal themselves, and contempt for authority are reflected in their defiance and/or indifference toward the therapist. The establishment of the therapeutic alliance is impeded. This requires specific interventions to engage these youngsters and lessen the power struggle.

## THE ANATOMY OF RESISTANCE

The inherent resistance to treatment may be of long-standing origin. Many of these youth have been angry for years and have learned to distrust adults. They may confuse our efforts to help them with an attempt to control them. Much of their energy gets invested in

avoiding the pain they feel. Their oppositional or antisocial behavior becomes the statement of protest. As long
as they stay angry, their distance from others is justified.
Therein lies the initial challenge of treatment.

Unfortunately, in their eyes, entering treatment is
tantamount to an admission that they are defective.
Since they deny having any problems, agreeing to attend
meetings would be like crying "Uncle." Their awareness
of their parents' insistence makes it all the more difficult.
As their identity is interwoven with their noncompliance
with society's expectations, they see treatment not only as
threatening, but as confining and senseless. It is against
this backdrop that treatment begins.

## TECHNIQUES TO DIFFUSE RESISTANCE

The challenge is to involve youngsters in the helping
process by enlisting their interest, helping them to feel at
ease, and offering them a relationship based on trust.
This calls for some ingenuity and a willingness to depart
from convention.

The anger, resistance, and complaints become the
starting point in the work. We acknowledge that they
have had a difficult life and have reason to distrust.
Although they protest treatment, they are reminded that
we are not responsible for their presence. Indeed, their
strongest wish is to be left alone with no one to hassle
them. I rarely challenge this and prefer to try to interest
them in finding ways to get people off their case. Perhaps
we are really on the same side and can accomplish
something useful.

Flanagan and Flanagan (1995) suggest that the adolescent's pursuit of freedom should be valued by the therapist. This will sometimes surprise the youngster, who is prepared to vehemently justify his or her actions. The therapist offers assistance to figure out legal and constructive behaviors to help adolescents get what they want out of life. Often they react suspiciously to this overture, but will listen carefully. They are reminded that they have nothing to lose.

## THE SILENT PATIENT

Sometimes we are faced with patients who are seemingly nonverbal. They do not speak spontaneously, often answer questions monosyllabically, and will sit in silence for lengthy periods. This is frustrating for the therapist and quite uncomfortable for the patients, who may be making a statement with their silence.

The therapist must quickly determine the function of the silence and guide the interventions accordingly. I distinguish between two categories of silence: *willful silence*, an active resistance that represents a deliberate attempt by the adolescent to undermine the therapy process, and, in contrast, *unintentional* or *natural silence*, characteristic of genuinely quiet or shy youngsters who just do not know how to converse or relate comfortably (Bernstein 1989).

### Genuinely Quiet Adolescents

This patient subgroup has typically been "quiet" for years. They had difficulty socializing when they were

younger and feel quite uncomfortable in situations calling for free-flowing conversation. In all probability they
are self-conscious, have difficulty asserting themselves,
and are at least mildly depressed. When questioned, they
will readily acknowledge their discomfort and directly
express a desire to be more outgoing.

Verbal psychotherapy is an unnatural situation for
these youngsters. They feel uneasy and are uncertain
about how to act in the office. It behooves us to actively
create situations that will facilitate dialogue. Direct questioning is often useful, but should focus on topics with
which the youngster is familiar. These might include
sporting events, television shows, rock concerts, or a
particular interest.

Other possible suggestions include telling a joke,
describing a news item in their own words, or sharing a
song that they like. We must enable genuinely quiet
adolescents to feel that they have something to say and
that it is acceptable to us. Some patients will accept a
solicitation to write or draw something. Others may
welcome the opportunity to respond to a brief but
interesting tape played for them in the therapist's office.
Any technique that facilitates dialogue is worth trying
with a silent and withdrawn patient.

It helps to acknowledge the youngster's discomfort
with talking and socializing. We can address some of
these feelings by sharing what others have felt in similar
situations. While accepting their silence, we convey that
there are often alternatives.

Some youngsters will be unable to talk despite our
best interventions. In these instances I suggest that
therapy be discontinued and other techniques considered. Social skills training has been demonstrably effec-

tive in helping noncommunicative youngsters to develop verbal skills (Lindsay 1987). It can be employed in either individual or group format. When the prerequisite verbal skills have been acquired, therapy may be resumed.

## Intentionally Silent Adolescents

This group chooses to protest treatment through their deliberate refusal to talk or otherwise cooperate. They are determined to prove they are unreachable and do not need help. The therapist's silence is often met with statements of anger, complaints that "this is a waste of time," and increased agitation or anxiety. Time is usually of the essence. These patients will be lost quickly if we don't intervene. The therapeutic task is to make it harder for them to stay quiet than to talk.

McHolland (1985) describes several strategies for interrupting silence. The therapist can comment: "You're very good at being silent. I'll bet if you were a POW the enemy couldn't get you to confess anything." Relabeling and admiring the silence should help to diffuse the resistance. A similar approach entails telling patients that you want them to remain silent while you discuss something with their parents, a rather difficult task for an angry adolescent. Finally, the therapist might say, "I'm going to ask you some questions. If the answer is yes do nothing, if no, nod your head." In each case the source of resistance is subtly challenged.

An approach I have found particularly useful is to point out that there is a struggle going on and that they will most likely win. I readily acknowledge that their will to remain silent may be stronger than my will to get them to talk. If the silence persists for several sessions, I propose an alternative. I ask that we try a four- to six-week trial period of talking about anything they want to. If they keep the bargain, at the end of the agreed-upon time period I will terminate therapy if they still do not wish to continue. This usually frees the youngster from the control battle and results in a more comfortable dialogue. Most often, they begrudgingly agree to continue at this point. A small percentage will insist that treatment be concluded as per the agreement. Of course I comply with their request. Interestingly, after several weeks have elapsed, they may return of their own volition, having considered the alternatives. A few patients will be lost, but they were unlikely to benefit from treatment at the time.

## ACTING-OUT ADOLESCENTS

These angry patients are both verbal and direct in expressing their resistance to treatment. They are often overtly provocative and make it clear that they neither trust adults nor wish to be close to them. They frequently test the limits and try our patience. I have been asked what I would do if they were to light up a joint in my office or drink a soda mixed with alcohol. They have gone to my desk and opened drawers, attempted to use my phone, and otherwise infringed upon my personal property.

Tests of our tenacity must be addressed immediately. Basically, we have three options. First, we can ignore the behavior, hoping the patient will lose interest, having failed to irritate us. Second, we can interpret the behavior, calling attention to the unconscious motive, with the intent of diffusing the provocation. Finally, we can simply set a limit, stating why we will not tolerate the action and specifying consequences if needed. In any case we must convey the message that we respect their rights and expect the same from them. We cannot allow ourselves to be taken advantage of.

## ALLIANCE BY ADMIRATION

In this approach therapists ally themselves with certain aspects of the youngster's pathology. We might marvel at their bravado, how they beat the system, or have made money illicitly. We stress our curiosity, being careful not to endorse the deviant behavior. It is also possible to comment on their determination not to be helped. The focus is on trying to understand how they have become adept in the particular area, thus facilitating communication and conveying acceptance of the person.

### Case Example

Damien was referred to treatment because of excessive aggressive behavior in school. He had been in numerous fights and insisted that he was just defending himself. During the early sessions he was uncooperative and contemptuous of the treatment process. The therapist attempted to ally with his bravado.

*Therapist*: Damien, I've heard that you're one of the toughest kids in your high school.

*Damien*: You've got that right, Doc.

*Therapist*: You're really not scared of anyone, are you?

*Damien*: Nope.

*Therapist*: I can see why. You're big, muscular, and even look mean. I'll bet you get a lot of respect from the other kids.

*Damien*: Yeah. They know better than to mess with me.

*Therapist*: Has it always been like this?

*Damien*: Pretty much; but when I was younger, some of the bigger kids used to pick on me.

*Therapist*: What did you do then?

*Damien*: I just learned to fight back. I wouldn't give them the satisfaction of crying or wimping out or anything.

*Therapist*: It must have been hard to keep all that inside you.

*Damien*: Yeah, but I had to.

*Therapist*: Why?

*Damien*: Well, there really wasn't anyone to help me out. I was pretty much on my own.

*Therapist*: You never even told your mother about it?

*Damien*: You've got to be kidding. She was out of it, you know, drinking all the time. It wouldn't have made a difference.

*Therapist*: Damien, I think I can understand how you've gotten to be this way. It's almost like you didn't have a choice.

*Damien*: Yeah.

*Therapist*: There's really a lot more to you than people see.

*Damien*: I guess so.

## CATCHING ADOLESCENTS OFF-GUARD

I find it useful to exaggerate the adolescent's unspoken feelings to prompt a reaction and loosen the flow of communication. The following comments serve to illustrate this: "I'll bet you think I'm a real dork," "I can see that you think therapy is a waste of time," or "I'm sure you feel that it's your parents who should be here and not you!" Each statement helps to relax the patient, allowing him or her to see that you can lightly touch on some of the strong, angry feelings behind the resistance and perhaps share the humor.

On occasion, something dramatic will circumvent the lack of cooperation. The therapist might be ranting and raving about an unrelated issue as the youngster arrives. This is likely to peak their curiosity and can lead to a productive discussion of life's annoyances. A variation would be to start talking spontaneously about a topic of interest, thus inviting comment from the patient. In either event we behave in a fashion inconsistent with their expectations.

## THERAPEUTIC ANECDOTES

At times it is useful to relate a story about another youngster's experience with a specific difficulty. This technique is particularly useful when dealing with those reluctant to disclose their fears, worries, or other secrets. Hearing that others have shared their experiences with you gives them subtle permission to do likewise. The anecdotes I share often represent a compilation of my experiences with other adolescents. If I feel strongly that a certain point needs to be made, I will embellish my story accordingly. On occasion, youngsters have challenged me on the accuracy of my account. I always confess to exaggerating if that is the case. Adolescents find this amusing and sometimes respond with admissions of their own distortions.

## TAPPING THE IMAGINATION

Adolescents often will respond to an opportunity to be imaginative. We propose to take turns making up a story that is of interest to them. The therapist might begin by telling about a boy who is very angry at his parents for the way they treat him. At the point where the character considers revenge, the therapist stops and asks the youngster to continue. The patient goes on for a minute or two and then passes the story back to the therapist. This process of interchange can continue for some time, enabling them to project their own feelings onto the story. It is nonthreatening and can be enjoyable at times.

Another technique I employ involves asking the youngsters to "strike a bargain with the devil." I tell them the story of Faust, an unhappy middle-aged man who traded his soul to Satan for the immediate pleasures of life. Would they consider such a deal or propose one of their own? We explore some of their wishes and ask what price they would pay to have them fulfilled. The ensuing discussion reveals their unmet needs and hope for a simple solution to their problems. Most troubled youth find this exercise interesting and thought provoking.

## Case Example

> Crystal was a 17-year-old conduct-disordered girl.
> She was amused by the thought of a pact with the
> devil. After some consideration she grew sad and
> stated, "My life is always hell. I guess if I were to
> make that trade, I'd ask for a lot of money. No, not
> really. I'd just want to stay out of trouble and maybe
> get along with my family. I'm really tired of all the
> hassles."
>
> "Anything else?" I queried.
>
> "Oh, yeah, I'd go with that cute guy Tim in my
> school."

## INVITING THE BEST FRIEND IN

Assuming that the sessions are not progressing satisfactorily and a patient remains guarded about his or her
feelings, we can utilize the patient's best friend effectively
in a therapeutic capacity. Adolescents generally confide
more in their best friend than in their parents or any
other adult. By acknowledging their importance and
indicating an interest in meeting this significant person,
the therapist opens up an additional avenue for communication.

Most youngsters cannot resist the opportunity to
have their "best friend" share in their experience. Although they imagine that the session will be great fun,
something rather different evolves. While attending the
session as a guest, the best friend usually winds up
assuming a different role, that of a junior therapist. Since
the focus of the sessions is not on the friends, they are

likely to disclose many of the patient's concerns, strong feelings, or idiosyncrasies in response to queries about what they are really like. This is readily accepted by troubled youngsters because, of course, friends are on their side. It greatly facilitates the flow of therapy by alerting us to the important issues that might not otherwise be discussed.

Over the years, I have learned of child abuse, suicidal intentions, and many dangerous actions through the disclosure of the confidant. This technique has served me well. The therapeutic alliance is indirectly strengthened and there is much new and useful information for future sessions. Two caveats are in order. First, state specifically that the friend's attendance is only a onetime occurrence so the situation is not abused. Second, make sure that the youngster informs his own parents as well as his friend's that such a meeting is being held.

A variation on this theme is to invite in an older peer who has successfully completed treatment. Patients are often able to relate to their ordeal and will listen with interest. As the veteran patient describes the process of change, the youngster may become less negative and more receptive to alternatives.

## PICKING UP ON NUANCES

At times subtle cues provide us with the opportunity to be helpful. Over the years, many youngsters have asked me what time it is during a session. This always struck me as odd since I keep a small clock visible on an end table between myself and the patient. On one occasion a 15-year-old boy was particularly adamant in his request.

Suddenly the obvious occurred to me. My clock was the old-fashioned type with hands. This unfortunate young man had never learned to tell time!

A window of opportunity had opened. I gently commented on his shortcoming, and of course he feigned indifference. "Look," I said, "since we're not accomplishing much during our meeting today, why don't I teach you how to tell time on this clock." He reluctantly agreed and I began to demonstrate how the minute and hour hands worked. After repeated practice he began to get the hang of it. He couldn't have been happier. After years of embarrassment he was finally able to tell time on a clock with hands. I had been helpful to him and he was appreciative. From that point the resistance lessened markedly and he was engaged in the treatment process.

Careful observation should reveal other cues to pursue. Some youngsters will keep their shoelaces untied, seemingly because it's cool. Questioning may reveal they never learned to tie them properly. Again we are in a position to be helpful. The same holds for ties that are not tied and disheveled hair. Any suggestions offered to enhance the appearance will be readily accepted.

Adolescents often ask how we like their new earring, freshly dyed blue hair, or other outrageous alteration of their appearance. They wonder about our tolerance and are curious about our reaction. It is helpful to comment that the change is striking without passing judgment. Most of these patients are pleased to be noticed. From that point we can proceed to explore the significance of their change in demeanor.

## SOME THERAPY AIDS

For some patients, sitting confined in an office is so uncomfortable that other options should be considered. Going for a walk can be useful in diffusing some of the anxiety. A simple destination such as a park or a snack bar will suffice. While outside, we may notice discarded beer cans, condom wrappers, and cars with missing hood ornaments. All of these provide impetus for discussion. Occasionally we can accompany youngsters to a juvenile courtroom, detention center, or jail. This can prove to be an eye-opener for youth who have denied the possible consequences of their behavior.

An obstacle course or game room can also be helpful to adolescents who are uncomfortable with verbal psychotherapy. This can introduce themes of competence, cooperation, and competition. When resources outside the office are not available, board games may be used. The Talking, Feeling, and Doing Game is particularly useful for young adolescents (Gardner 1973) and the Anger Control Game (Berg 1989) can be adapted for those a little older. Not all games will lead to a productive dialogue. Monopoly, Scrabble, Clue, and cards illustrate games that can inhibit conversation if the youngster gets too absorbed in the activity. Any choice should be influenced by our previous experience with patients. In general, games or other deviations from convention should be viewed as interim measures only. We must continue to encourage disclosure to the extent that it relates to the ongoing activity.

Sometimes I ask adolescents to write a letter to a person they are angry with. This could be a parent, a teacher, or a peer. For example, if a girl were upset with her boyfriend, we might sit down together to express the feelings on paper.

If the youngster's literacy is in question, the format of the exercise is changed. The patients are told that they will role-play dictating a letter while we are the recording secretary at work. As the letter is read back to them, we can note its impact and pursue a discussion.

## A JOB POSSIBILITY

Material possessions are of great interest to adolescents. Electronic gadgetry, CD players, and stylish clothing are often sought-after commodities. Conversations about their predilections will often lead to an exploration of how they might get additional spending money. Many youngsters indicate a willingness to work but believe that they cannot get a job. I use this opportunity to propose that we do something productive in our time together.

Why not conduct a job search right in the office? I take out the help wanted section of the local newspaper and we review the options. Some of the initial jobs available may be in a gas station, fast food restaurant, child care center, or sporting goods store. I encourage the patient to choose one to call as we sit together. They dial the number and suddenly panic! What shall I say? How should I handle this? Their lack of self-confidence and independence becomes readily apparent. I coach them through the process as best I can and the experience is usually positive. On two occasions, youngsters actually landed a job as a result of their telephone contact from my office!

I make it a point to seek my patients' advice every now and then. For instance, I might tell them that one of my children asked for a rap music CD for Christmas. Could they explain the difference between some of the current groups? Most adolescents will readily give this advice and are flattered that I ask. We reduce the one-sided nature of the helping process by supporting the notion that they have something useful to offer us. Patients are far more willing to accept our feedback when they feel we are interested in theirs.

## SHARED EXPERIENCE

Certain less conventional methods for diffusing resistance are worthy of mention. Outdoor trips such as hiking, rafting, or camping out have been used with this population. (Specific programs are discussed later in the book.) Removing youngsters from their daily routine can lift some of the prohibitions on talking openly. I have heard of therapists taking patients to concerts, sporting events, and shopping malls. Going to a thought-provoking movie can stimulate dialogue on any of a number of topics. Youngsters feel safer revealing themselves when they share an experience on an equal footing.

## FROM RESISTANCE TO COOPERATION

As the resistance lessens we can proceed to explore the benefits of change. Those with histories of failure and strained family relations may find it hard to imagine their lives differently. The reality is that they have been unhappy for some time. Their anger and frustration are readily apparent. If this is so, why would they want to perpetuate these patterns?

Their feelings of boredom and need for excitement are raised in this context. We remind them that it takes a great deal of energy to maintain a tough, noncaring facade. "After a while, people just expect you to behave that way. They assume that you won't change and treat you accordingly. To make matters worse, you play right into their hands. You get in trouble and they say, 'I told you so.' It must get stale eventually.

"I'll bet you could really shock people if you wanted to. Sometimes even the smallest changes will be noticed. Imagine how surprised your parents would be if you listened to them once in a while. They might give in more often if they saw you do the same. We've talked about your 'bad attitude' and some of the complaints about you. I know that you feel like everyone is on your case, but life could be easier if you did things a little differently. People might like you better and you would probably get your wish more often. I know this is hard to believe, but you can try it and find out. What have you got to lose?

"Now that we're meeting together we can talk about what is going on in your life. I'd like to improve your situation but will need your help. Sometimes I may ask you about your thoughts while other times we'll actually practice coping with the things that annoy you. I've been through this with many kids like you, and have found that once they make up their minds to work at it, things can change pretty quickly."

Conversations such as these are the forerunners of change. The motivation to work on issues evolves from the youth's increasing comfort with the relationship and the belief that someone is genuinely concerned with his or her happiness and well-being.

# 4

# A Model for Confrontation and Limit Setting

Initially, conduct-disordered youth see little or no need to change. As treatment unfolds, the alliance strengthens, which in turn makes them more receptive to our interventions. Dysfunctional behavior and thought must be challenged at the first opportunity. This is difficult because these adolescents are defensive and invested in maintaining the status quo. The pathway to change is through confrontation, where the bulk of the early therapeutic work is done.

Published clinical descriptions of confrontation range from subtle to forceful. Corwin (1973) describes a process of trying to get the patient's attention and produce a reaction in him. The process is active and direct. Adler and Myerson (1973) suggest that the therapist's expression of anger or other negative feelings communicate that they "mean business." Miller (1986) recommends a noncoercive but firm and empathic approach. Shepherd (1970) takes the less forceful position, that confrontation is best accomplished with a "feather" rather than with a "club." Patients are more likely to accept gentle confrontations, which they perceive as less threatening.

Sifneos (1973) discusses the countertransference problems of therapists who can only be gentle and permissive. He feels that they are struggling with omnipotent fantasies and do their patients a disservice. These overly tolerant therapists may have difficulty asserting any negative feelings directly as a result of either inexperience or fears of rejection. In contrast, Adler and Buie (1973) describe the destructive use of confrontation when it stems from the therapist's anger.

There are risks inherent in coming on too strong. Adolescent patients in particular are sensitive to any challenge to their integrity and are prone to overreact to comments that seem provocative. The process of confrontation must be tailored to the unique needs of the patient.

The Tough Love movement of the 1980s (York et al. 1982) sought to empower parents to take a stand with their defiant youngsters by challenging misbehavior, setting firm limits, and even evicting them if necessary. While successes were reported, in some cases the approach seemed to fuel additional acting out and further polarized fragmented families. This illustrates the difficulties associated with exclusive reliance on forceful confrontation without regard to the youngster's ability to tolerate it. Nonetheless, the Tough Love approach can provide vital support for parents who have lost control of the family situation.

Confrontation serves to call attention to something the patient is not talking about or dealing with effectively (Weiner 1975). The approach can vary from angry and assertive to calm and indirect. During the early stages of treatment, antisocial youngsters deny the seriousness of their problems and adamantly justify their actions. They have difficulty tolerating any challenge to their defensive structure. Consequently, our early interventions should focus on enhancing their thinking and self-reflection rather than provoking any actions that might interfere with the treatment process.

Therapeutic work requires a well-refined skill in presenting emotionally difficult material in a palatable fashion. This entails speaking in conversational tones with a nonjudgmental attitude. Our challenges should reflect curiosity and concern rather than intimidation. As these adolescents are often psychologically brittle and lack adequate resilience, strong confrontations are best reserved until there is an existing therapeutic alliance.

Confrontations should be based primarily on material we have acquired directly, either verbally or nonverbally. The interactions between ourselves and our patients provide ample material to call to their attention. Their basic attitude, style of relating, and overall appearance all provide grist for the mill. The more opinion-laden our observations, the greater the risk of triggering resistance. We must be certain that our confrontations are of potential therapeutic value rather than reactions to our own value system or discomfort.

Therapeutic confrontation differs markedly from what the youngster is accustomed to. These adolescents instinctively question authority and have trouble accepting adults' perceptions of them. They have endless capacities for bickering and can turn the most benign gesture into an affront. As their histories have been replete with unresolved power struggles, they remain poised for conflict.

In therapy we go to great lengths to confront behavior without setting up a win-lose proposition. Youngsters who feel cornered are likely to respond by striking back. Conversely, when a confrontation offers a variety of alternative thoughts and reactions, it becomes more tolerable. Ideally, both the patient and the therapist feel better as the result of an effective intervention. It conveys understanding and enables the patient to save face.

## THE SPECIFICS OF CONFRONTATION

The process begins with identifying feelings or behaviors that the youngster may not wish to address. Their resistance to therapy itself is often the arena in the early meetings. Why are they so convinced that they don't need help? Are they really happy with their current life and circumstance? Our early challenges need to subtly focus on their denial and avoidance. We are not disputing what they say; on the contrary, we are curious about it.

It is important to refrain from comments that are too threatening as these adolescents are easily offended and alienated. As mentioned previously, valuable observations are ones that can be supported by events within the session. The adolescent's approach to us, expectations about the relationship, attitude about treatment, and spontaneous comments are all useful. Speculating about the underlying significance of behavior should be approached cautiously unless we are asked. Although we might be privy to personal information about the adolescent (e.g., their sexuality or early history of abuse), raising it prematurely can result in defiance, indignation, or even refusal to attend further sessions.

The decision about what to confront should be governed in part by the solidity of the therapeutic relationship. The more stable the alliance, the more likely the patient is to benefit from the confrontation. Meier and Davis (1993) suggest that therapists should confront only as much as they have supported.

It has been said that "we give with one hand and take with the other." I make it a point to balance negative feedback with affirmative remarks. For example, I might tell a youngster how much I appreciate her dry sense of humor and quick wit before challenging her stubborn nature. When she sees that I appreciate and respect certain aspects of her personality, she is more likely to tolerate my commentary on her offensive traits. The goal of challenging these adolescents is to increase self-awareness and hopefully inspire a willingness to change. This is a slow and arduous process requiring tact and patience.

We must always be aware of the amount and type of discomfort the patient triggers in us. Those adolescents who make us uncomfortable likely have a similar effect on their parents, teachers, and other adults. By verbalizing these feelings directly to the adolescent, we increase their insight and present a model of forthrightness. It is striking how many antisocial youngsters lack any awareness of their impact on others. As they come to grasp not only the intended but the unintended consequences of their behavior, many are more receptive to change. After all, we know how crucial it is to them to feel in charge of themselves and their actions.

Some therapists are reluctant to confront for fear of strong reactions, criticism, or even premature termination. If this is the case, the therapist must address the relevant issues that impair his or her effectiveness. Peer supervision and personal psychotherapy can be particularly helpful in this regard. If confrontation remains intolerable despite this, one must question their suitability for working with this population.

An appropriate confrontation, comfortably and reasonably stated, serves only to gain respect, not lose it. We must strike a balance between allowing for a comfortable relationship and creating sufficient tension to foster meaningful interchanges. This process requires monitoring the patient's anxiety level to be certain that particular confrontations are tolerable.

Confrontations should be straightforward and presented without technical jargon. Patients should feel that we are interested in their well-being and their heightened self-awareness. Our aim is to strengthen the alliance, not to arbitrarily provoke authority conflicts. Confrontations should be just as routine as our questions. We might simply tell a youngster that his or her bravado makes us uncomfortable. This type of descriptive, nonjudgmental comment opens the door for dialogue. We lay the groundwork further by displaying ongoing curiosity about their reactions to our feedback. Any genuine, appropriate expression of their feelings is acceptable.

## SOME MINIMAL EXPECTATIONS

We must insist on regular attendance to sessions and tell adolescents that they are expected to come "straight," not drunk or high. Over the years I have had youngsters arrive in this condition. They deny it, of course, even when their altered state is obvious, offering a variety of excuses ranging from "someone spilled beer on me" to "my pupils are just dilated because I was looking at the sun too long." When their condition is apparent, I refuse to continue the session. They are usually shocked by my action and attempt to bargain. "What am I supposed to do for the next forty minutes?" "I don't have a ride home." "What will I tell my mother when I come out to the waiting room?" "Can't I just stay and talk?" "If you give me a chance, you'll see that I'm really okay." I have learned to stand firm about concluding the session. Adolescents must learn to take the treatment process seriously.

Some youngsters have actually brought marijuana, stolen goods, or other contraband to a session. Ostensibly, they just want to show me their new possession. In reality they are testing the boundaries of the relationship. Once they have displayed their possessions, I feel forced to challenge their action. They have put me in a difficult position and I tell them that. To simply observe without comment is to condone their wrongdoing. Consequently I remind them that if they bring something illegal to my office, I assume they are looking for a reaction and I will certainly confiscate it. Any additional consequences need to be decided on a case-by-case basis.

## UNNECESSARY CONFRONTATIONS

During one of my workshops several years ago, a high school guidance counselor expressed his discomfort with the fashion choices of many teenagers. He was distressed by some of their wild T-shirts, jeans that were torn and frayed, and boys who wore earrings. He wondered how he might challenge them and get them to conform.

Unfortunately, he seemed to have reached an impasse. His inability to tolerate the idiosyncrasies of the students in his school was hampering his counseling skills and rapport with students. I felt that he faced a difficult choice. He either had to find a way to work through some of his own discomfort or choose another population to work with.

Certain occurrences during therapy do not necessitate confrontation. Adolescents who rely heavily on jargon and use some profanity should not always be taken to task. Their speech, appearance, and style of relating are integrally involved with their identity. It is best to accept them initially as they are and refrain from confrontation unless they are being highly offensive and disrespectful. As the alliance strengthens, their provocative language often diminishes. If not, ample opportunities arise to call attention to distressing aspects of their behavior.

Sometimes patients intentionally create minor annoyances during a session. These may include aiming a rubber band slingshot at the therapist, making paper airplanes, or attempting to toss things into the wastebasket from a distance. These, of course, are tests of our resolve and should be dealt with accordingly. Challenging these disruptive actions may serve to fuel them, thus creating a contest between patient and therapist. Unless extreme, we would do well simply to ignore such behavior, conveying our expectation that they can control their own actions without our intervention. It is important to demonstrate that we are neither intimidated nor compelled to discipline them. Most often the provocative behavior dissipates rapidly, that is, they put down the rubber band or simply pick up the trash that has missed the wastebasket.

Some time ago a youngster accidentally shot me with a rubber band and knocked off my glasses. His reaction was instructive. Fearing I was hurt, he came over to me quickly, attempting to be of help. "Are you okay, Doc? I really didn't mean to do that. Don't worry, if they're broken, I'll replace them!" Clearly it was not his intention to hurt me and he had some capacity for remorse. He had intended only to check out my reaction when provoked.

## CHALLENGING THE DEFENSIVE STRUCTURE

Oppositional defiant and conduct-disordered youth are instinctively defensive. They rely heavily on denial, avoidance, rationalization, isolation of affect, and projection. Consequently they have great difficulty accepting any confrontation that could perforate their defensive structure. We must find ways to introduce them comfortably to this process. As we get to know one another, I often ask youngsters if they want me to be really forthright with them and if they can "take it." Most accept this challenge and agree that, although the truth is painful at times, they are usually better off knowing it. I prefer to begin with the most obvious observations.

At times youngsters arrive looking rather haggard, tired, irritated, or sad. When questioned, they state adamantly that they feel fine and nothing is bothering them. This discrepancy should be brought to their attention. Appearances rarely lie.

Certain adolescents will insist that they would be happy if everyone would just leave them alone. They state adamantly that they "don't care about anything" as tears well up in their eyes. When their pain is so close to the surface, the therapist again addresses the discrepancy between their words and appearance, but refrains from demanding that they open up before they feel ready.

Despite emerging signs of vulnerability, patients often cling steadfastly to their tough image. While acknowledging their bravado, it behooves us to explore what "tough" really means to them. Adolescents usually describe it in terms of being fearless or preventing others from taking advantage of them. I like to point out that they really are tough in many ways, but pain and fear are natural parts of being human. People can become hardened and deadened as a result of their experiences, but there is a price attached. The more we disguise ourselves and our pain and fears, the less people can get to know us. This can lead to feeling really lonely and isolated. Sometimes it takes a lot of guts to admit that something upsets us and that our lives are unhappy. I may ask them, "Are you strong enough to face the truth about what's going on inside you?"

By nature, adolescents are fairly self-absorbed. They are quite preoccupied with the details of their lives and at times give little thought to the lives of others. This must be challenged repeatedly as situations arise. When they place the blame for their behavior outside themselves, we must call attention to their role in both their difficulties and their successes. This is best accomplished through an active curiosity.

A youngster who constantly argues with his teacher

might be confronted by saying, "You know, you're always telling me about what a jerk Ms. Smith is, yet it's hard for me to believe that all of the disagreements are her fault. Usually both people have at least some part in the problem. Take a minute and think hard. What is there about your behavior that might provoke her anger?" Usually the youngster will reluctantly come up with something. If they totally deny any responsibility, then we should offer some possibilities. "Maybe when you get that stubborn and defiant attitude you've described, your teacher feels totally frustrated and under attack. After all, she's got a right to defend herself too. Have you ever thought about her side of things and what she might feel?"

Flanagan and Flanagan (1995) describe an interesting variation on increasing adolescents' self-awareness. Their approach involves wagering on new cognitions, such as telling the youngster, "I bet you can't think of any other explanations of why your teacher might have bugged you yesterday." This creates the opportunity to practice understanding someone else's motivation and diffuses some of the anger associated with the situation.

Youngsters' overall views of the world around them provide useful information. I like to ask some philosophical questions to get at this. "Are people basically good or bad?" "Is life fair?" "Are you optimistic about the future?" As these issues are discussed, valuable insights into their thought processes are revealed. Any negative interpretation of events or jaundiced views of life should be challenged. We must help our patients come to look objectively at the world around them and feel that they have some control over their own destiny.

## BETWEEN PATIENT AND THERAPIST

It is reasonable to expect that adolescents will be increasingly honest with you as the relationship evolves. Any signs of deceit, manipulation, or even unintentional distortions of situations should be brought to their awareness. On occasion I have had youngsters ask me to sign a note authorizing them to get out of school using some bogus excuse. I always want to know the reasons behind their doing this. Surely they must know that I will see through their attempt. The emphasis of the confrontation is placed on the patients' behavior rather than their character or worth. The reality is that our feelings also may be bruised, and we want to show them that they have an impact on us.

Any violations of trust should be called to their attention. We must explore their difficulty with closeness and their cynicism about relationships in general. Perhaps they are trying to drive us away by being overly demanding and entitled. Despite this, we make it clear that our concern about them is unwavering. Prior disappointments by significant others as well as the patient's distancing in current relationships must be confronted. Challenge them to consider what would happen if they really let someone get to know them.

## SOME ANTICIPATED CONFRONTATIONS

Certain predictable situations that recur during therapy sessions warrant immediate attention. Any blatant contradictions by an adolescent are pointed out in a nonjudgmental fashion. Differences between words and behavior are particularly rich sources of therapeutic material. Consider, for example, the patient who states that he is giving up alcohol and during the following session casually mentions that he got drunk last weekend. This must be challenged. Another example would be the youngster who speaks with conviction about doing well in school during the new marking period, yet continues to cut class and avoid doing homework. If their proclamations of self-improvement have evolved spontaneously, we must hold adolescents accountable for their words. How can they expect anyone to take them seriously if they cannot trust themselves to follow through?

It is a particularly useful technique to frame battles as occurring within the adolescent, rather than against someone else. When stripped of their ability to project blame, they can begin to take responsibility for what happens to them. This theme must be repeated throughout the treatment.

## CHALLENGING OPPOSITIONAL AND ANTISOCIAL BEHAVIOR

I like to talk to patients about the compelling and addictive nature of trouble. Here's how I usually present it. "Each time you get away with something, the temptation to do it again increases. I'll bet you love that feeling of excitement that comes over you just before you take a risk and then enjoy the satisfaction and relief afterward. After a while, you start to feel like you have to seek trouble just to keep your life interesting. It's similar to the high from drugs and drinking. Addicts always say that they could quit if they wanted to, yet it never seems to happen. Do you think that you could totally stop breaking rules if you chose to? Most kids say they could, but they keep right on doing it. How strong is the temptation for you?

"You've talked to me about the pleasure you get from beating the system. I can see that you've come to just assume that you'll get into trouble. Your parents, teachers, and friends also expect this, and you sure don't let them down. The problem is that you no longer have a mind of your own. You've become a trouble junkie. Anytime your friends are up to no good, they call you immediately. I guess you see that as being cool or tough, but I think you're a chicken in some ways. You've forgotten how to say no. Sometimes it takes guts to refuse to go along with the crowd."

Adolescents don't like this conversation but it provokes an immediate response. They generally see themselves as fiercely independent and strive to defend their actions. I encourage them to show me that they have some willpower and can think for themselves. They, of course, say that I'm trying to trick them into behaving. Nevertheless, they often come to the following meeting and proudly tell me how they resisted temptation just to prove me wrong. I see this as confrontation in a spirit of good will.

Our interventions are not always dramatic. There is much to be gained from confronting youngsters on seemingly trivial matters. Arriving five minutes late, wearing headphones, or persistent small talk can all become therapeutic opportunities. Adolescents often enjoy lively bickering despite their protests to the contrary. When we identify small examples of unacceptable behavior and hone in on them, we are allowing for a mildly heated but less threatening interchange. This process desensitizes the youngster to more forceful challenges and may prevent extreme reactions in the future. They come to see confrontation as an integral part of the relationship.

## LIMIT SETTING

Oppositional defiant and conduct-disordered adolescents have tremendous difficulty accepting limits. They routinely stretch rules and react negatively to any imposition of authority. Their lack of self-control fuels much of their deviant behavior. Friedman (1973) emphasizes the need for the therapist to compensate when there have been parental deficiencies in limit setting. At times we must take a position in opposition to the youngster's wishes or actions. To develop self-control, an adolescent must observe it in others in the surrounding environment and internalize it. The therapist must demonstrate that genuine concern and limit setting go hand in hand.

We must protect both the youngster and others from his destructive impulses. A loss of control can be scary and dangerous to all parties involved. In my inpatient work I have observed adolescents lose their capacity to reason and end up reacting violently against staff, peers, or themselves. Once a youngster has lost control, there is no verbal intervention sufficient to interrupt the sequence. It often becomes necessary to restrain or isolate them until they can settle down.

The challenge is to prevent adolescents from reaching the point of no return. This is best accomplished by anticipating the need for limits and applying them judiciously. In treatment we carefully monitor to determine which of the patient's requests or actions require an intervention. We also watch for signs of escalating emotions, hyperreactivity, and defensive posturing. Techniques to diffuse are central to this work.

Limits can be expressed in many ways. Verbal limits are almost always preferable to physical ones. The therapist states that an action or request is unacceptable and offers to explain why. Patients are then encouraged to express any negative feelings they might have in order to circumvent inappropriate discharges of anger. Physical limits should be imposed only when absolutely necessary. Should a youngster begin to deface property in our office or to aggress against us directly, we are forced to respond immediately. When uncertain about imposing physical restraints, do not attempt to do so. Walk out of the office or proceed to employ a symbolic limit. This might involve picking up a telephone to call for help or ringing a loud buzzer that signals distress. Actions such as these may startle the youngster into compliance. We must be certain that we can enforce a limit prior to setting it.

## Case Example

> While I was working in a day treatment center early in my career, a 12-year-old boy challenged my resolve. He was extremely active, agitated, and disruptive during a session. I insisted that he cease his actions or be escorted out of my office to cool off. He was enraged and threatened to jump from my window. Before I could react, he ran to the window, opened it, and attempted to escape. Since I took him

seriously, I raced there and grabbed him to prevent his dangerous exit. He screamed at me to get my hands off him so he could jump. I refused to let go and held on tightly. He told me that he hated me and uttered a few other choice words. I insisted that I was holding him because I cared and wouldn't let him hurt himself. "No, you don't," he replied, "you're just like everyone else." By this point I felt that I had to restrain him until he could assure me by climbing down from the window ledge. We struggled for almost a half hour as I held onto him. Eventually he settled down and I could relax my grip. He was teary and we were both exhausted. We had survived a difficult time together and the experience was the source of many subsequent discussions that proved extremely fruitful.

The risk involved with setting a firm limit is that the patient may refuse to continue in treatment afterward. Alternatively, leaving dangerous behavior unchallenged is unsafe and jeopardizes the therapy process. Thus it is always necessary to stand firm within the context of the session.

The rationale for limits should be discussed at the first available opportunity. Try and point out that we are siding with the patient's own healthier side and striving to uphold his or her best interests. Limits will be imposed when we feel that there are no other options. If possible, involve patients in the process. What do they feel the limits should be? Can they control themselves so that we don't have to intervene?

I like to remind youngsters that they have much more power than they realize. The more responsibly they behave, the less need there is for control by others. For example: "If you don't like being hassled about skipping school, you can get people off your case by attending regularly. There is always a choice open to you!"

## A CLOSE CALL

The scariest event of my career occurred early in my outpatient practice. It serves to illustrate both the potential danger of unchecked behavior and a spontaneous and less than optimal approach to limit setting in a crisis situation.

I had been seeing a 16-year-old boy for several weeks in individual and family therapy. He had initially been referred to me because of school difficulties, acting-out behavior, and aggression. He was guarded and cynical about the therapy process. This young man experienced frequent conflict with his parents, particularly his stepfather, who was in law enforcement. Many of their arguments seemed to center around control issues.

Shortly after we had begun one of our individual sessions, he reached into his book bag, took out his stepfather's gun, and pointed it at me. "When I get home tonight, I'm going to blow my father's brains out," he stated angrily. Struggling to contain my own anxiety, I thought quickly about what might help this young man and ensure my own safety simultaneously. A discussion of his anger at his father might be useful, but was risky as he was holding an ostensibly loaded gun. I felt that making this a control issue by demanding the gun might exacerbate the situation. I chose a more tempered approach that had served me well in the past.

I shared how anxious I was knowing he had a gun and told him that I could not continue the session under those circumstances. At that point I offered what I felt were the only alternatives and asked for his reaction. The first was to simply notify the police and have them take appropriate action. He was adamant in his rejection of this idea. My second suggestion involved calling his stepfather, letting him know what was happening, and asking him to come by and pick up his gun, which I would be holding onto for him. This proposal was also unacceptable, although he was less adamant in his resistance. I asked if he had any better ideas but he just shrugged. Finally I stated that if these options were unacceptable, my only other thought was to keep the gun myself for safekeeping until we could figure out what should be done. Thankfully, this was an acceptable alternative. He handed me the gun and I placed it carefully in my desk drawer.

I kept the gun in my possession until the next meeting. He arrived cheerfully and began making small talk. I had expected that he might raise the looming issue but my hopes faded quickly. That put the onus on me, but this time I was prepared. I told him I had thought about how to resolve this situation and had come up with a good idea. During our upcoming family session I would tell his parents what had happened, emphasizing his cooperation and good judgment in turning the gun over to me. He reluctantly agreed to go along with my suggestion.

When the family arrived, I wasted no time in sharing the incident as we had planned. His mother burst into tears, while his father got a look of shock and consternation on his face. He asked for the gun and proceeded to unload several bullets from the chamber!

"Well, I guess this is a good outcome," the stepfather remarked.

"It sure is," I replied with a sigh of relief. The parents were able to give their son some support for turning in the weapon on his own and the meeting went on to be constructive in many ways. Therapy proceeded reasonably well from that point.

I must confess that if this gun episode were to occur again, I would handle it very differently. Rather than keep the gun, I would notify the police and the parents immediately. Although this might contaminate the therapeutic relationship, I would first attend to the safety of myself and the patient's potential victim. In retrospect, my actions were impulsive and potentially dangerous, but were prompted by the belief that he would not have brought the gun to the session if he had truly intended to use it. Indeed, he was inviting me to set limits for him.

Although this event was quite extreme, it underscores the need for preparedness. Youngsters may show up with knives, baseball bats, or other weapons from time to time. We must have a repertoire of alternatives available to deter their actions, allowing them to save face and preserve their self-respect if possible. It is always best to be prepared for the unexpected.

# 5

# The Role of Therapist Self-Disclosure

The area of self-disclosure has received little attention in clinical work with behaviorally disordered youth. In general, there is a wide range of opinion concerning the appropriate amount of self-disclosure in treatment. Encounter group leaders suggest extreme amounts, while traditional psychoanalysts espouse almost none (Flaherty 1979). A therapist sharing personal information and feelings affects patients in a range of ways, varying from productive to disruptive. I see self-disclosure as a potentially powerful agent of change. An elaboration of this process as a therapeutic tool should clarify how and why to use it.

Orlinsky and Howard (1978) suggest that the relationship bond between client and counselor exerts a greater role in the process of change than do therapeutic techniques. Self-disclosure should be an integral part of any treatment process based on mutuality. Carter and Motta (1988) found that patients saw their therapists as more trustworthy when they were both informal and open. This is particularly applicable to an adolescent population.

My experience has been that most youngsters benefit from some degree of therapist disclosure when appropriate to their needs and emotional state. Weiner (1972) states that when an adolescent wants to see us as real people, we should accommodate their wish for historical information. Many of the patients we deal with have never had an intimate relationship based on trust. They have become self-protective and suspicious of the motives of others. The result is a reluctance to share any personal information that might cast them in a negative light. Appropriate self-disclosure can serve as a model for a mature adult and gives patients permission to share their own fallibilities.

Most training programs devote little attention to the role of personal variables in the treatment process. This may leave us ill-equipped to deal with the unique demands of this population. Adolescent work demands some degree of self-comfort and an ability to understand the patient's experience. Lewis (1978) feels that therapist empathy emerges from the recollection of personal experiences that relate to the patient's experiences. The reexperience of the associated emotions enables us to convey compassion and understanding. Needless to say, the therapist must have worked through his own adolescent developmental issues to minimize potential interference.

The therapist's personality style influences the process significantly. Our approach to anger, threats, and self-assertion will be quickly communicated as our patients challenge us. We must be sufficiently comfortable with ourselves to take an active and directive role in treatment. This often means foregoing neutrality in order to reveal our position on pertinent issues. Our therapeutic stance should be an accurate reflection of who we are. Disturbed adolescents need to borrow from our sense of self to develop their own.

A question often arises about exactly what should be shared with an adolescent. As a rule of thumb, the patient's ability to benefit from a disclosure should govern both the nature and the content. The strength of the therapeutic alliance bears directly on the youngster's ability to tolerate increasing levels of intimacy. Andersen and Andersen (1989) surveyed counselors on their relative comfort with different levels of disclosure. Expressions of positive affect toward the client were most frequently cited as the preferred disclosure. Imagery and metaphors, although less personal, were also employed often. Disclosures revealing either the therapist's attitude or a personal weakness were the areas of greatest discomfort.

I feel that certain personal information should be revealed in response to direct questioning. Queries about our training, age, or marital and family status reflect legitimate curiosity and should be responded to accordingly. Given our desire to foster an atmosphere of sharing, any reluctance to do so on our part may give a mixed message to these youngsters. On the other hand, before volunteering information spontaneously, we should consider the potential impact.

Gorkin (1987) points out that therapist disclosure can be a burden at times. Certain patients prefer that their therapist remain anonymous to ensure their own emotional safety. Those who have been abandoned, abused, or neglected might feel more comfortable getting personal at their own pace. On the other extreme are patients who ask questions that are clearly intrusive or inappropriate. This requires us to share our discomfort, set appropriate limits, and inquire why they are curious. Are they simply trying to make us uncomfortable, or do they lack any sense of personal boundaries?

In my experience, adolescents have expressed repeated interest in certain themes. They often wonder how we would handle misbehavior or wrongdoing in our children since they may lack appropriate role models. The underlying wish is for an indirect expression of limits and parental authority. I often reflect such questions back to the patient, inquiring what they would do if they were the parent. The ensuing dialogue is usually productive.

Frequently this population puts us on the spot by asking us if we have ever smoked pot or engaged in any other illicit activity. Caution is in order here. Would it be useful for the youngster to have this information? Does the question reflect an evolving trust or is it a manifestation of continued resistance? I am reluctant to answer this directly but acknowledge that I know how it feels to experiment with breaking rules. Sometimes I will tell them that I went to school in the '60s and early '70s, an era of protest. The reference seems to satisfy them. As long as they see that we are genuine and avoid proselytizing, they will accept the limits of our disclosure.

Other inquiries will be less threatening and are suggestive of a genuine curiosity. I have had many patients ask me why I have chosen to work with kids like them. They wonder what it takes to become a psychotherapist and are interested in how much money we make. I consider this a legitimate question and try to provide helpful information without disclosing specifics. Troubled youngsters often feel that their experiences could be helpful to others and wonder if they could do this type of work. Other questions I have been asked include: "How old were you the first time you had sex?" "What kind of car do you drive?" "Were you a good student when you were my age?" Again, our responses should be governed by the basis for the youngster's inquiries and the potential usefulness of our answers.

Certain youngsters are curious about our perceptions of themselves or their family. They might ask what we think causes their parent to drink, neglect them, or behave punitively. While this may be difficult to approach, it is potentially useful. Their hope is that we will favor them and condemn their parents. The reality is that family problems are multidetermined and each member must reflect on his or her own contribution. Our answers to these questions may help them to see that we can be objective and nonjudgmental. We may be their only link to a realistic perspective.

Generally, adolescents prefer not to hear about our personal idiosyncrasies. It is rarely helpful to them and places an unnecessary burden on the therapeutic relationship. Our political and religious beliefs can also be potentially disruptive. We must be especially careful about disclosing information not relevant to their own difficulties.

Despite attempts to be reasonably open, some adolescents may never ask us personal questions. I am always curious about why this is the case. When queried, these patients offer some interesting explanations. Some volunteer that their parents had always told them it was none of their business when they sought information.

Others just assumed that we would not answer the questions. In either case, when given the opportunity, many will raise appropriate questions. Some will decline the offer and, of course, their wish must be respected.

## REACTIONS TO HOW WE COME ACROSS

Adolescents will sometimes comment on our appearance, wondering why we look sad, tired, sick, or otherwise distracted. If their observations are accurate, we need to acknowledge their concern and decide whether sharing what's going on will benefit the relationship. When done at the right time in the right way, an exposure of vulnerability can foster trust, empathy, and, ultimately, the therapeutic alliance. Bear in mind that adolescents may assume that our moods are a rejection of them in the absence of evidence to the contrary. Conversely, if an adolescent's comment is clearly unrelated to our physical or emotional state, we must explore the significance. Why might the youngster assume we are tired or otherwise preoccupied? Perhaps it relates to something going on with themselves or in their own family.

At times events occur in our lives that may interfere with the effectiveness of our work. Serious illness, death of a loved one, or even divorce may be nearly impossible to conceal before they are worked through. This requires a difficult decision on our part. Will sharing our feelings about the experience enhance the relationship or burden the patient?

My most poignant experience with self-disclosure

occurred a number of years ago in a rather unexpected situation. I had been seeing a mildly depressed, oppositional defiant, 17-year-old girl for several weeks. We had not made much headway toward establishing an alliance. During that time my mother died rather suddenly and I left town for a week to deal with the tragedy. My patients were informed that there was a family emergency and the week's appointments were canceled. I returned to work continuing to struggle with the enormity of my experience. During the first session after my return, my young patient commented that I looked very sad and concluded that something must be wrong. It seemed unfair to deny my emotional state so I proceeded to acknowledge what had happened. She looked at me knowingly and compassionately and said, "I don't know how you can expect to talk about me when all this has gone on with you." Her point was well taken.

We proceeded to discuss my ordeal a bit more and I saw a side of her that had not been revealed previously. She was sensitive, sympathetic, and quite capable of relating to difficult and painful issues. Toward the end of our meeting, she told me that she knew exactly how I felt. She painfully recalled the loss of her grandmother who was "the only person who ever really loved me." Following this session, our relationship was greatly strengthened. She was far more willing to disclose difficult personal material and seemed much more accepting of my interventions.

Without question, exposing our vulnerability can evoke strong feelings in the patient. While my experience with loss was a discretionary disclosure, some instances are obvious and impossible to avoid. Early in my career

I broke my leg skiing and spent six weeks in a cast. I vividly recall the reaction of my adolescent group upon seeing me for the first time. Initially there was nervous laughter and comments about my helplessness. One youngster actually grabbed my crutches and ran out of the office with them. I did not respond and he returned shortly.

The discomfort quickly gave way to curiosity about how it felt to break a leg. I shared how painful it was with the group and told them about lying in the snow and waiting for help. They were fascinated by my account and wanted to know more. Was I afraid? Did I cry? How did it happen? Did people really come to help out? It was clear that many issues lay under their questions. They were grappling with my vulnerability and the related dependency issues. We spent most of the session talking about how it felt to be scared, helpless, and uncertain about an outcome. Some of the youngsters were able to share their own experiences and a productive discussion ensued. Clearly the catalyst was the self-disclosure around my injury that led to a focus on the group's curiosity and fears. I felt it was important for the adolescents to see me model the behavior I was seeking in them.

Certain other instances necessitate disclosure and discussion. Pregnancy is a specific event that breaks the anonymity of the therapist (Flaherty 1979). Physical disabilities that are conspicuous should also be discussed. We must assume that any observable characteristic, surgery, speech impediment, or even habit affects the therapeutic relationship. Our willingness to raise and explore the obvious can lead to an enhanced alliance based on mutual disclosure.

## THE FEELINGS ADOLESCENTS EVOKE

Over the course of time, deviant adolescents will evoke a wide range of emotions in us. The impact of their behavior and experiences on us is an important part of the work. Not only must we be aware of the positive or negative feelings they generate, we must determine which of our reactions to share and how. Generally, the more tentative the relationship is, the greater the need for tact in disclosure. A solid therapeutic alliance permits more open discussion; however, objective observations are usually more readily accepted than inferences about their emotional state.

Acting-out behavior is often more amenable to confrontation than either passivity or shyness. The actively provocative, recalcitrant patient mobilizes us and, in effect, forces us to deal with the presenting behavior. Passive and quiet patients often bring up more subtle feelings in us. They may lessen our spontaneity or, worse yet, lull us into complacency.

### Case Example

David was an 18-year-old mildly depressed, conduct-disordered young man I saw several years ago. He was often in fights and had great difficulty accepting authority. David's affect was flat; he was guarded and quite detached. He had no major objection to coming to therapy, but our conversations rarely deviated from the mundane. Therapy was moving rather slowly.

After several sessions I found myself becoming

increasingly aware of the difficulty I had focusing on this young man during our meetings. In fact, I was sleepy and struggled to keep my eyes open. Things had reached the point where I dreaded the sessions and actually experienced an anticipatory drowsiness. Something had to give.

I gave the matter considerable thought and could not avoid the conclusion that I found this young man boring. I imagined that he was, at the very least, aware of my inattentiveness and perhaps even resentful. The only approach that I felt would be useful to both of us was to share what I was feeling.

At the start of one of our sessions, I said something like this: "David, this is very hard for me to tell you but I feel that I must. You may have noticed that I seem sleepy at times. To be truthful, I often find you boring and just don't know how to be of help!"

David was silent for a moment. Then he burst into tears, sobbing that he had always known this, but no one had ever told him directly. He sadly recalled his childhood memories of trying to talk to his father and having him fall asleep during the conversation. "Even my dog would walk away when I tried to be friendly," he added. His history was filled with recollections of people turning off to him. I felt terrible as this young man opened up to me. There I was behaving in the same rejecting fashion that was so familiar to him. I shared this connection and the fact that I felt bad, but told him that he seemed so much more real to me now that he had shared some genuine feelings. Following this session, our work together progressed rapidly as I was more tuned in and he was more receptive to feedback and strategies for change. I shudder to think what would have happened if I had not faced up to what was going on with me.

Ferenczi (1955) points out that when a therapist cannot tolerate certain features of a patient, the only useful approach is to admit and discuss the feelings. These situations are likely to arise frequently in our work with antisocial youth. Their lack of morality often challenges our value system and may evoke contempt for their actions. While we may not express our disdain directly, it often gets conveyed subtly in our reactions. Consequently, we must be able to share our discomfort without rejecting the patient. As an example, consider a youngster who recalls having snatched a purse from an elderly woman. Rather than labeling it a despicable act, we might comment that personally we couldn't imagine doing something like that, or acknowledge our shock and rage if that happened to someone close to us.

Certain other characteristics are often difficult to tolerate. Youngsters who are bigoted, abusive toward others, or contemptuous of the treatment process often evoke strong countertransference reactions in therapists. In all instances we must find a way to deal with our own feelings and remain objective toward the patient. Sometimes this might necessitate our own psychotherapy or peer supervision. It is extremely difficult to work with this population in isolation.

Youngsters with lengthy histories of conflict can often discern our discomfort or a judgmental stance. Ultimately one must develop a thick skin and learn to keep the long-term goals in mind. In a sense, the therapist must learn to delay gratification in the same way that the patient is expected to. Many fluctuations and disappointments are likely during the course of treatment.

## THE BOUNDARIES OF TREATMENT

At times these patients will elicit strong compassionate feelings in us. When one considers their feelings of rejection and some of their histories of neglect and abuse, this is not surprising. We may find ourselves wanting to nurture them and somehow help to satisfy their needs to compensate for their losses. The question is how to display concern and caring without contaminating the therapeutic relationship. Any physical expression of affection is risky. Adolescents are highly sexualized and prone to misinterpret or abuse our overtures.

Several years ago I was working with a group of early adolescent boys on an inpatient psychiatric unit. They were assigned to a particular nurse who was responsible for their daily care. This woman was competent, compassionate, and nurturing. She informed the group that if they ever felt they needed a hug, they should just stop by and ask. On one occasion I overheard the boys talking to one another in their room. "I'm going to go to the nurses' station and get me some," a 13-year-old joked. He proceeded to his destination and received a big hug from his well-meaning caretaker. I watched as he quickly returned to his room grinning and flaunting his erection. Therein lies the risk of misinterpretation and overstimulation. My feeling is that we do better to comfort with our words rather than our actions. It has served me well over the years.

Adolescents may dress and act seductively at times. They may arrive in our office scantily clothed and determined to gain our attention. This is not easily ignored but must be approached judiciously. Pretending we don't notice only reflects our discomfort with the situation or, worse yet, escalates the provocative behavior. This behavior must be dealt with directly and quickly. My approach has been to hold up a mirror to the youngster, that is, to simply describe my observation without judgment or interpretation. I might comment to a young lady that her blouse is unbuttoned, revealing her breasts. Usually this leads to an apologetic or explanatory response without creating excess uneasiness in the patient. The issue has been addressed and is less likely to recur. More often than not, our patients could not tolerate an exploration of the sexualized aspects of the relationship.

## CONTACTS OUTSIDE THE OFFICE

Theoretically, the therapist–patient relationship should be confined to the office. In reality, events frequently arise that necessitate our continued contact in a different setting. Consider a youngster who is placed in a detention center, psychiatric facility, or drug treatment center. When possible, we should maintain our association for the sake of continuity and effective treatment. In most cases we certainly don't want to convey the message that if their behavior worsens, our relationship ends. I have almost always felt welcomed when visiting a patient in a treatment facility. They view me as their link with the outside world and readily share their experiences. These frequently include their complaints about the program and assurances to me that they will do much better after discharge. The one exception would be when I hospitalize a youngster against his will. Then I must first deal with their associated anger before returning to the business of the relationship. In all cases I directly express my feelings about why the placement was indicated and propose specific goals for discharge.

On occasion we encounter our patients in a more relaxed setting. Shopping malls, restaurants, and movie theaters are some of the possibilities. If the youngster sees and approaches me first, I am always friendly and willing to chat briefly. Should I see the youngster when they are unaware of my presence, I will not approach them. I feel respectful of their boundaries and do not wish to create unnecessary discomfort. Occasionally our eyes will meet, but I leave the choice to them. In either case, I always raise the chance encounter in our next therapy session. If they have seen me with my children, it arouses many feelings of curiosity and necessitates certain disclosures. I always try to be mindful of the patient's needs.

Every so often a youngster will invite me to attend an event in their life. Over the years these have included graduations, plays, games, funerals, and orchestra recitals. This clearly is flattering and reflects a strengthening alliance. I am always open to the possibility but feel it necessary to discuss their motives first. If they are legitimate and time permits, I attend. I have yet to regret such an action.

When I doubt the therapeutic value of participating in an outside event or cannot attend, I often ask the youngster to bring me pictures or a tape. This facilitates discussion and provides me with the indirect opportunity to share in their lives. I believe that behavior-disordered adolescents need the experience of a real relationship to facilitate the process of change.

## SOME PERSONAL BOUNDARIES

Therapists need a certain amount of distance to insulate themselves from intrusions into their personal life. When I was starting out in the field, I often gave patients my home telephone number so they could call me if needed. My rescue fantasies were strong and my personal boundaries were weak. I soon learned why this was contraindicated. One Saturday night about 2:00 A.M. I was startled by the ring of my telephone. It was an adolescent female I was treating, so I immediately feared for her safety. She proceeded to explain that she was having trouble sleeping that night and just felt like talking. After all, I had told her to telephone if she needed me! From that point on, my home number has been unpublished. I tell patients that if they need to reach me they can simply leave a message with my answering service. I check it regularly and return important calls within a few hours.

I feel equally strong about giving out my home address. Adolescents are prone toward impulsive behavior and I certainly would not want to encourage any unexpected visits. The situation is more complicated if you see patients in a home office. Clearly the issue of boundaries must be dealt with early on in the treatment. Questions continually arise about how much personal information a youngster can handle and what are our own needs for privacy.

## THE RISKS OF SELF-DISCLOSURE

Sharing personal material is not without its risks. While the patient can safely assume that the therapist will uphold the bond of confidentiality, the therapist must be cognizant of information leaks. Antisocial youth will be tempted to use personal information to their advantage. For example, an adolescent might tell his parents that the therapist confessed to getting drunk when he was in high school. This could be done to justify his actions or weaken the therapist's credibility.

In general, we should not share any personal experiences that we do not want repeated. Parents may misinterpret the motive for the disclosure or disapprove of the therapist's actions. When the issues revolve around religious beliefs or personal values, it gets even more complicated. This raises questions about the extent to which a therapist should either affirm or refute a family's beliefs. It is usually safer to remain neutral on these sensitive issues. The exception would be a situation in which the belief system is pathological and interferes with the developmental tasks of adolescence.

When a therapist's disclosure has been repeated outside the session, the event must be explored. Why did the youngster take such an action? How does he or she think it made the therapist feel? The implications for the dyadic relationship are significant. Technically, a patient sharing material from an individual session is not breaching confidence. If the disclosure was unintentional, it is certainly understandable. Otherwise, the motives should be interpreted as a statement about the nature of the therapeutic alliance.


## AS TERMINATION NEARS

The amount of self-disclosure generally increases with the closeness of the therapeutic relationship. As patient and therapist finally grow comfortable with one another, termination must be considered. Adolescents must be encouraged to separate from the treatment process when sufficient progress has occurred. We do not want to foster unnecessary dependence and must attend to the subtle signs of readiness to terminate. Forgotten appointments and comments about busy schedules suggest that the patient is beginning to break away. If the youngster does not raise the issue directly, we must. This is particularly difficult for some, as it may be their first relationship based on mutuality, respect, and trust.

I try to be forthright about any observable behavior changes and express my increased positive regard for them. My yardstick for progress is their emerging ability to enjoy themselves in a nondestructive fashion, think about the future, and assert themselves appropriately. Since there is a certain sadness that accompanies the end of any relationship, I often share some of my relevant experiences. I believe that after a good relationship ends, either through loss, moving, or termination, we carry around a part of that special person inside us. In a sense they are there for us when we need them. To illustrate this point, I might describe a hypothetical situation in which their parents wouldn't allow them to go to a concert or special event. I ask them what advice they think I would offer and have them role-play. Invariably their perceptions are right on target. This convinces them that they really do know my thoughts and are able to function independently. I am available if they need me, of course, and can easily be reached.

When self-disclosure has been judiciously employed, it can enhance trust and serve as a model for a healthy relationship. Therapists must be mindful of youngsters' boundaries and provide information they can readily digest. The emerging bond between them should enable adolescents to develop other meaningful relationships outside the treatment setting. This in turn will reduce their isolation and provide the impetus for further change.

# 6

# The Road to Self-Control

Jerry was no stranger to the principal's office. At age 15 he was the veteran of many skirmishes with both teachers and students. It was never his fault, of course. The teachers were "critical," "bossy," and blamed him for things he "didn't do." He overreacted to any commentary on his behavior. He cursed out school personnel, threw down chairs, and slammed doors on his way out of the classroom. Multiple detentions were unsuccessful in deterring his behavior. He had been suspended for fighting on two occasions and was on probation for bringing a pocket-sized baseball bat to school. He insisted it was to protect himself from other students' attacks.

Jerry's developmental history was punctuated by episodes of aggressive behavior dating back to the first grade. His parents reported that he had always been hard to manage. There were frequent arguments with his siblings, temper outbursts, and general noncompliance with rules. Efforts to discipline him often led to conflicts that escalated to the point that the parents ultimately gave in to keep the peace. His father was harsh and punitive while his mother was protective. Both were generally inconsistent and agreed that none of their efforts had been successful.

By adolescence, Jerry's behavior had worsened markedly. Teachers and counselors had raised the possibility of ADHD; however, a psychiatric consultation did not recommend psychostimulant medication. Jerry readily acknowledged his difficulty getting along with others, but felt that he "just couldn't help it." He minimized his problems, claiming they were the result of others' provocation and mistreatment. His school grades were deteriorating and he was spending more and more time with an undesirable group of friends.

Jerry's story is a familiar one. A constellation of self-control problems fueled by impulsivity, negative attribution, and an inability to manage anger. Lochman and colleagues (1991) found that aggressive boys often overperceive their peers' aggressiveness and place a high value on dominance and revenge. They justify their lack of self-control and anger by placing blame outside themselves.

Many youngsters describe a rapidly intensifying feeling of tension prior to blowing up. They do not believe that they can exercise control over their anger and impulses. Often-heard comments include, "I couldn't help it; it just happened before I knew what I was doing," or "I always react that way when someone gets me mad." Some adolescents report that they get warning signals before exploding; others describe it as spontaneous. The net result is the same. Overreactions lead to intensified conflict with others. When questioned, they readily acknowledge their reputation as someone with "a bad attitude" who "goes off too easily."

I have heard many stories about these youngsters punching holes in walls and breaking windows, locks, and family possessions. Their frustration tolerance is low and they are prone to "take off" when they cannot have their way. Their parents lament that they just can't talk to them about anything. Anger and impulsive behavior seem to permeate their existence.

Any treatment of the disruptive behavior disorders must include a component focused on self-control. Cognitive behavior therapy has been the dominant approach to modifying anger and aggression (Wilson 1984). My experience has been that this is maximally effective when combined with a focus on the need for change and the direct benefits to the youngster. Initially, patients must learn to discuss their anger to benefit from a program to alter it. Any attempt to short-circuit this process can undermine the treatment effort.

Most youngsters will readily acknowledge their difficulty with anger, although they rarely take responsibility for it. I often ask them whether, if they could simply push a button to make their temper go away, would they do so? Most youngsters smile and say yes! A few are not sure, but are willing to consider the issue. We then spend some time exploring the advantages of better self-control.

I usually tell them something like this:

> When your reactions to situations are measured and predictable, people will feel more comfortable around you. This often leads to increased acceptance and popularity. The fact is that hot tempers can result in trouble or even

violence. If you can't think clearly when you're under pressure, you're at a disadvantage. The other person is in a position to influence your behavior by simply provoking you. Furthermore, when you get extremely upset, your thoughts and actions become irrational and you may regret doing something afterwards. As you develop emotional control and learn to monitor your own behavior, adults will not need to tell you what to do. Ultimately you'll have the satisfaction of knowing that things can be on your terms; that is, you're initiating rather than reacting.

Adolescents are intrigued by the thought of having more power over their environment. When they are approached with an offer to strengthen their position, they readily agree to try. This, of course, presupposes some degree of trust between patient and therapist.

## LEARNING TO DEAL WITH ANGER

Everyone gets angry at times. It is the most human of emotions. The appropriate expression of anger can help to resolve conflicts and call others' attention to our feelings. Most oppositional and conduct-disordered youth have not learned to express their anger appropriately. This must be brought to their attention at the first opportunity. Of course they are entitled to their feelings, but they rarely succeed in getting their point across. There is an excessive focus on their self-righteous perceptions and a lack of awareness of anyone else's feelings.

The therapeutic task is to help them differentiate between the legitimate aspects of their anger and the illogical extensions that lead to unnecessary conflicts. Those who have been neglected, abused, or raised in dysfunctional families have good reason to be angry and to distrust others. To expect otherwise would be to block their opportunity for the expression of negative affect. Faulty family communication and poor role models have not prepared these adolescents to ventilate their feelings appropriately and listen to the shared feelings of others.

Although difficult, we must present the advantages of expressing anger appropriately; that is, making sure that someone hears our feelings. Tavris (1982) points out that anger is effective only when it leads to changes in the other person's behavior. Simply blowing off steam may feel good in the short run, but it rarely serves a useful purpose. I tell youngsters that a reciprocal exchange of emotions is more likely to get their point across than a tirade. It is a major challenge to convince them that words can be safer and more effective than actions.

A role-playing exercise is useful in this regard. It is based on the assumption that anger is legitimate and should be expressed. The focus is on the present situation rather than an enumeration of past hurts.

I ask an adolescent boy to imagine a situation in which a teacher has just criticized him because he did not turn in a homework assignment. He feels humiliated in front of the class but knows that he has a legitimate excuse. On the previous evening, his brother had sustained head injuries, and they spent several hours in the emergency room waiting for treatment. How would he handle the situation?

I remind him that he has been through this before.

In the past he had made wisecracks or angrily stormed out of the classroom without offering an explanation. The task here is to express himself without reacting angrily to the unwarranted accusation. I assume the role of the teacher and ask him to show me how he might respond.

> *Dr. B*: David, I see you've not done your homework again. This is the fourth time I've had to talk to you and we're only three weeks into the quarter.
>
> *David*: Forget you, I'm out of here!
>
> *Dr. B*: Wait a minute, David. What good will that do? Remember, you didn't do anything wrong. Getting angry won't help, and worse yet, it makes you seem guilty when you're not. What else could you say?
>
> *David*: Oh. Well, listen, Mrs. Smith. This time is different. There was sort of a family emergency. Can I talk to you about it after class?
>
> *Dr. B*: Well, if you want to.
>
> *Dr. B*: (*Ending role play*) David, that was really good. You avoided a potential blowup and a trip to the principal's office. See what I mean?
>
> *David*: Yeah.
>
> *Dr. B*: But what if Mrs. Smith said, "I don't want to hear about it" when you tried to explain.
>
> *David*: Then I'd take off.
>
> *Dr. B*: Hold it; this raises another situation that we're all forced to face occasionally.
>
> *David*: What's that?
>
> *Dr. B*: Sometimes we just have to bite the bullet. We have something important to say, but the other

person won't listen. There may not be anything we can do.

*David*: That happens to me a lot.

*Dr. B*: That's a tough one. I guess you just have to choose your battles sometimes. Maybe there'll be a chance to say something later. Do you think you can try that?

*David*: I don't know. I hate it when people get on my case. It makes me angry and I want to strike back.

*Dr. B*: I understand that, but can we just practice not reacting?

*David*: If you really think it will help.

## USING ANGER CONSTRUCTIVELY

We can often talk to kids about how they can make their anger work for them. When they feel insulted, hurt, or misunderstood, they instinctively strike back. This leads to further conflict, of course, which rarely gets resolved. Why can't they do something that will help to get their point across?

Suppose a coach cuts them from a team, or a teacher tells them that they'll never amount to anything. Sure, that makes them angry, but wouldn't it give them great pleasure to prove the other person wrong? Why give them the satisfaction of being able to say "I told you so"?

Although difficult, we can press adolescents to put their strong feelings to use. Ask them to imagine their coach's face when he sees them playing well for another team. Have them think about how that critical teacher will react when she learns about another teacher who enjoys having them in class.

I try to get adolescents to picture all of their anger as a force of energy. I tell them: "It's just a question of how you want to use it. Why don't we try an experiment. The next time your parents bug you about something, don't snap back at them. Instead, find a way to demonstrate that their comments are unnecessary. Just do things on your own and prove that you don't need their supervision. It'll make you feel better and get them off your back."

## Case Example

Jane was a 16-year-old girl who took pride in her punk hairstyle. After dyeing her hair orange, she received approval from her few friends. The majority of her peers told her it looked stupid.

Jane was really angry and upset. "Who are they to judge me?" she lamented. After several altercations at school, she expressed her frustration tearfully. I asked her if she thought her individuality was worth the price she was paying. She acknowledged that she wasn't sure, but would not change her hair just to satisfy those "preppy idiots."

"Well, there's got to be a better way to show your anger," I commented. "What can you do to prove your point?"

She thought about it for a while and suddenly the idea hit her. "I know! I'll take a picture of myself, blow it up, and then use it on a poster. You know that school election coming up? I'll run for office.

Yeah, my friends will all help. I probably won't win, but it'll be worth it."

"What will your campaign slogan be?" I queried.

"Dare to be different," she answered proudly.

"I like that!" I told her.

Well, she went on to lose the election, but it turned out to be a useful experience. A week later she dyed her hair back to her natural color. The case was closed.

## NEGATIVE ATTRIBUTION

The majority of behaviorally disordered adolescents do not take responsibility for their behavior. They attribute hostile motives to the actions of others and justify their aggression accordingly (Kendall et al. 1990). Often they interpret neutral situations as threatening and then react angrily and defensively. For example, a teacher may ask a student to sit down so that she can begin the class. The teenager takes this as criticism, snaps back at her, and refuses to comply. The stage has been set for a negative interaction.

This population responds impulsively in the absence of sufficient information. They believe that aggressive behavior strengthens their image and feel that self-protection is necessary. When questioned, they are likely to insist that the other person got what they deserved. This propensity to interpret ambiguous situations as provocative must be challenged. These patients need to learn how to correctly infer others' thoughts and actions.

We should make a brief assessment of their perception of events. I like to present hypothetical situations and ask that they share their reactions to them. For example, I tell an adolescent boy to imagine that he is standing on line at McDonald's and notices that another boy is staring at him. Which explanation would he feel is the most likely?

1. The boy thinks he knows you from somewhere.
2. He's looking at you because he likes the shirt that you're wearing.
3. He's thinking that you're wimpy and challenging you to react.

Clearly, the third choice infers hostile attribution; the other choices are relatively benign.

A second illustration involves a mother asking her child to take the garbage out. The possible explanations are:

1. She needs some help around the house.
2. She's picking on you and could have asked your brother.
3. She's just tired and doesn't feel like doing it.

Again, it is the interpretation of intent that we are interested in. Similar situations should be presented and discussed at length. Adolescents seem to enjoy doing this and can benefit from an analysis of the motives of other people. The goal is to improve their ability to interpret events accurately.

Ferguson and Rule (1988) describe several types of provocation. These can be readily adapted to help young-sters to discern the motives of others. An example of an *accidental provocation* would be someone tripping and spilling their drink on you. While this might be upsetting, it is clearly unintentional. Most antisocial youth will acknowledge this, although they would get angry just the same. They can usually see the rationale for forgiving in this situation.

*Foreseeable harm* is a circumstance in which harm was unintended but avoidable. Someone backing their car into yours would be careless but not premeditated. Certainly the anger would be understandable, but retaliation is still an overreaction. This is somewhat harder for certain youngsters to see as they believe the perpetrator should be taught a lesson.

*Justifiably intended harm* occurs when a youngster beats up someone because they hurt his little sister. Most patients would have trouble seeing anything wrong with this action. They would insist that the aggressor got what was coming to him.

Finally, *unjustifiably intended harm* would be a violent attack on someone for no reason. Of course, the youngsters would feel strongly that anything goes in this situation. Self-protection and vengeance are among the most frequently cited themes here, with no remorse whatsoever expressed.

Attributional change can be facilitated by getting youth to consider alternative explanations for the seemingly hostile actions of others. They should be encouraged to consider the person's motivations, the circumstances, and the avoidability of the event. Did the person seem genuinely angry at the time? What were the cues that inferred offensive action? Did the youngster have any previous experience with the alleged aggressor? The more we can foster introspection and discussion, the less likely is the risk of misinterpretation.

Adolescents should be taught to check out their observations before jumping to conclusions. They can either ask direct questions or tell the person that he or she sounds angry or critical. The response should help them to determine the appropriate action. Patients sometimes feel that this is silly, but I persist in challenging them on the result of assuming the worst. In effect it makes someone seem like a negative or pessimistic person, and few of us want to be viewed that way. Finally, I inquire how they might feel if people continually misinterpreted their actions. It would be frustrating, annoying, and provocative. We spend considerable time working on situations in which they feel another's intent is unclear.

## Case Example

June was certain that most of the ninth grade girls talked about her behind her back. She was defiant and adamant about not "taking stuff from anyone." She was frequently in arguments and felt compelled to defend herself. It made her angry when people ignored her. I was curious about why she was so convinced that others were against her. The evidence was meager. "Well, they don't say hello, and I can just tell by the expressions on their faces," she lamented. "Besides, I think they avoid me."

"Maybe they're just afraid of you," I commented. "Is that what you really want?" June grew quiet.

I challenged her to test out her assumptions. Could she try being friendly to one of the girls in her class? What if she asked someone why they avoided her or if they felt angry at her? It seemed there was nothing to lose.

Ironically, June used to be friendly with these girls and had drifted away over the past year or so. Family conflicts and an agitated depression had intensified her oppositional behavior. The aggressive posture was the outgrowth of her perceived rejection and misinterpretation of social cues. As it turned out, the other girls had misread June as well, assuming that she did not want to be friends anymore. Although awkward at first, she finally approached them and was surprised to learn that they felt little if any hostility.

## ANGER MANAGEMENT TRAINING

The predominant approach to directly treating anger and aggression is cognitive behavior therapy. Novaco (1975) found that anger is maintained and enhanced by self-statements. Consequently, teaching individuals to regulate arousal should facilitate the development of self-management skills. Feindler and Ecton (1986) built upon Novaco's early work to develop a comprehensive anger control program for adolescents, which was validated experimentally. I employ an adaptation of their work as an integral part of enhancing self-control in a behavior-disordered population.

Anger management techniques can be utilized in either an individual or a group format. Simply telling these youngsters that we are going to teach them better self-control is unlikely to motivate them. Their bravado, short attention span, and need for excitement often fuel resistance to treatment. They may complain that a cognitive behavioral format is stupid and boring. Consequently we must find ways to capture their attention and enlist their cooperation. This is best accomplished by making treatment interesting, spontaneous, and perhaps even fun.

In a group format the approach can be introduced by a dramatic demonstration of conflict. Before the initial meeting my cotherapist and I will plan to stage an altercation at the start of the first group. Typically, I would be sitting and chatting with the youngsters as I hold a pen to my chin. Moments later my cotherapist enters and seizes the pen from me, rudely stating, "Give me that. I have to write something down."

I get angry and shout, "You've got a lot of nerve, grabbing the pen like that."

He retorts, "I'm getting sick and tired of your attitude. I don't have to take this stuff from you."

I stand up and angrily walk toward him, shouting, with fists clenched. The group is mesmerized. They are not quite sure what is going on, but certainly relish the opportunity to watch a good fight.

Suddenly we cease our argument and look toward the group. After a few moments they realize it was a charade and laugh heartily. Who do you think started the fight, I ask? One kid shouts, "You did, when you overreacted." Another corrects him, "No, it was the cotherapist's fault. He provoked Dr. B." The divergence of opinion is readily apparent. We proceed to explore the occurrence to determine who was at fault. The discussion quickly leads to an exploration of anger and the related aspects of self-control. Anger management training has been introduced painlessly.

Differences between good and bad self-control are readily distinguished. The group is asked to name some celebrities or sports figures who have consistently demonstrated a positive attitude and good self-control. Michael Jordan's name comes up often. Basketball players are always trying to prove themselves when competing against him and he takes it in stride. He doesn't overreact when he gets fouled or taunted on the court. Outside the sports arena he tries to keep a low profile in his personal life. Sugar Ray Leonard, the former middleweight boxing champion, is also mentioned. A man of patience and temperance, he is noted for his generosity, sportsmanlike conduct, and avoidance of trouble.

The youngsters are quite eager to point out the rich and famous who lack self-control. Sean Penn, the volatile actor and ex-husband of Madonna, is often in skirmishes. Mike Tyson, former world champion, has been convicted of rape, and is known for his violent temper. Sports personality O. J. Simpson was abusive toward his wife, and acquitted of murder after a lengthy and much publicized trial. What differentiates those who have good control from those who lack it?

These examples lend themselves to further discussion of how one develops self-control and learns to manage anger effectively. A cognitive-behavioral model of anger management is presented in simple terms. The group is told that our bodies signal our distress in response to certain cues from the environment. When we interpret these cues as hostile or provocative, we respond angrily. What we say to ourselves determines the extent of our reaction. Any negative interpretation of events can ignite our fuse. To alert the youngsters to these signals, we discuss situations likely to arouse their anger. Parents criticizing them, peers challenging them, and teachers disciplining them are frequently occurring catalysts.

Adolescents are encouraged to listen to their bodies for signals of anger arousal. The physical cues described include a tightened stomach, flushed face, pounding heart, and arms getting pumped up. Each youngster must identify the signals most familiar to him or her. When they have learned to do this, they can begin to recognize the point at which they must interrupt the sequence. Some will insist that they blow up without warning, of course. They must learn to anticipate troublesome situations.

Patients can be asked to keep a record of hassles occurring during the previous few weeks (Feindler and Ecton 1986). Their reports are then discussed and analyzed by the group. A behavioral model is employed to focus on the antecedents, behavior, and consequences. The youngsters are asked to identify the events immediately preceding the run-in, describe their reaction, and note the immediate consequences. This increases their objectivity and creates an opportunity for intervention. Unfortunately, many adolescents will not complete their assignments at home. The similarity to schoolwork is too great and they resist instinctively. When this is the case, a few minutes should be set aside at the beginning of group so they can complete their records without fanfare.

I find it useful to show movie clips from time to time. The action is often fast paced and realistic, thereby promoting discussion. I try to choose scenes that depict a variety of responses to anger and provocation. After showing a portion of the segment, I stop the tape and ask the group to anticipate what will happen next. This often serves as an entree for the discussion of events in their own lives. The movie *Boyz N the Hood* is one tape that both holds their interest and provides ample material for discussion.

When the group can successfully identify the precipitants of anger and differentiate between appropriate and inappropriate coping responses, the concept of self-talk is introduced. Youngsters are told that we all speak a private language composed of what we think and say to ourselves (Pope et al. 1988). Others are not aware of this, yet it influences all our feelings and actions. Negative or irrational thoughts and self-statements can lead to extremes of behavior. A young man who convinces himself that others are trying to put him down is likely to react angrily to any remark directed toward him.

Angry youth can be taught self-talk so that they can settle themselves down when provoked. The group should be encouraged to generate calming statements to be used in stressful situations. For example, repeating "I won't let him get to me" or "Calm down, man" can help to diffuse anger. Youngsters must develop their own repertoire of self-statements to employ when agitated. Some prefer to imagine themselves as someone famous who keeps his cool, and then emulate the behavior. Others may tell themselves that they've been through this drill before and can control themselves if they want to.

The importance of determination and willpower should be stressed. It's like getting in a fight and winning against the odds. You just have to keep talking to yourself until you can calm down. These self-statements should be practiced out loud so that others can judge their effectiveness. The individuals in the group function as coaches for one another as they role-play situations.

## THOUGHT STOPPING

Adolescents can also be taught to control their angry thoughts by employing basic relaxation techniques. Many have observed professional athletes or entertainers taking a deep breath and exhaling before a performance. This is easily demonstrated and practiced in a group or individual setting. Youngsters generally find this simple and easy to apply in stressful situations. If their interest has been sustained, we can go on to teach them to tense and relax various muscle groups in a progressive fashion.

Counting backwards is another cognitive technique familiar to many adolescents. Youngsters are instructed to close their eyes and try to focus exclusively on the numbers in their mind. Some find it helpful to visualize counting their CDs, attractive peers, or days left before their next school vacation. The more they can get absorbed with their thoughts, the better. Again, the task is to shift their focus away from the provocative thought or stimulus.

Visual imagery is an extension of this exercise. I ask patients to take a minute and try to imagine something they did in the past year that was really enjoyable and exciting. They are then given the opportunity to share their memory with the group and explore the accompanying effect on them. Most readily state that it makes them feel good when they recall the pleasant incident. It is important to ask them to clarify what "feel good" means. Patients usually make references to relaxed, happy, or peaceful. I explain that those feelings of pleasure or relaxation can be used to mitigate their angry states. When they feel themselves getting uptight, they can simply imagine their scene for a minute or so, and feel themselves chilling out.

The relaxation techniques are practiced in the group until they are mastered. Patients are encouraged to adapt them to their own style and find what works for them. We discuss and role-play situations likely to occur in their lives, emphasizing the importance of their doing something to control their angry state. As their familiarity with the new skills increases, they become more likely to think about and apply alternatives.

## NEUTRALIZING THE OPPOSITION

Another useful self-control technique is to teach patients to lessen the significance of the provocative behavior of others. The most obvious way is simply to ignore someone's challenge, thereby removing any satisfaction they might get. This is a hard sell. Antisocial youngsters sometimes find it hard to just let it go. The discussion must return to the advantages to them. Learning to roll with something can make life easier.

*Fogging* is a response intended to play down the significance of another's taunt (Feindler and Ecton 1986). For example, if someone were to say, "You're a nerd," the response would be, "You're right. I'm a nerd." The trick is to handle any provocative comment without a retort. Many teenagers prefer to use humor as an outlet in these situations. So long as their response does not escalate the conflict, it can be useful.

I also help the impulse-prone to practice freezing in their tracks. This improves self-control by delaying their immediate reaction to a perceived provocation. I ask them to imagine that they are filming an action scene (e.g., a conflict sequence) when the director suddenly yells "Cut." Their job is to stop what they're doing no matter what. Adolescents find this exercise amusing and readily comply with the guidelines.

## A DRESS REHEARSAL

When patients feel comfortable with the various skills they have learned, they are told that we want to test their resolve by trying to provoke them. Our goal is to get them angry; theirs is to prevent us from doing so by using their newly acquired abilities. Each patient is tested individually with provocative comments. I might say, "Where did you get those cheap shoes?" or "Your hairstyle is really ugly." At first their discomfort is apparent, but they manage to control their anger by applying of one of these techniques. Occasionally they can't refrain and will snap back angrily with an insult. The group often laughs, realizing what has happened, and then encourages the offender to keep his cool. After a second trial of provocation, the patient usually succeeds in deflecting it or calming down.

After everyone has been challenged and has triumphed, we move to a more difficult phase. I tell the kids they've won the first round, but haven't been tested by the real experts yet. They, of course, are the real masters of insult. The only rule is that they attempt to provoke another member verbally, not physically. One by one they take their turns making provocative remarks to each other. Their comments are incisive and frequently refer to someone's mother, anatomical parts, or a personal vulnerability. Somehow the youngsters manage to withstand the temptation to overreact and are quite pleased with themselves.

Further test of their resolve is to provoke them while they are engaged in a task that requires concentration. A youngster might be asked to build a house of cards while others try to distract him with provocative remarks. Again, the challenge is to stay relaxed and focused in the face of disruption. It is good practice for situations they are likely to face outside the office.

## THINK BEFORE YOU ACT

Impulsive behavior accompanies self-control problems. As patients develop new ways to manage their anger, the tendency to overreact decreases. Their cognitive assessment of situations may not change as readily. I use an exercise that I refer to as the "What Would You Do If" game. The intention is to get the youngsters to think before they act so as to anticipate the consequences of their behavior. They are presented with a series of hypothetical dilemmas they might be faced with in real life. The task is to blurt out the first response that comes to mind.

One situation I present is the following:

> You are standing in the checkout line of the grocery store. The woman in front of you unknowingly drops her change purse at your feet. You notice that a $20 bill has fallen out. What would you do?

Some youngsters react quickly, saying that they would grab it if they could get away with it. Others want more information. Is she a rich lady or a poor lady? Is there a hidden camera in the store? After some discussion the group usually concludes that it is best to call it to her attention. After all, it is the right thing to do, and you might even get a reward.

Another illustration:

> You are walking down the hallway at school with your friends. A much younger boy who is visiting for the day runs down the corridor without looking. He accidentally crashes into you and knocks the books out of your arms. What would your first reaction be?

Impulsive and angry youth are inclined to throw him to the ground to teach him a lesson. The group reminds them that he's just a little boy. After some consideration it is agreed that he should be told to watch where he is going and then be allowed to walk away.

Finally, I ask older adolescents what they would do if they were driving a car approaching an intersection when the traffic signal turned yellow. Many blurt out that they would slam their foot on the accelerator and go through the light. Group members readily bring up the risks. You could get in an accident. If the cops catch you for speeding, you can get additional points on your license and perhaps lose it. Is it worth the risk? I use a series of related critical incidents to stimulate dialogue. Patients are then encouraged to share their recollections of situations in which they responded impulsively and how they might have done otherwise.

## BROADENING THE GAINS IN SELF-CONTROL

After adolescents acquire new skills in a therapeutic context, they must be helped to extend them to other situations. It is useful to contact teachers, staff, family, and others who deal with them daily. They are informed of the patient's progress and asked to cooperate in testing them out with minor provocations. I tell the youngsters this and encourage them to be prepared. As they face these minor annoyances, they begin instinctively to apply their anger control techniques in day-to-day situations. They are asked to report on these experiences and discuss them with their peers.

It is important to support, praise, and recognize these accomplishments. As others notice their improved self-control, a naturally occurring reinforcement process evolves. Their feelings of mastery gradually lead to increased pride in themselves and a reduction in the frequency of acting out. They can then teach both friends and family their newly acquired skills. This helps to consolidate their treatment gains and lays the groundwork for further concomitant interventions.

# 7

# Developing the Necessary Interpersonal Skills

Behavior-disordered youth often misread social cues and assume an aggressive posture. Most are uncomfortable in social situations and lack the ability to establish meaningful relationships. Much time is spent seeking excitement in an attempt to avoid boredom. They justify their misbehavior by placing blame on others and see little reason to change. Consequently, considerable energy is devoted to saving face, keeping a safe distance from others, and avoiding feelings.

Adolescents who violate social norms do not possess the necessary interpersonal skills to achieve their desired goals through legitimate means (Hazel et al. 1983). Their histories are replete with examples of inconsistent parenting, poor family communication, and a failure to resolve problems without resorting to aggression. Social inexperience results in unpopularity, which increases the risk for delinquency and conduct problems (Kazdin 1985). These social skills deficiencies lead youngsters to rely on action-oriented solutions rather than dialogue. Despite their denial of any social discomfort, observations reveal that they do not make conversation easily and have difficulty managing stressful situations.

Although they genuinely need help with their interpersonal skills, the majority of this group deny their shortcomings and resist interventions. They view training in social skills as "dumb" since it's "kid stuff" and they "can deal with other people fine when I want to." Some have learned to work the system by being polite and saying the right things; however, their relationships are shallow and short-lived. Others find themselves in continued conflict with peers and adults but do not relate it to their own deficits.

Social skills training is a behavioral approach to remediation that focuses on teaching the prosocial skills needed to interact comfortably on a daily basis. It can be employed in either an individual or a group format; however, the group setting more closely resembles real life and provides the opportunity for role-plays with peers. The training is psychoeducational by design and identifies the behavior deficits fueling conflicts with others. It involves teaching, modeling, role-playing, feedback, and reinforcement techniques.

## OVERCOMING RESISTANCE

These adolescents initially balk at therapeutic interventions designed to enhance their skills. Despite their difficulties, they describe themselves as socially competent and deny the need for assistance. Any introduction to the training must provide a demonstration of appropriate behavior and somehow whet their appetite for change. Therapist modeling (Dowd and Tierney 1992, Goldstein et al. 1980, Liberman et al. 1989) has often been employed to introduce the process. I have found it useful to precede any demonstration by showing video-tapes of both awkward adolescents and "smooth opera-tors." Adolescents readily critique the situations, thereby getting involved in the training process. Rather than pressing them to acknowledge their shortcomings, it is better to encourage them to sharpen their already exist-ing skills. Any opportunity to save face will be welcomed.

It would be simplistic to suggest that presenting interesting social scenes would ensure compliance. Some time must be spent discussing the rationale for training in social skills. A dynamic, interesting, and humorous presentation helps to engage the group. Examples rel-evant to their lives and to current adolescent culture should be liberally employed.

A trainer can begin by appealing to the youngsters' frustration and anger with those around them. "You know, it can be a real hassle when other people get on you all the time and don't take you seriously. How would you like it if you could get them to do what you wanted? Life would be a lot easier, wouldn't it?

"Well, there really are some skills that you can learn to help influence those around you. That's what we are going to start working on today. When you've gotten the hang of it, it should be easier to meet interesting kids and even get your parents to chill a little bit. You'll also get better at communicating your needs and learning to say no when you want to. Once you have learned how to handle other people, you should be able to stay out of trouble. This all leads to better self-confidence, which is something we could all benefit from."

## THE LEADER'S ROLE

Conducting social skills groups requires a high energy level, spontaneity, and a willingness to deviate from convention. The leader's personality characteristics often determine the pulse of the group. When creative teaching techniques are employed in a spirit of good will, the likelihood of a successful experience is increased. The leader must be thoroughly familiar with a behavioral approach and provide illustrations of the skills to be attained. Although a presentation of behavior principles can be rather dry and uninspiring, it is possible to orchestrate a challenging and absorbing experience. Leaders are advised to stay on their feet, move around the room, and respond quickly to any disruptions. Once the youngsters sense that the leaders are competent, flexible, and not easily ruffled, they are more apt to participate in the exercise.

The leadership role should be approached from the perspective of a theater director. Various gestures are employed to coach the youngsters through their role plays. Liberman and colleagues (1989) use a finger across the throat to prompt youngsters to cut the action when needed. Slowing down might be suggested by gently moving the hands up and down. Speeding up the action is accomplished by rolling the hands in a circle quickly. Adolescents seem to enjoy this type of nonverbal direction. A finger over the lips communicates the need to be quiet; a hand to the ear prompts speaking louder.

The leader's approval can be expressed nonverbally as well. Thumbs up conveys pleasure as does silent clapping. Pointing and smiling simultaneously serves to reinforce behavior. Disapproval can be expressed by rolling the eyes, throwing up one's arms, or simply shaking the head back and forth. Again, the emphasis is placed on providing feedback in an acceptable, non-threatening fashion.

## THE NECESSARY INGREDIENTS

Goldstein and colleagues (1980) and Lindsay (1987) have presented an extensive social skills training program. The steps are carefully specified and easily followed. The initial technique generally employed is modeling. The leader and co-leader begin by carefully demonstrating the execution of a useful social skill, making certain to break it down into its component parts. The group observes, listens, and prepares to role-play the newly presented skill. Several members are then chosen as participants. They are encouraged to emulate the leader's presentation carefully and try to act as if they are in a real-life situation. The other members observe their interactions and prepare to offer feedback upon completion of the task.

It is essential that the leaders employ praise liberally. Minor accomplishments should be noted and expanded. Adolescents are prone to joke around, criticize, and belittle the seriousness of the exercises. This is in part due to their performance anxiety and uncertainty about their competence. A spirit of camaraderie must be developed, and the role players acknowledged for their courage and risk taking. It is particularly helpful when a member is forthright about a personal deficiency. Self-disclosure is strongly encouraged and rewarded. It is critical that the youngsters come to feel safe in the setting.

Oppositional and antisocial youth are instinctively suspicious and reluctant to acknowledge their areas of insecurity. Despite their insistence that they "already know how to," we observe otherwise. An approach presented as a way to "make them even better" or "more expert" is accepted more readily. When the leader can enable youngsters to save face, yet simultaneously participate, genuine progress has occurred.

## SKILL SEQUENCING

While grouping youngsters by skill deficits is desirable, it is often impractical. Since we must work with the limited selection of patients in our treatment setting—sometimes including those who have been mandated—it is often necessary to deal with adolescents with various deficits. This in fact has some advantages, since behavior-disordered youth display a wide range of social competencies and deficits that others in the group might learn from.

In my experience most youth are amenable to working on basic conversation skills when the format is interesting. Choosing the lowest common denominator in the group allows everyone to participate readily and observe others with varying levels of competence. As adolescents grow more comfortable with the process and "learn to learn," the group can readily progress to more complex behaviors. Social skills should be presented in an ascending order of difficulty so that previous gains may be broadened

For example, if conversation skills were presented initially, the group proceeds to work on more advanced interactive skills such as dealing with directions and learning to influence others. Still higher levels would include learning to deal with feelings and managing stressful situations (Goldstein et al. 1980).

## THE ART OF CONVERSATION

As previously suggested, basic conversation skills are the logical place to begin social skills training. The steps entailed in the learning process are illustrated by describing the acquisition of a particular skill. For example, the group might be asked how they would teach a peer to play basketball. Where would they begin? Dribbling is a fundamental skill that involves bouncing a ball up and down with the fingertips. This can easily be demonstrated. An explanation of passing the basketball follows. Finally, the process of shooting would be described and modeled. The point of this drill is to break down the skill of basketball into its component parts. The more specific and detailed they can be, the better.

Once the group grasps the concept of skill building, the art of conversation is introduced. They have already observed a video or role-play and have some familiarity with the process. Resistance is minimized by a dynamic presentation promoting a high interest level. The leader asks the group to list some of the basic steps in starting a conversation. This should not be threatening as it is something they do on a daily basis with varying degrees of success.

Following the discussion, the group is told that everyone has his or her own way of doing things and may operate on different skill levels. They are asked to bear with us if it seems simple, and volunteer to role-play if they are familiar with the steps in the sequence. The remaining group members are asked to be coaches and judges of the role-plays, attempting to give feedback when indicated.

The nonverbal aspects of conversation are introduced first. Members are instructed about body language and encouraged to interpret the leader's modeling. For example someone sitting with arms and legs clasped might be uptight as compared to another person with a more relaxed posture. The group practices these variations to sharpen their discrimination of others' emotional states.

This proceeds to an exercise during which they are asked to communicate a range of emotions nonverbally. Although they find this somewhat humorous at first, they generally comply. Some basic emotions to role-play include anger, sadness, joy, fear, and curiosity. Behavior-disordered youth often have difficulty accurately reading the feelings of others. One at a time they are asked to role-play each of the aforementioned mood states. The group then attempts to read them correctly. Feedback is given and they are encouraged to make the necessary adjustments. This process helps the group to increase their awareness of how both they and others come across.

As they grow more proficient at utilizing and interpreting nonverbal cues, the basics of conversation are introduced. Those uncomfortable with any dialogue are asked to begin by simply describing something. This could range from objects in the room to relating an event they have seen on the news or heard about recently. As their comfort increases, they are encouraged to talk about the thoughts and feelings that accompany their description of an event. For example, when they heard about a recent plane crash, what went through their mind?

When it is clear that the group members can talk descriptively, the leaders proceed to model the basic conversation skills. A chance social encounter between two acquaintances serves as a useful illustration. The leaders make certain to demonstrate all of the steps in the process for the purpose of discussion. To begin with, conversations should open with an appropriate greeting to the other person. This includes making and maintaining eye contact, smiling, and conveying a friendly attitude.

Some youngsters complain that it is difficult for them to make small talk. They should be offered concrete suggestions to initiate and stimulate conversation. Complimenting a person often serves to break the ice. Some aggressive youth have difficulty with this as they are more familiar with criticism and negative interactions. They must practice flattering one another in the group, much the same as they did with provocation in anger management training.

Initiating a conversation is easier when you feel you have something to offer. Youngsters should be encouraged to keep up with current trends so that they have interesting tidbits at their fingertips. People are more likely to respond when they are familiar with the topic at hand. School, contemporary music, movies, and clothing, all present the opportunity for discussion with peers. Adolescents are encouraged to comment on a topic of interest, ask a question, or seek the other person's opinion. The importance of asking open-ended rather than yes-or-no questions is stressed. In conversation with adults they can build on current events or information pertinent to the relationship.

One must learn to balance the amount of time they spend between talking and listening. This is especially difficult for impulsive and distractible adolescents. Attention is conveyed by nodding, making affirming sounds, and maintaining eye contact. The leader demonstrates how to interject opinions appropriately and pick up on another's comments. Our goal is to help these adolescents refine their judgment about when and how to use particular skills.

Antisocial youth have difficulty gauging what is appropriate to disclose. They lack a clear sense of the boundaries of relationships and need coaching in what to share about themselves and what information to seek from others. This too should be practiced in the group format.

Finally, the groups work on how to tactfully end a particular conversation. For example, one could change the topic when the other person finishes talking, or excuse themselves by saying, "I really have to be going, but it has been nice talking to you." Any abrupt endings should be discouraged so that the door can be left open for future conversations.

## AN ILLUSTRATIVE GROUP SEGMENT

I often set up the following role-play situation to engage youngsters in the learning process. "Imagine that you are about to enter a new class and notice that there is just one seat available. It happens to be next to the best-looking girl in tenth grade. Show us exactly what you would do and how you would go about starting a conversation.

"Let's try to make this as realistic as possible. I need a boy and girl to volunteer for this exercise. The rest of you will be the coaches. Offer suggestions to the participants and help them to do this as well as they possibly can." Mike and Jenny volunteer after some bantering in the group.

> *Dr. B:* Okay, I'm putting two chairs in the middle of our room. Jenny, you have a seat here. Mike, I want you to leave the room and enter as if this is really happening. Ready to roll? Great, you're on the air!
>
> *Mike:* (*Enters the room and takes a seat next to Jenny*) Hey, baby, what are you doing this Saturday night?
>
> *Dr. B:* (*Interrupting the group's laughter*) Jenny, what would you do if a total stranger sat next to you and said that?
>
> *Jenny:* Well, I might slap his face or ignore him or something. I sure wouldn't go out with him!
>
> *Dr. B:* Mike, that might have sounded cool and funny but it sure won't get her to talk to you. Try and think of the things we've discussed

here. How about it, group? What else could he use for an opening line?

*David*: Well, how about asking her if she's new in the school. Tell her you've never seen her before.

*Joe*: Compliment her on the top she's wearing. Maybe that'll loosen her up!

*Dr. B*: Not bad. These ideas could actually work. Why don't we just try it again? Be a sport, Mike. Why don't you leave the room and start over?

*Mike*: Whatever. (*Leaves the room, reenters, and takes the seat again.*)

*Mike*: So, how are you doing? I've never seen you around the hallways. Just move here or something?

*Jenny*: Well, actually we moved here at the end of the summer. I've been in town about a month now.

*Mike*: Great, I'll give you a tour of the neighborhood later.

*Laura*: Mike, wait a minute. You just met her. Lighten up a little bit.

*Mike*: Oh, okay. Well, Jenny, have you met many kids yet?

*Jenny*: Not really. A boy from school lives down the street from me and two girls in my homeroom introduced themselves.

*Mike*: Well, what are you into, Jenny? I mean, what do you like to do?

*Dr. B*: Mike, you're really getting the hang of this. Stay with it.

*Jenny*: I listen to music a lot and I played soccer in my old school.

*Mike*: Cool! Are you into heavy metal at all?

*Jenny*: Well, yeah, there are a few groups I listen to.

*Mike*: Like who?

*Jenny*: Well, I've always liked Metallica and recently I've gotten into some of the hard-core rap groups also. I just got a Snoop Doggy Dog CD.

*Mike*: Great, I know their stuff.

*Dr. B*: (*Interrupting*) You guys are doing really well at this. Let's assume class is about to start. How can you close this conversation, Mike?

*Mike*: Hey, Jenny, it's been good talking to you. Can you, uh, write your number down on my hand. Maybe I can call you sometime.

*Jenny*: (*Slightly awkward*) I guess so.

*Dr. B*: (*To group*) Well, how do you think they did? It's time to critique the action.

*Laura*: Well, it seemed pretty real, but Mike, you should have gotten her to talk more. You know, maybe asked her more questions.

*Mike*: I didn't have that much time.

*David*: Jenny, you think you'd really go out with someone if they talked to you like that?

*Jenny*: I might.

*Dr. B*: As far as I'm concerned this was a darned good role-play. Let's get two other people to play this scene again and see what else we can come up with.

## INTEGRATING ASSERTIVENESS SKILLS

As youngsters learn to converse comfortably and begin to reap the benefits, we can readily progress to more complex skills. Given their propensity to impulsive and aggressive reactions, it is essential to familiarize them with more appropriate assertiveness skills. I suggest to the group that there are better ways to get what we want than demanding, overreacting, and violating other people's rights. Assertive behavior is a way to express our personal rights without denying those of others. It falls midway between passive behavior and aggression (Forman 1993). These skills can be learned easily and applied in many situations.

Both appropriate and inappropriate assertiveness skills are demonstrated to the group. First the leaders model a situation in which someone cuts in line at the movie theater. This role-play depicts shoving and cursing at the offender, clearly aggressive behavior. In the second illustration the person is ignored and allowed to get away with it (passive behavior). Finally the offender is told: "Excuse me, you've just cut in front of me. Could you go to the end of the line?" (assertive response). The group can easily grasp the distinction but is often interested in what would happen if the person refused to move. At this point it becomes necessary to escalate the assertive responses sequentially. One begins with a statement that "you really can't stay here" and progresses to calling the manager if necessary. Any aggressive or violent approach must be strongly discouraged, of course.

Members must be clear on the distinction between assertive and aggressive responses. They are encouraged to develop and practice alternatives through role-play exercises. Feedback is given frequently to teach the adolescents how to evaluate their own performance. The practice situations must closely resemble those they are likely to encounter in their daily lives.

Here are some questions that can be used to determine how well kids are able to stand up for themselves in an appropriate fashion (Hipp 1985). They can be posed to the group and discussed prior to the assertiveness exercises.

1. When a friend arrives very late to meet you, do you say anything?
2. If someone borrows a CD from you and doesn't return it, do you ask for it back?
3. If you wanted to see a movie and none of your friends were interested, would you go anyway?
4. If your teacher is taking attendance and doesn't call your name, would you say anything?

Adolescents are told that several "no" answers suggest that they need to be more assertive. During the discussion a number of related issues may arise. Themes of anger, rejection, and self-confidence all tie in with the issue of assertiveness. They should be addressed briefly but the group must return to the task at hand.

Following is an excerpt from a group session focused on assertiveness training.

> *Dr. B*: Okay, today we are going to work on putting those assertiveness skills that we have been talking about to use. Here's the situation. Imagine that you're at home, in your room, listening to music. All of a sudden your mom barges in, screaming that your little brother is crying because you took his headphones. Now, you've done a lot of stuff before, but this time you really didn't do it. How would you handle it? I

need two volunteers here. One to be the mother, another the accused son. (*Molly and Jeff raise their hands*) Okay, let's roll.

*Molly* (mother): Jeff, I'm sick and tired of you bugging your brother all the time. Where are his headphones? If you don't turn them over right now, you're grounded this weekend!

*Jeff* (son): (*Screaming*) Forget you. He's a punk. Get out of my room!

*Dr. B*: Wait a minute here. Jeff, you didn't even do anything wrong. Why would you possibly react like that?

*Jeff*: (*Smiling innocently*) Sorry, I got carried away. It sounded a lot like what goes on in my house.

*Dr. B*: Come on, group, help him out.

*Harry*: Jeff, why don't you tell her she's overreacting. You didn't do anything wrong and it's not fair to always blame you.

*John*: Yeah, get her to listen to you.

*Jeff*: Well, uh, Mom, wait a minute. I didn't do it this time. You've got to give me a chance to explain.

*Molly*: Well, what have you got to say for yourself?

*Jeff*: It upsets me when I always get blamed for bugging my brother. Sometimes he really starts it. I wish you'd listen to my side of the story more often.

*Molly*: Well, it's hard to. Your brother gets so emotional and you know how it gets to me.

*Jeff*: Yeah, well, I know that, Mom, but sometimes I bug him just because he gets off easier than me.

*Molly*: I never knew that.

*Jeff*: That's all I have to say (*getting sad*).

*Molly*: All right, Jeff, let's just forget it this time. Maybe I did overreact a little.

*Jeff*: Thanks, Mom.

*Dr. B*: (*To group*) This is a good example of how you can express your feelings without overreacting and get the other person to listen. That's really important when someone is bugging you. Can anyone think of any real situations that happened to them? Maybe we can figure out some better ways to handle those.

## SOCIAL PROBLEM SOLVING

Pope and colleagues (1988) emphasize that youth who employ social problem-solving skills cope more effectively with stress and frustration. When assertiveness skills have been practiced sufficiently, the training should be broadened to include other aspects of social competence. The adolescents are reminded that problems are an unavoidable part of daily life. Those with oppositional defiant and conduct disorders report an inordinate number of hassles with others. Any discussion must focus on ways to make their lives easier.

The group is presented with examples of situations that are difficult for them to deal with. Parental restrictions, teacher criticisms, peer pressures, and boredom are frequently encountered in their daily lives. The Adolescent Problems Inventory (Freedman et al. 1978) includes an extensive list of topics for discussion. Group members are encouraged to share their personal encounters with annoying and upsetting situations. Social problem solving can then be introduced as a way to make coping easier.

The sequence is presented in much the same way as other social skills. It is broken down into small steps so that group members can rehearse each separately. Forman (1993) and Pope and colleagues (1988) describe the necessary steps in the social problem-solving process. Initially the adolescents learn to identify the problem from the perspective of both parties. They focus on how it started, what the accompanying emotions are, and their desired outcome. Alternatives are then considered carefully in a nonjudgmental fashion. What are the likely consequences of each possibility? Following this, the youngsters must choose the alternative most likely to benefit them and then ultimately evaluate the outcome.

It is helpful to have the important steps posted on a blackboard or listed on a handout so that group members can remind themselves of the sequence. The leaders then present a social dilemma and the adolescents are asked to take turns trying to resolve it.

Illustrative situation:

> Imagine that you are out with your friends one night and you have nothing to do. Someone proposes that you all go to the local grocery store and steal some beer. Although they only ask you to stand watch, you are a little worried because you have already been in trouble with the police on two separate occasions. If you get caught, it would most certainly mean a return to court. You want to go along with the crowd but something tells you it's not worth the risk.

Each group member is asked to apply one of the steps in the problem-solving sequence. The problem is identified as one of good judgment. The adolescent wants to be one of the guys but is afraid of getting caught. He also fears rejection by his peers if he declines and is uncertain how to bow out gracefully. The goal here is to stay out of trouble and simultaneously save face. The group proposes the following alternatives:

1.  He can simply state he is not feeling well and has decided to go home.
2.  He is straight with his friends, telling them that he'd like to go along with it, but just can't take the chance of getting in further trouble.
3.  He agrees to just be the lookout, but stands as far away from the store as he possibly can.

They then proceed to discuss the possible consequences. It seems likely that he could get away with it but you never know who might be watching. If they got caught stealing beer, the police would most certainly be summoned. From that point it would be hard to know if the store would press charges. Ultimately the group agrees that he would be better off avoiding the situation. They choose the option of being straight with his friends about why he can't do it, concluding that "if they were really your friends, they would understand."

## EXTENDING THE BENEFITS OF TRAINING

There is an extensive list of social skills that are beneficial to this population. Group leaders must make practical decisions as to how many can be worked on and to what extent. Tisdelle and St. Lawrence (1986) point out that no single isolated intervention is sufficient to produce social competency in impaired youth.

Goldstein and colleagues (1980) and Dowd and Tierney (1992) provide a comprehensive listing of social skills that can be taught by applying the learning principles previously discussed. The specific skills I have found most helpful in working with oppositional defiant and conduct-disordered adolescents include:

Asking for help
Apologizing
Accepting decisions of authority
Negotiating
Making a complaint
Accepting defeat
Choosing appropriate friends
Compromising with others
Dealing with boredom
Appropriate risk taking
Avoiding temptation

As youth increase their repertoire of social skills they begin to interact more appropriately with those around them. To a certain extent there are naturally occurring reinforcers that help to maintain the newly acquired behaviors. For example, an adolescent who learns to converse comfortably will find that others include him in their plans. When coupled with assertiveness skills, he becomes better equipped to resolve conflicts and relate more comfortably to others.

One recurrent problem, however, is that peers outside the group may reward antisocial rather than prosocial behavior. This situation must be anticipated and addressed to whatever extent possible. Time devoted to resisting peer pressure and making new friends is well spent. Opportunities to conduct interventions in the school and family settings should be sought. The adolescents must ultimately come to believe that their newly developed skills will make their lives easier, thus increasing self-satisfaction and the motivation to change.

# 8

# Building
# Self-Esteem

It is difficult to like oneself in the face of criticism, rejection, and ongoing conflicts with others. Coercive parenting practices and school failure also serve to erode self-esteem over the years. Despite their protests to the contrary, these youth are unhappy with their lives but feel at a loss to change them. Their bravado and indifference have evolved at great cost. Painful experiences have been repressed and replaced by anger, hostility, and avoidance of close relationships. In effect, they have lost touch with themselves.

Self-esteem is essential for psychological survival (McKay and Fanning 1987). When it is low, it predisposes us to negative expectations, self-deprecation, fear of change, and a distrust of relationships. Positive self-esteem is defined as the match between the perceived self and the ideal self (Pope et al. 1988).

Behavior-disordered adolescents often deny their discomfort and avoid an honest look at themselves because they might not like what they see. As trust develops and self-disclosure increases, a portrait of their negative self-perception emerges. Their ideal self—that is, the person they would like to be—is often very vague to them. Former positive aspirations have been clouded by a history of repeated failures. The therapeutic task is to help the youngster develop a realistic self-view and to formulate achievable goals.

Most antisocial adolescents do not readily share their negative self-perceptions. It is safer to begin by talking with them about the importance of pride or self-confidence. Although they insist that they like themselves, their definitions of confidence are rather narrow. Some declare that when you have confidence "you don't take stuff from anyone," "you do what you want," or "you get girls." This narcissistic position reflects a lack of social competence, empathy for others, and self-awareness.

## ASSESSING SELF-ESTEEM

The process begins with a careful look at the central areas of their lives. The adolescents are told that we all conduct ourselves a little differently in each situation. We are interested in their own perceptions of their behavior as well as the perceptions of others. A useful assessment tool is the Test of Self-Esteem for Children (Pope et al. 1988). This provides sixty self-statements that the adolescent rates to determine how often he or she feels that way. Several variations I have employed in early sessions are:

1. I believe that I am a likable person.
2. My family feels that I am important to them.

3. I will do anything I can to avoid losing.
4. I wish I could be someone else.
5. If it would keep me out of trouble, I would blame someone else for something I did wrong.

After they respond they are asked how an important other might answer that question about them (e.g., friend, parent, or teacher). Many youngsters will agree to fill out self-report inventories but their truthfulness varies with the strength of the therapeutic alliance.

Initially we explore their perceptions of their social sphere, family, school experience, and physical appearance. How do they feel about their friendships and interactions with others? What might someone else say about them? While most of these youth describe themselves as competent, this is often not the case. They are reminded that no one is perfect and that everyone has something that could stand improvement. Could they come up with at least one shortcoming?

Their behavior, performance, and attitude about school are carefully examined. Do they see themselves as capable of doing the work but choose not to? What might their teachers say about them? How would their peers characterize their school attitude? To whatever extent possible, we want to understand how the school experience has influenced the development of their self-esteem.

What about life in their family? Do they feel accepted by their parents and able to communicate with them? Most often the answer will be no. Adolescents frequently cite family conflicts as the most distressing aspect of their lives. They are quite willing to voice complaints that reflect the negative impact of the home environment. We want to learn more about the role that they play in their family. What about their behavior at home might be different from the way they are in other situations?

Finally, we try to learn how they feel about their "image" or physical appearance. Again there is a tendency to minimize their concerns and feign satisfaction. Adolescents are notoriously self-conscious and tune into the slightest irregularities of their complexion, features, and mood states. Disclosure is easily facilitated by sharing the concerns of other youngsters and then asking for their opinions. Often the greater the self-dissatisfaction, the more likely the youngster is to avoid dealing with the issue. Harper and Marshall (1991) found that adolescent girls reported lower self-esteem than boys. While this may in part be due to their greater willingness to acknowledge shortcomings, it was noteworthy that the girls were more concerned with their appearance and relationships, while the boys stressed financial and vocational worries.

Clearly, adolescence is a time of fluctuating self-esteem. During the course of a week, a youngster is likely to report both elated and depressed mood states. Their suggestibility and resilience are both high. Seemingly minor events may trigger extreme reactions, albeit short-lived. A thorough assessment must include the youngsters' global self-esteem; that is, their composite view of themselves based on all aspects of their lives.

## SOME DETERMINANTS OF SELF-ESTEEM

The internal yardstick by which we measure ourselves influences our degree of self-satisfaction. One's experience of an event as a success or failure reflects the idiosyncratic processing of information (Pope et al. 1988). Youngsters must be encouraged to verbalize and scrutinize the standards they set for themselves. Those with behavior disorders have lowered their expectations to avert further disappointments. In effect they have abandoned any effort to alter their situations. The lessened expectations enable them to justify their failures and misbehavior.

Certain adolescents will deny that they have any internal standards whatsoever. Indeed, their peer group may be their only frame of reference. Any denial of standards or excessively low expectations are clinically significant. Adolescents naturally compare themselves to others and often feel they are being watched. How often have we heard them say, "What are you staring at?" Despite their insistence on their independence, the youngsters are quite concerned with what their peers think of them.

Antisocial youth must frequently deal with failure and disappointment. Their interpretation of events reflects their low self-esteem. Failures, for example, may be attributed to a skill deficiency rather than recognized as the result of unrealistic standards.

## Case Example

John was a 15-year-old boy in frequent conflict with his teachers and parents. His school performance was poor but he excelled in basketball, which was a source of pride for him. At the start of the ninth grade John tried out for the freshman basketball team. Although he was quite talented, he skipped two practices and was ultimately cut from the team. This was quite upsetting but he rationalized that he didn't care because he just played basketball for fun.

As his rejection was explored, it became quite evident that John's internal standards were unrealistic. He acknowledged that he compared himself to the older players in the schoolyard and assumed that he just wasn't good enough for the team. It took considerable discussion to get him to see that his disappointment was the result of nonattendance rather than skill deficiency. Ultimately he was persuaded to talk to the coach about why he was cut from the team. This helped him to take responsibility for his failure and redirect his energies.

In discussing disappointments with patients, they are urged to define what constitutes a success or a failure. Harsh standards are likely to result in dejection as these adolescents usually feel they can't measure up. The adolescent who feels he always screws up may stop trying altogether and reject any offers of help. Sometimes they are angered by others' high expectations of them and refuse to make an effort as a statement of protest. The therapeutic task is to help these adolescents set realistic standards and attainable goals for themselves. Somehow they must come to see that failure is not the end of the world, that circumstances can change and other opportunities will arise.

# THE POWER OF NEGATIVE THINKING

How youngsters talk to themselves influences both their feelings and their outlook. Negative self-statements eventually erode self-esteem if they are not challenged. A girl who keeps telling herself she is unattractive will feel bad about herself and act accordingly. A boy who believes his parents don't want him around may behave as if the world is constantly rejecting him. Those who learn to challenge their negative thinking through objective assessment develop a more positive self-esteem.

Cognitive-behavior therapy attempts to modify how a youngster thinks about himself, his experiences, and the future (Wilkes et al. 1994). The approach is direct, short term, and well suited to those with a negative self-image. In essence, the task is to help adolescents to identify the distortions in their thinking that affect their interactions, mood states, and self-esteem.

The challenge is to get this population to share their negative thoughts in a safe atmosphere. Assuming that the resistance has been at least partially diffused, the dialogue should be flowing fairly smoothly. At this point the patient is told that everyone has a private language that we speak to ourselves. Our feelings are influenced by what we say and how we say it. For example, if a teenage girl repeatedly tells herself she is overweight, she may begin to avoid social contacts. A boy who believes he is popular will readily approach other youngsters. All of us have a private side we rarely share and a public self that is the image presented to others. Ask adolescents if they feel that anyone really knows them. If they say yes, inquire about who it is and what he or she might say about them (Rosenberg 1979). The ensuing discussion focuses on how difficult it is to trust others, particularly with our most personal feelings.

"It takes a great deal of courage to let someone get to know us and see our more vulnerable side. We spend considerable energy pretending we feel fine when we actually may not. It is perfectly natural to have a down side. I think I could help you to feel better if you are willing to share some of the negative thoughts about yourself that go through your head. I know this seems unfamiliar to you, but I'd like to ask that you bear with me until you get the hang of it."

Most youth will tentatively share some of their personal thoughts at this point. Efforts are made to empathize, universalize, and disclose some of our own relevant experience. Youth are naturally suspicious that this process will not bring relief, so it is helpful to construct an agenda for them. What areas of their life would they want to change? We try to collaborate with them to formulate goals. Usually these are reflections of their daily concerns: getting someone to like them, influencing their parents, or surviving a difficult class. The focus is on how their negative thinking causes them discomfort and makes them feel worse.

Belsher and Wilkes (1994) provide an excellent description of the elements of cognitive therapy with adolescents. The process is introduced by asking them to identify daily thoughts that cause them distress. They go on to describe an upsetting situation, note how they feel, and what they say to themselves.

For example, Alan recalled his mother's insistence that he empty the dishwasher one evening. It made him angry because he thought "she always sticks me with jobs and lets my brother off the hook." In another example,

Susan described a school situation in which a boy she was interested in walked by her without acknowledging her. This saddened her and led her to conclude that no one in her grade liked her.

Another way to tap into negative thinking is to ask youth to predict future events. What do they imagine will happen when their parents see their report card? Are they prepared for the worst? Automatic thinking that anticipates failure, disappointment, or conflict can become a self-fulfilling prophecy. Again adolescents are asked to record distressing situations and to note their accompanying thoughts (Belsher and Wilkes 1994). During the session it is useful to offer a written list of some examples of other teenagers' thoughts. They are then asked to complete several blanks with experiences of their own. Antisocial youth often report automatic thoughts that justify their behavior and reflect their poor self-esteem. Table 8–1 provides some examples of this type of thinking.

When automatic thoughts are examined, the accompanying moods should also be described. Have the youngsters evaluate how their day went and describe what made it good or bad. One student who cut a class in school might see it as an accomplishment; another might consider it a failure.

Clearly the mood is an outgrowth of the interpretation of the event. Adolescents must be questioned about their beliefs to determine what thoughts underlie them. As they describe incidents in their lives, encourage them to offer their own explanations. Their characteristically negative thinking should be identified and analyzed. Most often their beliefs are of longstanding origin and occur almost automatically. As they learn to evaluate

## TABLE 8–1

| SITUATION | AUTOMATIC THOUGHT |
|---|---|
| 1. I failed my last English test. | 1. The teacher will fail me for the semester so there's no point in trying. |
| 2. My parents have restricted me for the next two weekends. | 2. I might as well sneak out of the house. They're always punishing me. |
| 3. I got caught stealing something from the store. | 3. I'm a fuck-up. I can never do anything right. |
| 4. This girl that I like shot me down. | 4. I'll never get a date. |
| 5. My soccer team lost its third straight game. | 5. It was my fault. I might as well quit. |

their thought processes objectively, they can begin to consider alternative explanations for events.

Cognitive distortions are at the root of a sad mood state. Antisocial adolescents often misinterpret social cues and display characteristic rigidity in their thought processes. Burns (1980) has described the major thinking errors that take place. Several are particularly applicable to this population. In *binocular magnifying* things are made to seem much worse than they are. The statement "All my teachers are out to get me" illustrates this type of thinking. When the adolescent denies a success by refusing any credit, *binocular shrinking* has occurred. A boy elected class representative might explain away his victory by claiming that everyone felt sorry for him. *Black and white thinking* is also prevalent and is illustrated by comments that parents are either all good or all bad.

Finally, some youngsters practice *mind reading*, that is, they predict others' thoughts without any evidence to support their beliefs. For example, Terry recalled that when she got a rather short haircut, she stayed home from school the next day feeling certain that everyone would look at her and think how ugly she looked. Indeed, negative thinking can influence all aspects of one's life.

## CHALLENGING MALADAPTIVE COGNITIONS

The initial task is to bring these cognitive distortions to the adolescent's attention. I sometimes joke that they are quite proficient at seeing the negative side of situations and have great difficulty in looking at the positive aspects. As I get them to share events in their daily lives, they are challenged to look objectively at their own behavior and that of others.

Joe, for example, spoke frequently about his parents' bugging him and trying to control him. When questioned, he insisted that "they did it for no reason and probably enjoyed it." He was encouraged to look at other possible motives for their annoying behavior. Perhaps they really cared about him and felt at a loss as to what to do. More important, the point was raised about Joe's feeling powerless to stop them. He was challenged to see that if he chose to behave responsibly and less provocatively, they wouldn't have much reason to harass him. That, in fact, would give him a lot more power. This reframing technique is used to get youth to view things from a different perspective. Alternative explanations for

behavior are always explored. How would another teenager look at the same situation? Comparing their thoughts
to those of others can help them to gain a realistic perspective on a situation.

Cognitive distortions should be systematically challenged and dismantled. When a negative automatic
thought is first identified, it should be recorded on a
chart. Following that, the youngster is helped to generate
a more rational set of responses.

Steve, for example, was quite upset when he called a
girl he liked, left a message, and did not hear from her.
He concluded that she felt that he wasn't cool and didn't
want to talk with him. A discussion of this event turned
up several other possibilities. She may not have received
his message, might have been very busy, or couldn't make
up her mind what to do. Steve ultimately concluded that
he had no way of knowing what she really thought. He
had assumed the worst and needed to investigate his
assumptions further. When asked what a really popular
boy would think, he replied, "Oh, she'd call back sooner
or later; he'd have nothing to worry about!"

Negative thinking is not always a distortion of the
facts. Youngsters who have legitimate concerns about
their appearance because they are short, overweight,
have severe acne, or are otherwise considered unattractive must be approached differently. Their self-esteem is
poor because of their inability to accept or compensate
for their shortcomings. This group needs help in identifying other positive qualities about themselves. A good
personality, athletic ability, a particular talent, or unique
appearance are all strengths to build upon.

I've developed an exercise called "Name that Nerd"
that I use with many of these youth. They are shown old

pictures of awkward adolescents who have become famous as adults and then asked to identify them. Most are shocked when they learn who they are and what they look like today. This is a graphic illustration that appearances can change drastically. The ensuing discussion focuses on what they can do to improve their image or make the make the most of what they have.

I also like to tell youngsters brief stories about famous people who succeeded against the odds. Did you know that

- Beethoven's music teacher told him he was hopeless as a composer.
- Cher had learning disabilities as a child.
- Sylvester Stallone was a juvenile delinquent.
- Thomas Edison's teachers said he was too stupid to learn anything.
- Michael Jordan was cut from his high school basketball team.
- Walt Disney was fired by a newspaper editor for lack of ideas.

All of these facts can serve as springboards for discussion. Everyone has a right to their dreams and should be encouraged to project ahead and imagine a positive outcome. If someone strongly believes that things will never change, they probably won't. Those who forecast doom should be challenged on their thinking. Conversely, youth who believe that things will magically be different the next day or year or when they go off to college must be confronted on their denial of the realities.

Thought-stopping techniques can also help to interrupt the pattern of negative thinking. In this technique individuals are instructed to do something to distract themselves from their recurrent thoughts. They might engage in an absorbing physical activity such as running or swimming. They can also try to think about something that is incompatible with the distressing thought (e.g., a party or a good movie). The focus is on getting absorbed with the present moment to avoid interfering ruminations. Flicking a rubber band on the wrist serves a similar function. The patients are instructed to concentrate on the sensation rather than the disruptive thought.

McKay and Fanning (1987) suggest that we view negative thoughts as our internal critic and encourage people to talk back to that inner voice. When the self-recriminations begin, one might tell their internal critic to "cut this crap," "shut up," or "don't even think about that." The goal is to help the youngster feel in control of the thought, rather than feeling like the thought is controlling him.

Wexler (1991) employs an interesting group exercise called "the protective shell" to further challenge negative thinking. A youngster is asked to identify a particularly distressing thought or self-perception for discussion. Several group members are then assigned the role of an assault team to attack the youngster with his own negative thinking. The others are instructed to form a "protective shell" around the member under fire. Their job is to protect the youngster from attack by coming up with powerful arguments to counteract the negative assault. When effectively executed, this exercise actively helps the youth to feel more valued and empowered.

## IMPACT OF THE THERAPEUTIC RELATIONSHIP

When adolescents feel respected and accepted, they are more likely to display their vulnerability. Their lives have often been filled with rejection, disappointment, emptiness, and suspicion. The trust that evolves from a close relationship enables them to face their weaknesses and begin to make positive changes. In a way, they borrow from the therapist's sense of self as they begin to develop their own. The process of challenging negative thinking, confronting maladaptive behavior, and helping to make their feelings important ultimately contributes to improved self-esteem.

Change does not occur in a vacuum. As adolescents improve their interpersonal skills, learn to modulate their impulses, and begin to think differently, they can discard old maladaptive behavior patterns. This is not to suggest that the many failures and losses are easily overcome. A broad array of interventions must be employed to get at the multiple determinants of their problems.


## EXPERIENTIAL AND INDUCTIVE TECHNIQUES

Many behaviorally disordered adolescents have lacked adequate role models, mentors, or anyone who could consistently support them in their lives. Wexler (1991) presents a detailed process for teaching troubled adolescents to self-soothe. I have found his exercises to be quite helpful after a therapeutic alliance has been established. The work has its origins in the techniques of Milton Erickson, a brilliant psychotherapist and strategist.

Wexler (1991) introduces youngsters to the concept of an ally. The goal is to create an internalized image of someone who can be there to comfort them when they feel insecure, alone, or under great stress. Initially they are asked to recall someone from their past who was special to them in a unique way. They are given instructions to lean back, relax, and breathe deeply until they feel comfortable. As they become free of distractions, the therapist asks them to imagine that special person and describe them as best they can. Careful attention is paid to nuances such as this individual's tone of voice, how he or she touched them, and any distinguishing characteristics. When the youngsters feel they can clearly imagine the presence of that special person, they are encouraged to talk with their ally. What might the person say to help them feel comforted? What would they want to be able to tell him?

## Case Example

Jim agreed to try this exercise after some initial skepticism. The ally he envisioned was his grandfather, who had passed away several years previously. After setting the stage for a conversation with him, Jim was first asked what he'd want to tell his grandfather. Sadly, he said, "I guess I'd want him to know that I'm really sorry."

"For what?" I queried.

"For all the problems I've caused everyone," he said.

"Why tell your grandfather that?"

"Well, he was the only one who ever really

listened to me when I was a kid. I remember getting hurt sometimes. My parents would always say it was no big deal. To him it was. He'd always say he wanted to hear all about it. He used to tell me I was his favorite. We played a lot, did some fun stuff. I never felt like he was in a hurry. Even when I got in trouble, Grandpa would want to talk to me. He always said that he wanted to hear my side of the story. I never lied to him, you know. And then he died. I guess I was around 13."

*Therapist*: Well, he's here right now. What would he say about the problems you've been having lately? How could he make you feel better?

*Jim*: I think he'd put his arm around me first. Tell me he really cares about me and ask what he could do to help. He'd never say I was a bad person. You know, a loser.

*Therapist*: Just sort of be there for you.

*Jim*: Yes.

*Therapist*: Anything else he'd tell you?

*Jim*: Well, I guess he'd tell me not to give up. He always used to talk about just doing the best you can. I liked that.

*Therapist*: In a sense, your grandfather is still here for you. You can call on him when you need to. If you're in a rut, you can talk to him. Try and think about the things he'd say and let yourself feel him comforting you. I think it'll help.

*Jim*: Yeah, I guess I can try this again sometime.

A surprisingly large group of kids cannot think of someone from their past who might fill the shoes of an ally.

They must be helped to describe the qualities that such an imaginary person would have. This is not always easy as many have trouble identifying and expressing their needs. When reminded that this confidential exercise is designed to help them to feel better, most will reluctantly comply. The answers are usually interesting. The ally would be someone who would keep them company, give them reassurance, and listen to their thoughts without telling them what to do. Clearly their expectations have been diminished by their negative experiences. Some time should devoted to exploring what a "good ally" could offer them so they can broaden their awareness of what closeness means. The therapeutic relationship should be discussed as a possible example of this.

Another exercise I use to assess the "real" self involves asking them to imagine themselves appearing before a tribunal on judgment day. What would the charges be and how might they defend themselves? Their good and bad points are discussed at some length with an emphasis on the adolescents' perspective. They are asked to evaluate their life to date and consider any changes they might care to make before the final verdict is in. Who could be of help to them at this point? Some antisocial youth will insist that they "really don't care." Reminding them that this is their script, however they'd like to write it, sometimes helps to engage them.

## A RECIPE FOR SELF-ESTEEM

Adolescents who lack self-definition complain frequently of boredom. They report few interests and lack any sense of purpose to their lives. Any possible excitement is strongly associated with risk taking and courting trouble. This pattern is firmly established since the youngster assumes that no other options are available to him. These beliefs must be challenged and alternatives presented.

Inquire about what hobbies or interests the youngsters had when they were younger. Perhaps they collected comic books, stamps, or baseball cards. There are many interesting stories about kids discovering old baseball cards of considerable value in their closet. Needless to say, the thought of making easy money has great appeal to them. They should be encouraged to resurrect old interests and discover new ones.

On one occasion I brought a lawn and leaf bag filled with old sports cards to a group session. I told the members that I had placed a fairly valuable old Michael Jordan card in the bag and they were invited to search for it. The group spent the better part of an hour going through several thousand cards until it was discovered. They enjoyed the experience and were exposed to a hobby. This approach can be applied to many different ideas to whet their appetites. One youngster proudly brought in a metal detector he had received the previous Christmas. It was the topic of some discussion. Again, the task is to broaden their horizons and assist them in finding new interests and activities.

Adolescents should also be asked if they have had any enjoyment that did not violate rules. Some will insist that they can't think of anything but with assistance and prompting they begin to generate ideas. Many recall having fun at amusement parks, going on the thrill rides and feeling excited. Riding waves in the ocean comes up often, as does skiing and skate boarding. It helps to have a variety of ideas to present for discussion. Following this, youngsters are instructed to do something that is legal and "really fun" outside the treatment setting. The assignments are discussed in the next session.

Other avenues for channeling aggression should be explored. Some youngsters will participate in sports programs when directly invited, while others prefer outdoor activities of a noncompetitive nature. Opportunities for volunteer work should be sought and presented. Exposing them to those in need (e.g., individuals in nursing homes, hospitals, or shelters) can sensitize troubled youth to the feelings of others and bolster self-esteem by making them feel wanted. Interestingly, this population is often amenable to joining community protection groups as an alternative outlet.

In effect, self-esteem reflects a sense of control over one's life. It is acquired gradually through a sequence of affirming experiences. As youth acquire new cognitive, affective, and behavioral skills, the seeds of confidence are planted. Those who develop a sense of pride are better able to resist trouble and make good choices. Ultimately the remediation of deficits in the self will contribute to durable behavior change.

# 9

# Developing
# Empathy,
# Morality, and
# Vulnerability

Several years ago a 17-year-old patient, John, told me the following story without blinking an eyelash. He and his friends had been hanging out in front of an apartment building the previous Saturday evening. A young man leaving the building with his girlfriend walked past them, looked at one of his friends, and said, "Hey, man, what's doing?" The friend did not like his look or his tone of voice. He got up, walked over to him, and punched him in the face, knocking him to the ground.

At this point the four others in the group decided their friend needed help and joined the fracas. They began kicking and punching the man who was down. Despite the girlfriend's screams, the assault continued. While the victim put up a fight, this served only to make them angrier. One of his friends picked up a brick and started beating the man on the head with it. It was not long before he lay motionless on the ground.

The group decided he had had enough and left him

lying there in a pool of blood. The girlfriend called the police and an ambulance. Tragically, the youngster was dead on arrival at the hospital. As I listened to this story I felt a sense of pathos. I shared this with John in the hope that he could understand. His reaction shocked me. "Dr. B., you shouldn't feel bad. He got what was coming to him. He should never have talked to my friend like that!"

Sadly, within this group, there was a marked lack of empathy, a belief in the legitimacy of their actions, and peer approval for this random act of violence. It was difficult to get this 17-year-old to look at the situation from any different perspective. He had been hardened by life at home and on the streets. If there were legal consequences for their actions, then so be it. Unfortunately, there is no redeeming quality or epilogue to this story. The fact is that some youth are so entrenched in their ways that change is extremely difficult.

Adolescents who regularly violate social norms display inadequate moral development and an impaired capacity to empathize. Two schools of thought represent the current formulations. Hoffman's (1983) affective socialization theory suggests that empathic responding inhibits the tendency to engage in antisocial and aggressive acts. Consequently, the task is to help youth to develop feelings for others and to experience guilt. Kohlberg (1984) emphasizes the role of delays in sociomoral development in the etiology of antisocial behavior. The acquisition of moral reasoning and empathy skills is essential to the socialization process. They reduce the likelihood of violating social norms and joining a deviant peer group.

Contempt for rules and authority reflect undersocialization and poor parental role modeling. When the parents have failed to sensitize their children to the feelings of others, and simultaneously provide little warmth and support, the seeds have been planted. Youngsters must be taught why their actions are inappropriate and learn to take the victim's perspective. Those not directed to attend to other's distress will lack the empathy-based guilt necessary to avert wrongdoing.

There is a striking egocentricity in this population. They view the world through their self-serving needs and those who attempt to thwart them are the enemy. They believe that rules are for other people, not for them. Punitive consequences serve only to worsen the situation and strengthen their resolve. The antisocial youth is unable to display weakness, kindness, and a need for others. Their victims are often described as stupid people who got in their way. Blame is assigned to others and the explanations for their transgressions are typically superficial and immature.

Kohlberg's (1984) stages of moral reasoning are helpful in conceptualizing the developmental process and pinpointing the adolescent's cognitive deficits. Stage one represents the least mature and most superficial moral view. In essence, it is the law of the jungle. Individuals comply with authority if those in power are physically superior—and keep their word so they won't get beat up. There is little awareness of the mutuality of needs.

Stage two is somewhat more pragmatic. The focus is on the satisfaction of needs and the avoidance of negative consequences. The basis for doing something is the expectation that another will return the favor. A sense of decency has not yet evolved; however, adolescents will not violate the rights of someone who has done a favor for them. A high percentage of conduct-disordered youth function at this stage of moral reasoning.

The movement to stage three represents a more mature grasp of society's expectations. Those functioning on this level display an ability to establish relationships and see things from another's perspective. A stage three adolescent would experience guilt after wrongdoing, which reduces the likelihood of his or her doing wrong. Finally, those who have achieved stage four moral reasoning reflect an understanding of and respect for conventional standards. One might say that such an adolescent is well socialized and respectful of others.

## SETTING THE TONE FOR CHANGE

Despite the pronounced absence of guilt, compassion, and age-appropriate moral reasoning, antisocial youth do not see themselves as bad people. Treatment interventions not only must identify these deficits, they must offer a rationale for change. From the adolescents' perspective, increased empathy and improved moral reasoning are not important goals. Their primary incentive is to get others off their back. When empathic understanding is presented as a tool to influence others, the youngsters will display some interest. Most will acknowledge an awareness of others' feelings; however, they do not allow this to influence their actions. Although they feign indifference, the idea of being well liked has some appeal. I often tell youngsters that they're more real when they feel. Ultimately, an increased sensitivity to others will lead to better judgment and less conflict. This in turn should result in increased acceptance.

Some youngsters must be motivated by extrinsic reinforcers, school pressure, or court mandates. The content of any curriculum or therapeutic program should be highly interesting and relevant. The greater a program's similarity to their own lives, the more likely is the youngster's participation. Attendance in the group must be mandatory and active involvement expected for the program to be completed.

Discussions of famous and infamous people will help to illustrate the extremes of morality and empathy. Mother Teresa and Abraham Lincoln come to mind as great humanitarians who were highly empathic and had a marked impact on their country. Conversely, Jack the Ripper, Saddam Hussein, and Adolph Hitler serve as heinous examples of the depravity of mankind. Antisocial adolescents are often fascinated by accounts of moral deterioration that make their own wrongdoing pale by comparison. Even the most hardened youth have sometimes been able to acknowledge that genocide is immoral and should never be condoned.

Mobilizing peer pressure is no easy task. Some youth have lacked exposure to compassionate role models and must be challenged to take a different perspective. If one is to reject deviant behavior, a more viable alternative must be available. Mixing youth with varying degrees of disturbance creates the opportunity for modeling and challenging to occur.

When an entire group (i.e., a gang) lacks any sense of morality or compassion, the task is far more difficult. At times a concentrated effort to solicit the leader's cooperation can pay off. This can be accomplished by developing an alliance outside the group session. I often tell influential peers that they have a great deal of power and that I need their help. Sometimes we can strike a bargain that involves my helping them to get something they want in return for their cooperation with the group task. This reduces their resistance and opens them to the possibility of change. While it is a nonconventional approach, I believe that in this instance the means justify the end.

## DEVELOPING SOCIOMORAL REASONING

Kohlberg (1984) describes his work with antisocial youth as a sequential process designed to raise their moral reasoning ability to a higher level. If successful, the likelihood of antisocial behavior decreases. The goals of the group are accomplished primarily through discussions of moral dilemmas. Adolescents are presented with various problem situations and are asked to come up with the best solution. The group's task is to reach consensus on the appropriate course of action. Members are encouraged to challenge one another's reasoning and try to see the dilemma from the other person's perspective. The leaders help them to express their thoughts clearly and actively listen to the other members' views.

When possible, it is desirable to mix youngsters who are at different stages of moral development. A stage three adolescent is far more likely to challenge stage two thinking, thereby creating the opportunity for movement to a higher level. Homogeneous groupings of adolescents at the lower stages will reduce the likelihood of intra-group confrontation as they often reinforce each other's immature and self-centered thinking. These situations require the leaders to take an active and directive role in challenging the patients on their myopic views.

Arbuthnot (1992) recommends that group leaders vigorously question members to be certain that their perceptions of the moral dilemma are accurate. Vague statements should be labeled as such and the patients encouraged to explain the reasons for their thinking. Under what circumstances might a certain behavior be acceptable? What if everyone always did what they felt like? Compelling arguments are presented to try and sway youngsters from their rigid position.

Following are the discussions of several moral dilemmas I have posed to my groups.

*Theme One—Theft.* Several of your friends notice a woman double-park her car with the keys still in the ignition. As she runs into the cleaners, they decide to take the car for a joyride. They insist it will only be for a few minutes so you decide to go along, despite the fact that the lady looked familiar. As they prepare to abandon the car in another neighborhood, your friend notices her purse on the floor and grabs it on the way out. While you're all taking off, you recall who the woman was. She is a single mother of three children who lives down the street from you. You know that she is really struggling to make ends meet and you figure that the $150 in the purse was grocery money for her children.

As you return to the neighborhood you notice her talking to the police and crying about what happened. The thought crosses your mind that you could return the purse later with the explanation that you found it in the street. This is complicated because the friend who has taken the money is pleased about it. He has always been a good friend to you, and in fact has helped you out of several jams. What might you do in such a situation?

*Discussion.* The group strongly agreed that she was stupid to leave her keys in the car. Several members felt she deserved what she got (stage two reasoning), but others argued that the boys still broke the law and, worse yet, were causing additional hardship to her family (stage three reasoning). There was some discussion as to what the boy would do with the money he had taken in contrast to the woman's need. Two of the members felt strongly that he should return the purse since it was the right thing to do (stage three). Another pointed out that since he vaguely knew the woman from the neighborhood "he should cut her some slack" (stage two/three). Several members expressed concern about getting caught when he returned the purse, but reluctantly agreed. Ultimately, the group decided that the purse should be returned, but had trouble deciding on the best way to do so.

*Theme Two—Domestic Violence.* One night a girl's parents got into a huge argument over money. During the altercation she observed her father (who had been drinking) strike her mother and knock her to the ground. Her mother did not appear hurt but screamed that she would not take this and proceeded to call 911. The police were dispatched to the house.

Upon arrival they asked for the girl's account of what had happened as she had witnessed the incident. The daughter felt close to her father but knew this was not the first time he had hit her mother. On the other hand, the mother had always been openly critical of the father, at times provoking his angry reactions. The girl felt that her father was in the wrong but worried that if charges were pressed, he might be removed from the home.

*Discussion.* This issue generated heated debate in the group. Several of the more antisocial members insisted that anything goes in a fight. They had difficulty accepting that the woman was physically inferior and emphasized that she had provoked him (stage two). Others felt equally convinced that any type of physical abuse was wrong and should be punished (stage three). This topic was especially poignant because several of the youngsters had been abused as children.

The question of whether the daughter should be truthful with the police split the group down the middle. Most of them were interested in exploring whether there were any mitigating circumstances and if the mother was really hurt. Two felt that because he was a "good father," it would be wrong of her to turn him in. One young man picked up on the father's drinking problem and suggested that this made him prone to violence. Following a lengthy discussion, all but one member were able to agree that the daughter should tell the police what had happened. The group felt strongly that her father loved her and would understand. In addition, they emphasized that this might be the only way the father could get help.

## SELF-SERVING THOUGHTS

Certain cognitive distortions impede the development of an objective moral perspective. These self-serving thoughts enable youth to rationalize wrongdoing and thus avoid responsibility for their actions. Antisocial youth view the world from an egocentric perspective. A sense of entitlement permeates their thinking. A boy questioned about why he stole something responded: "Because I wanted it." When asked why he beat up someone, another adamantly stated that "I felt like it." These are not intended to be sarcastic answers. The youngsters genuinely believe what they say, despite the superficiality of the content.

Minimizing is sometimes used to justify inappropriate behavior. Joe was suspended from school for beating up another student. When questioned by his principal, Joe wondered why everyone was making such a big deal of the incident. He had simply hurt someone "who deserved what they got."

"It serves him right," Joe added; "he shouldn't have tried to fight me."

This playing down of the significance of an event comes rather naturally. Youth avoid looking at the implications of their behavior and routinely offer a variety of self-serving explanations. They regularly place blame for their difficulties on others. A fight with a teacher occurs because the teacher provoked them. They don't get along with their parents because their parents are out of touch. A youngster caught stealing angrily exclaims that the store owner shouldn't have gone to the restroom.

As is the case with negative thinking, these specific distortions must be challenged. It is not acceptable to steal just because you can get away with it. In fact, it is stupid. Sooner or later you will get caught. Fighting may earn you a reputation for being tough, but it won't get you very far in life. People will get tired of your blaming everyone else for your problems; eventually they'll just avoid you.

Emphasis should be placed on the long-term consequences of their behaviors. In the group context members must be encouraged to identify egocentric thinking. As they grow better at challenging one another, their perspectives broaden. After all, their peers know their tricks. When rationalizations are no longer tolerated, the accountability increases. Ultimately, the self-centered pattern of thinking gives way to a more other-oriented approach.

## DEVELOPING EMPATHY

Antisocial adolescents must shift from their narcissistic perspective to a broad-based understanding of the needs and feelings of others. When behavior disorders progress from oppositional defiant to conduct disorder, the capacity to empathize seems to decrease. Samenow (1984) noted that youthful criminal offenders suppress empathic feelings by taking an impersonal view of others. They lack an understanding of what friendship is because trust and sharing are incompatible with their lifestyle. This absence of compassion and social perspective enables them to violate societal norms without remorse. Ed explained his antisocial actions by emphasizing that "I just don't think about what the victim might feel."

"What if you did?" I queried.

"It might be harder to do some of the shit I pull off," he replied.

Repeatedly inducing empathy and empathy-based guilt should help to prompt consideration of others' feelings (Gibbs 1987). Those who avoid any thought of the potential consequences of their behavior must be confronted in both individual and group treatment.

Feshbach and Feshbach (1982) define empathy as an affective response involving the ability to accurately perceive a social situation and take the role of another. The empathic youth is less likely to misinterpret someone's behavior and get angry. This capacity to understand what another feels is essential to the development of morality and guilt. The therapeutic goal is to get youngsters to look outside themselves and develop the foundation for caring.

Sociomoral reasoning groups should be integrated with specific empathy-induction exercises in order to alter immature and self-centered reasoning. As youth become increasingly able to appreciate the feelings of others as different from their own, the propensity toward antisocial behavior is reduced. Their capacity to experience empathy is assessed while treatment is introduced.

Duggan (1978) devised a series of stories with follow-up questions to determine the adolescent's reasoning skills, interpretation of events, and empathic capacity. Following is one of the stories I have used to stimulate discussion and assess empathy.

Zack had lived in the same neighborhood for the past eleven years. Although he was not doing well in high school, he liked the kids he hung out with and felt that he "really knew the ropes." He had been going with the same girl for three months now. Zack's parents argued frequently and he avoided being home whenever possible.

One day his mother sadly approached him and

told him she just couldn't take life with his father anymore. Her intention was to move out of their house and stay with her parents until she figured out what to do next. She imagined it would be several months before she found her own place and wanted Zack and his sister to join her. Unfortunately, Zack's grandparents lived about an hour away.

Zack got along reasonably well with his mother, but had little to do with his father, who was rather quiet. He was certain that his father would stay in the house and allow him to remain if he chose. His sister was leaving for college in a few months and said she'd go wherever Mom did. Zack realized that if he moved, he would seldom see his friends and girlfriend. He felt that his mother really needed him and knew that she would be easier to get along with.

The following questions are posed to the youngsters:

1. How do you think Zack feels?
2. Have you ever been through a similar situation or known someone who has?
3. What would you do if you were in Zack's place?
4. How does it make you feel to think about it?

Their responses indicate their ability to place themselves in someone else's shoes and to "feel" for what he was going through. Those who "really don't care what happens" or comment that they "don't see what the big deal is" will need considerable assistance.

## EXERCISES TO DEVELOP EMPATHY
## AND CONSCIENCE

The ability to identify and describe emotional states is a prerequisite to empathy. Adolescents observe a role-play of situations illustrating sadness, fear, joy, and anger. They are then encouraged to offer personal examples for each of the emotions. This process of sensitizing them to others' feelings can be expanded to include perspective taking. One nonthreatening approach is to ask youngsters to try and see things through another person's eyes. What might it be like to be Shaquille O'Neal? How does the world look to a seven foot, three hundred pound man? Can they imagine the pressure that a President lives with?

Those stuck in an early stage of moral development will need a rather concrete demonstration of feeling. An analogy can be drawn between physical and emotional pain. Someone hits you and it hurts. You feel the pain directly and react automatically. Different levels of pain are demonstrated by titrating the intensity of the impact.

Emotional pain is more complex. We experience it internally and may or may not express it. Some people are clearly distressed or have been through a great deal and readily evoke sympathy. Even hardened youth will acknowledge the plight of the homeless or victims of tragedy such as earthquakes or plane crashes (sometimes there is just no explanation). They should be asked to describe how they think the victims might feel.

Moral norms should be discussed at length. Why must a society have laws to operate efficiently? What if everyone just did what they felt like all of the time? Youngsters find these topics stimulating but initially resist anything symbolic of authority. Gradually, through continued dialogue and challenges to their egocentric views, many come to accept the need for some externally imposed structure.

Youth should be asked to describe their own exposure to morality. Who were their role models? How do they figure the role models developed their sense of values? As they share their stories, much of their residual pain becomes apparent, and their values and beliefs are more readily understood.

Movie clips can be used to elicit empathy in "unfeeling" youngsters. The Dickens classic *A Christmas Carol* illustrates the evolution of compassion in Ebenezer Scrooge. The recent movie *Boyz N the Hood* depicts a well-liked "cool kid" getting shot because of gang vengeance. Teenagers who watch this scene are often moved to tears and sometimes question the street mentality. Groups should be encouraged to come up with their own stories illustrating both the presence and the absence of empathy. As group cohesion develops, the interactions and feedback will reward disclosure and vulnerability.

Duggan (1978) developed a childcare apprenticeship program to pair troubled adolescents with needy children. Having them help these children on a regular basis resulted in increased levels of empathy and understanding. When possible, we can require youth to engage in other benevolent acts such as work with the elderly, terminally ill, or homeless. This can further sensitize them to the plight of others. There must first be an initial mandate or incentive to ensure cooperation, of course. The assignment of alternative community service is particularly helpful for antisocial youth. Many have never felt appreciated in their lives and begin to see themselves in a different light, that is, in a helping role, rather than that of a troublemaker. Caring responses can also be modeled to help adolescents to develop an appropriate frame of reference.

Exercises in perspective taking are essential to the development of empathy and the generation of guilt. I have found it useful to play tapes of victims expressing their sadness, outrage, and humiliation following acts of aggression against them. As they listen to the words of their peers or adults whom they can relate to, their eyes are opened just a little further. Here's a synopsis of one of the recordings I have played.

> Danny was a 15-year-old boy who was beaten and robbed by several rough kids in his neighborhood. He spoke at length about how terrified he was while he was trapped and mugged. "The boys jumped me from behind and threw me to the ground. I was crying and begging them to just take my wallet and leave me alone. They laughed and kept harassing me. I think they were probably drunk or something. It felt like it would never end.
>
> "Now when I think about it I get angry. What they did was really wrong. I can't believe they could get away with it. I was upset for weeks after that. I had trouble sleeping and would react to any strange noises. It's a terrible feeling to be embarrassed about something and be totally helpless. I guess I'll never forget that experience."

As antisocial youth listen to recordings like these, their first reaction is often amusement. They must be challenged to try and understand what the victim is

feeling. What does fear feel like? How about the humiliation of being publicly abused by others? Surely some of
them can recall being victimized in their own lives. They
are encouraged to share these experiences with the group
so they can make the connection to a victim's pain. The
greater their capacity to empathize with the victim, the
less the propensity to victimize.

Another exercise that is useful with juvenile offenders is the reenactment of their crime before a group of
their peers (Gibbs et al. 1995). The perpetrator is asked to
role-play the incident with the help of several group
members. Attention is focused on the thoughts of both
the offender and the victim before and during the act of
aggression.

Afterwards, the offender is asked to hang around to
observe the victim's reactions. This experience can increase
the empathic responsiveness to the victim, thereby reduc-
ing the likelihood of further incidents. It should be used
in conjunction with other empathic induction exercises
to maximize effectiveness.

## Case Example

> Curtis was asked to reenact his mugging of an
> elderly woman in the parking lot of a grocery store.
> He was reluctant at first, but agreed after some
> urging by his group. Jane volunteered to role-play
> his victim.
>
> Curtis began by sneaking up on her from be-
> hind and attempting to grab her purse. "Shall I fight
> back, or what?" Jane queried.

"Well, she screamed and held on to her purse," Curtis replied.

"What did you do?" another member asked.

"I told her: 'Just give me the damn purse and you won't get hurt.'"

The therapist interjected: "Okay, Jane, why don't you scream and fight a little?"

Curtis immediately interrupted: "This is just too weird. I can't do it."

"You did it in the parking lot," one member yelled angrily.

"All right, dickhead! If that's what you really want . . ." Curtis retorted. He proceeded to shove Jane down and pretended to grab and run away with the purse.

Afterwards, Jane screamed and cried as she imagined the woman did. Curtis seemed embarrassed and somewhat shocked by this, but did not respond. Another female member shouted: "You know, Curtis? You're a real pig! I don't know how you could do that."

Curtis was silent briefly and then stated that "somehow it seems different now."

"It makes you more aware of what you did, doesn't it, Curtis?" the therapist commented.

"Yeah, I guess so," he replied nonchalantly. "Maybe it wasn't too cool."

"You've got that right!" another member retorted.

"She was an old lady, man! It was a sorry thing to do."

"All right!" Curtis screamed. "I get the point!"

Ironically, the histories of many of these youngsters are replete with themes of loss, neglect, abuse, and disappointment. Getting them to share these feelings requires patience, modeling, and a little ingenuity. These common experiences should be discussed with emphasis on the accompanying rage. Some feel that no one ever felt sorry for them, so why should they empathize? Others vividly recall the painful memories and the feelings of hopelessness. Members should be encouraged to support one another, and the therapist must maintain an objective, nonjudgmental stance.

At times I encounter youngsters who adamantly insist that they have never felt the pain of a victim. Their attachments seem shallow while their rage is extensive. When dealing with these "hardened" youth one must help them to retrieve any possible memory of a painful experience they had. Such a recollection can lead to increased awareness of the victim's perspective.

On one occasion I had been unsuccessful in evoking any empathic feelings in a conduct-disordered youth. He was cynical, tough, and prone to minimizing his difficulties. After some thought I recalled that just before our first meeting I had seen him in the lobby of my office building. At that time he was petting a little puppy rather tenderly. I shared my recollection and commented that he must like dogs.

"Yeah, so what?" he replied.

"Well, I was just wondering if you have ever had a dog. You've never mentioned one."

He grew quiet, somewhat sad, and then spoke softly. "I did once."

"Whatever happened to him?" I queried.

"He got run over. You know, killed."

I commented on what a terrible experience that must have been. "Can you recall how you felt at the time?" I asked gently.

With tearful eyes he answered, "Yeah, I guess I'll never forget it. It was like someone ripped something out from inside of me. I felt really empty. I didn't want to see or talk to anyone for a while. It lasted a long time."

"You know, you were a victim back then," I commented. "That person who ran over your dog without stopping the car was really wrong."

Here was the connection for this young man. Those strong feelings he had experienced paralleled those of a victim. At last he could understand how someone else felt. The incident was particularly useful in planting the seeds of empathy. He needed to reexperience some of his own pain to gain another's emotional perspective. This is precisely the process we must engineer to encourage meaningful dialogue with this population. Everyone has some feeling, somewhere, an island of residual pain that has been untapped. We need only to find the way to open the doors.

Ultimately, discussions can focus on the inherent shred of decency in most people. Youth should be asked what kind of person they feel they are. Even those with antisocial tendencies are capable of some emotion, although initially it may be shallow and limited to their friends. These feelings must be uncovered and expanded to induce empathy-based guilt. We must try to convince youth that they will see themselves in a more positive light after they "have done the right thing." Although they may have gone to great lengths to avoid any guilt about their transgressions, they need to accept that it is the most human of emotions. Those who can acknowledge any second thoughts or regrets over wrongdoing should be encouraged to use this awareness to prevent further incidents.

Hollin (1989) cites research that suggests that reparation is useful in curbing antisocial behavior. Those youngsters who are forced to face their victims afterward are less likely to repeat the offense. The experience of listening to the pain they have caused and then apologizing for their actions increases sensitivity. This is probably more effective for youth who are held accountable early in their cycle of offending.

A court appearance can also be helpful in getting youngsters to take their actions seriously. Their apprehension about the possible consequences can reduce the likelihood of future offending. Discussions about detention centers, probation, and community service should be routinely initiated. Unfortunately, some parents take action to get their youngsters off the hook by hiring shrewd lawyers. This rarely serves a useful purpose. In fact, adolescents may get the message that getting into trouble is not serious because there is always a way out. For this reason I encourage parents to let the charges stand so their child will learn something useful from the process.

## EXTENDING TREATMENT GAINS

Developing sociomoral reasoning and fostering empathy in a therapeutic setting is one thing; broadening the gains to the natural environment is another. Certain youth are able to express the correct thing to do in a discussion of a moral dilemma, but do not practice it.

They can identify what a victim feels, yet do not experience any guilt for wrongdoing. This subgroup must be challenged repeatedly on the inconsistencies between their words and their behavior. Who do they think they are fooling, anyway? A rather firm approach is necessary with those who are intent on beating the system. Careful observation and extensive collaboration will help to track the youngster's progress. Some type of system of accountability must be put in place if these youth are ever to change.

Often the school or neighborhood peer group encourages deviant behavior. Its own norms violate conventional moral standards and interfere with the capacity to empathize (Kohlberg and Higgins 1987). Before treatment is completed we must develop in our patients resistance to peer pressure, and help them to form different friendships. This is accomplished by helping them develop a new image, rekindling their former interests, and sometimes suggesting a school change. In short, empathy and morality must become socially acceptable.

# 10

# Guidelines for Managing Behavior Problems

To suggest that the parents of oppositional and conduct-disordered youth are frustrated, angry, and drained would be an understatement. Many dread going home and feel that their lives are markedly disrupted by the presence of their defiant adolescent. I have been called upon frequently by schools, PTAs, and other civic organizations to speak about the daily management of disruptive behavior. It seems that everyone is in search of practical solutions to these complex problems.

Those who must live with these youngsters need a framework from which to operate. The therapeutic principles employed in a treatment setting must be translated into understandable and readily applicable interventions for this population. The amount of time spent in treatment is a drop in the bucket compared to that spent in the natural environment. A mixture of common sense, knowledge of adolescent normative behavior, and some self-discipline is required of those seeking to alter the difficult daily behavior patterns.

I propose that there is a state of mind that predisposes parents, teachers, and others to react to challenges appropriately. Several assumptions underlie this conviction. First, they must genuinely believe that they will not be intimidated, controlled, or taken advantage of. Self-respect is imperative. This does not imply harshness, retaliation, or rejection. It simply means that they have certain rights regarding their person, property, and values that must not be infringed upon. Second, they must continue to care despite the persistent trials and tribulations. Although difficult to sustain at times, youth must be reminded that the adult's position is based on a deep-rooted concern for their well-being. Finally, it is important to assume that adolescents are capable of change under the right conditions. This optimistic outlook should be conveyed to them whenever the opportunity presents itself.

## LIVING WITH DIFFICULT BEHAVIOR

The concept of negative attitude needs no introduction. One gets the feeling that talking to these youngsters is an imposition. They display pronounced irritability and are easily annoyed by "stupid questions." Abrupt mood shifts are not uncommon and any adult curiosity about them generates suspicion. It is frequently difficult to initiate any dialogue to learn about what's going on with them. Parents and teachers are particularly cognizant of this. A typical conversation might sound like this:

| "Where are you going?" | "Out." |
|---|---|
| "How was school today?" | "Okay." |
| "What's the matter?" | "I don't know." |
| "I'm angry at you!" | "That's cool." |
| "Later." | "I'm out of here!" |

Unfortunately, neither talking nor listening may be socially acceptable. Parents must learn to cut through the defensive posture and persist in initiating conversation. I advise them to share stories of their own adolescence and freely acknowledge any vulnerabilities that may be obvious. The kids may not immediately pick up on this, but it gives them subtle permission to talk about their lives. Giving the youngster the third degree usually pushes them in the wrong direction.

Rather than direct questioning, I recommend that the parent simply make inferences. They might say, you look sad, tired, or upset, and then leave the rest up to the adolescent. When the silence persists, one can intentionally guess the wrong feeling. The youngster might feel compelled to correct you. When we must ask, it is often better to inquire about their friends or other teenagers. Many will feel safer talking about the feelings of others and may give us valuable information in the process.

Some adolescents are downright rude and provocative toward those around them. While it is tempting to respond in like fashion, this usually worsens the situation. For instance, John's father asked him where he was going as he was leaving the house one evening. "It's none of your business," John replied. His father grew angry.

"If you don't tell me, you can't leave the house."

"What are you going to do if I walk out," taunted

John. "You can't make me stay." He angrily stormed out and slammed the door.

Now this father certainly had a right to know where his son was going. What might he have said differently when faced with his son's challenge?

Here's another dialogue, with a different result. Assuming that John has already refused to account for his destination, the father begins by saying that he can't force John to tell, but he won't be able to trust him if he doesn't provide any information.

> *Father*: Look, John, I understand your need for privacy, but it's not that big a deal to let us know. It's not like we're following you anywhere. When you tell us more, we worry less. It's not that much to ask. How about it?
>
> *John*: All right, Mike's house, bye!

It's rarely that simple, of course, but it is important to minimize control battles. There are no winners in escalating conflicts. When possible, youngsters should be offered alternatives to help them feel they have some power. Otherwise they become more defiant in the face of rigid authority. It is best to interpret most provocations as misguided declarations of independence. The need for autonomy takes many guises and should be recognized as such.

Parents often express concern about their children's attire and appearance? To what extent should they attempt to exert influence? Torn jeans, baseball caps, tee-shirts with slogans, and ultra-baggy pants are today's uniform, often accompanied by earrings, partially shaved heads, and dyed hair. While this may not be pleasing to the adult eye, it nonetheless makes a statement of non-conformity (at least in the eyes of the teenager). The need to buck convention is very important to these youth. Although a more radical appearance does not in itself constitute trouble, extremity of dress can be reflective of the child's emotional state.

Before forbidding a youngster to dress in certain clothing (assuming it can be controlled), a parent must assess what is to be gained. One might make the case that more conventional dress leads to less rebellious behavior; however, experience has not borne this out. Forbidding self-expression seems only to shift the battleground. Adolescents find other ways to irritate adults and reject parental expectations. Some are far more dangerous than choice of clothing.

My perspective is that radical dress is a developmental phase that is likely to pass. Ironically, parents who roll with it, by participating in the choice of something outrageous for their child or at least accepting it nonchalantly, are likely to reduce the compulsion to protest. The case is different when a school dress code prohibits certain clothing. In this instance the parents must support the system and emphasize the importance of accepting rules whether or not we like them.

Today's music also raises some interesting questions about parental censorship. Some lyrics are sexually provocative, rebellious, and violent. Some research suggests that youth who listen regularly to heavy metal and rap music are more prone to trouble (Took and Weiss 1994). That is not to say that the music itself causes the problems; more likely, certain youngsters gravitate toward it. Restricting listening habits is a difficult matter, but parents should feel free to express their opinions. Certainly they can refuse to buy anything that advocates violence and anarchy.

The adolescent's bedroom often becomes another family battleground. The parents complain that their child lives in a pigsty and must keep it clean. Teenagers insist that it's their room, it looks fine, and their parents are making too big a deal of it. Provided that the youngster's mess does not spread to other areas of the house, I recommend that parents settle for some semblance of order rather than insisting on total compliance. This is not a battle worth fighting on an ongoing basis.

Several years ago a father told me an amusing story about how their daughter was shocked into keeping her room tidier. For months the parents had complained about food and dishes littering her room. Threats about the filth attracting roaches were summarily dismissed by the girl. One day the father decided to take matters into his own hands. He collected a number of cockroaches in a jar and distributed them in his daughter's room. Her shock at the "gross sight" when she entered the room that evening prompted her to take neatness far more seriously after that incident. A seminatural annoyance at work!

While the adolescent's room should be respected as a private place, at times the boundaries must be violated. If the parents suspect substance abuse or the presence of stolen merchandise, they should reserve the right to search and seize. Adolescents who violate social norms cannot be allowed to involve the family as accomplices. They forgo their right to privacy when they place themselves or others at risk. When held accountable for their transgressions, they are less likely to commit future offenses.

Choice of friends is also a frequent topic of conversation and discord. Parents are naturally suspicious when their children associate with others who are often in trouble. As a rule, the greater the youngster's need for secrecy, the more the parents should worry. I feel that parents ought to encourage their children to bring their friends home despite any misgivings. This deflates some of the magical appeal of the forbidden peers. Friends who are invited to the home regularly are more likely to feel somewhat accountable. It's harder to deceive someone who knows you and has been nice to you. In addition, it is better to have the social group gather under your roof than roaming the streets looking for action. In many instances initially adversarial peers turn out to be the parents' allies after they feel welcomed in the home.

Adolescents often invoke their friends' freedoms as proof that their parents should allow them to stay out late, attend rock concerts, or go to the beach unescorted. Angry parents may retort, "I don't care what everyone else is doing." I'm with the parents on this one. Kids are notorious for coming up with the one overly permissive parent within a twenty-mile radius. They must be reminded continually that "in this family" trust evolves from the demonstration of responsibility, not the intensity of the demand. Parental limits should be reasonable, of course, and consistent with age-appropriate norms.

## LIFE AT THE BARGAINING TABLE

With great exasperation many parents lament: "Nothing is ever simple with our teenager. She disagrees with almost everything we say and can never take no for an answer. Each day brings new hassles. Some of her demands are actually ridiculous. Yet she argues as if her very life depends on it. There are times when we feel she truly enjoys it. Frankly, it is really wearing us down. We sometimes find ourselves giving in just to keep the peace."

Indeed, oppositional youngsters feel compelled to argue. They lack the skills needed to resolve conflict through negotiation. Despite this, parents must insist on discussing issues before making decisions. The youngster will undoubtedly be impatient and demand an answer "now." Although this is difficult, the parents must remain resolute, setting firm but reasonable limits while maintaining some degree of flexibility.

Arguments often revolve around rules, curfews, and privileges. Adolescents are determined to have their way and will argue their case desperately. Although extreme demands should be denied, the bargaining process itself can be therapeutic. When we tell kids that we're willing to listen to their position but will then have to think about it, the intensity of the demand can be diffused. They may persist in debating, but will usually back off somewhat.

Advance planning is certainly desirable and often possible, although occasionally a spur of the moment decision is required. As a rule, I suggest that the parents negotiate up, not down. By this I mean that if the teenager demands a 2:00 A.M. weekend curfew and the parents feel 12:00 A.M. is more reasonable, they should offer 11:00 P.M. The youngster, of course, will disagree vehemently, but is more likely to accept 12:00, feeling that something has been gained.

## NONCOMPLIANCE

Overt defiance is difficult for anyone to deal with. Negative, angry, and provocative behavior may develop quickly and seemingly without warning. The youngsters justify their actions through hostile attribution, claiming that the other person wronged them in some way and "deserved it." Their impulsivity and self-righteousness make them difficult to reason with. It is quite hard for them to let things go. When challenged on their actions, they become defensive and may flee the situation abruptly.

Alex, for example, was having an altercation with his brother when their father entered the room and insisted that Alex leave his brother alone. Alex screamed, "I always get blamed for things" and refused to comply. There seemed to be no stopping him. Tempers flared and the father attempted to pull the boys apart. This led to increased conflict and a physical scuffle between the father and son. Ultimately Alex cursed his father and stormed angrily out of the house.

Incidents such as these are commonplace in this population. Adults must learn to maintain a sense of composure under fire, taking pains to avoid retaliation and stooping to the child's level. At times it may be necessary to teach anger control techniques to the parents as well as their child. When up against the wall, most of these adolescents are unable to give in. The savvy parent offers face-saving alternatives to diffuse a heated situation. The youngster can be asked either to take a ten-minute break or to talk about why they're so angry while the parent listens nonjudgementally.

Once someone has lost control, of course, little can be accomplished immediately. Concerns about safety must take precedence. We can employ restraints as a last resort, but extreme caution is necessary. A failed attempt at physical control may only worsen the situation since the youngster is no longer rational. The more prudent approach may be simply to leave the room and give the youngster time to calm down by himself. If any damage occurs, he should be held responsible afterwards.

Following the clash, the participants need to discuss the event in order to avoid a recurrence. Youth often begin by insisting that they were innocent and end by asking for one more chance. Some will express remorse afterwards and promise that it won't happen again. The goal is to get them to look at their role in the situation, understand their impact on others, and propose alternative solutions. They should be reminded that others do not wish to control them. In fact, when they take charge of themselves, they are, in effect, more in control of the world around them.

While there should be consequences for extremes of behavior, I believe they should be constructive. For example, we might require that the offender devote several hours to productive family service such as cleaning, painting, or lawn mowing. The subsequent sense of accomplishment helps bring the youngster back into the family with a minimum of humiliation.

More punitive actions are far more complex. The antisocial youths' immunity to consequences often makes effective punishment difficult. I sometimes hear of youngsters being restricted for several months to teach them a lesson. Unfortunately, they usually manage to sneak out of the house, talk their parents into special exceptions, or otherwise violate the punishment. The result is that little or nothing has been learned from the experience.

To effectively have an impact on behavior, a punishment must be consistent, meaningful, and enforceable. The proof is in the outcome. If the youngster continues to engage in the undesirable behavior, the punishment has probably been ineffective. This is illustrated by the coercive family process described by Patterson (1982).

Over the years, I have asked adolescents to describe the characteristics of the people they respect in their daily lives: teachers, parents, coaches, or others. Their answers are revealing. When they perceive an adult as proud and self-confident, they are less threatened by them and more likely to comply with their expectations. A consistent and nonauthoritarian approach seems most effective. Youth speak highly of those who have a good sense of humor, capture their interest, and are fun to be around. They gravitate toward adults who convey an appreciation of their uniqueness. Conversely, they have trouble with those who try too hard to be cool or have a bossy attitude.

## PASSIVE-AGGRESSIVE BEHAVIOR

Not everyone can express anger directly. Some youth display their negative affect through symbolic protests. For example, a boy who is angry with his parents might conveniently forget to do his chores or homework. When asked to do things, he agrees cheerfully, but has no intention of complying. This pattern of passive aggression is both annoying and puzzling to adults. It may be of longstanding origin and is unlikely to dissipate without intervention.

The task is to help adolescents identify what they feel

and express it directly. Initially their behavior patterns must be called to their attention. Those who deny the underlying anger need to be challenged on their avoidance. They may make vague statements about their feelings and have difficulty clarifying the meaning.

I suggest talking about more appropriate, direct, and mature ways to resist and protest. I might use the following approach. "Everyone gets mad sometimes and has a right to express their anger directly. When feelings are bottled up, they fester and weigh us down. Worse yet, we never have the satisfaction of knowing that the other person is even aware of our hurt. This virtually eliminates any chance of getting them to change their behavior or at least to know our side of the issue."

Although those oppositional youth see themselves as tough, their behavior should be framed as "wimpy." Such a challenge often leads to a heated argument about their personality style. They maintain that they are not afraid to speak up for themselves, yet their behavior states otherwise. When they are asked to describe some of the things that really get to them, nagging and criticism frequently top the list. What do they usually do when their parents keep bugging them about the same thing? Is their annoyance expressed directly or do they withdraw, sulk, and slam doors? These daily issues should become springboards for discussion. It must be stressed that there are always alternatives to passive aggressive behavior. In particular, exercises designed to role-play more assertive behavior should be helpful.

## Case Example

Tina was a 14-year-old girl with considerable rage toward her mother. She felt that her mother worried excessively and treated her like a child. Despite these feelings, Tina was often compliant and fairly docile. She was aware that her mother had to raise her alone and was struggling to make ends meet. Tina rarely expressed her anger because of her guilt and fear that her mother couldn't handle it. Instead, she often slammed her door, turned the music up loud, and monopolized the telephone. This, of course, greatly irritated her mother.

When her behavior patterns were called to her attention, Tina initially denied there was any connection. She was encouraged to discuss all the things that bothered her, identify her immediate responses, and consider the impact of a forthright conversation with her mother. A role-play was designed to help her express her anger and need for independence. Although she felt awkward at first, Tina verbalized these concerns, adding that nothing could really change her situation. After some discussion it was agreed that her mother would be invited to attend a session. During the meeting the mother initially displayed little awareness of Tina's feelings and rationalized them as typically adolescent. The ensuing dialogue led to increased understanding and empowered Tina to protest more directly. Ultimately she was encouraged to use her newly acquired skills in other situations as well.

Parents must be expecially vigilant in identifying passive aggression as it is often the precursor to more serious problems. When manifestations of it occur regularly, they should be scrutinized and challenged. This is best accomplished through inferences or direct questioning. If the youngster denies the significance of his or her actions, the parents can model more appropriate behavior as well as disclose some of their own pet peeves and encourage him or her to do the same.

## DEALING WITH ANTISOCIAL BEHAVIOR

What must a parent do when their child violates rules or social norms? The more established the pattern, the greater the importance of challenging even the smallest infractions. Firmness, consistency, and accountability are essentials here. As discussed, the parents of antisocial youth often revert to extremes of discipline that are usually ineffective. The poor family communication blocks the opportunity for any constructive dialogue after incidents occur.

I do not mean to suggest a simplistic solution for complex behavior problems. However, there are some basic guidelines to be followed. For example, stealing should be dealt with firmly and directly. It is against the law and cannot be justified under any circumstances. The offender must return the stolen item and meaningful consequences must then be imposed. As a logical result of the infraction, the adolescent's credibility is weakened and his behavior will require increased scrutiny in the future. If something suspicious occurs (e.g., money disappearing from the house), he or she will most likely be presumed responsible, with little weight given to arguments about innocence.

When a deceitful pattern has persisted over time, the cycle can sometimes be broken by granting temporary immunity. In effect, youth are told that they will have the opportunity to confess any wrongdoing with no consequences attached. If they comply with the offer, they can start fresh and begin to regain trust.

A similar approach should be taken with vandalism, arson, and any physical assault against others. All actions that violate social norms must be challenged and the perpetrator made aware of the harm inflicted upon others. Parents should not cover up for their children and would be well advised to allow the natural consequences to unfold. Despite claims that it won't happen again, all incidents must be taken seriously.·

## THE BOTTOM LINE

When the pattern of antisocial behavior is longstanding, it will be difficult for parents to break the cycle. Nonetheless, they must begin to enforce limits consistently and convey the message that the present situation is no longer tolerable. Simply getting tough is not enough. The adolescent must be convinced that the family loves him or her but will no longer tolerate negative attitudes, lack of cooperation, aggressive posture, and illicit activities. Minimal conditions must be established for the child to remain at home, attend the same school, and spend time with the same friends. A line must be drawn in the sand. Will youngsters try to comply with the requests presented or risk placement in a far less desirable atmosphere? The choice is theirs.

Antisocial youth will most certainly test the parents'

resolve. It is necessary that they maintain a no-nonsense attitude. Parents should be told that they will need considerable support and determination to withstand the adolescent's protests. Although control issues (e.g., rules and curfews) will be the initial battleground, the adolescent's underlying need for nurturance and positive self-regard will quickly emerge.

## COLLATERAL ISSUES

Runaways pose a unique set of issues. Some youth leave home for self-serving reasons. They actively seek excitement and thrive on risk taking and deviance. Others have intolerable home situations and they search desperately for acceptance elsewhere. Family disagreements and chronic fights may precipitate impulsive actions by these adolescents. This group displays little awareness of their own role in problems and frequently present themselves as helpless victims. They often lack a clearly defined identity and may gravitate toward cults, gangs, and vagrants.

Parents must set limits on any type of runaway behavior. The police should be notified if the child has been gone for more than twenty-four hours. Youth can often be located rather quickly and incidents can be dealt with. Ensuing discussions should focus on (1) identifying what precipitated the running away and (2) generating alternative solutions for future conflicts. Adolescents who refuse to remain at home under any circumstances must be placed in an appropriate facility (i.e., detention or group home).

Genuine emergencies (e.g., suicide attempts, drug

overdoses, or domestic violence) must be dealt with immediately. There is little time for discussion and it is essential to ensure the safety of all parties. The parents must be instructed to either call 911 or go directly to an emergency room. I have never heard regrets expressed about prompt action, while avoidance or extended delays have sometimes resulted in dire consequences.

# 11

# Challenging Poor School Performance and Other Failures to Thrive

I really can't stand my high school. The teachers are boring, the classes are dumb, and the work is too hard. Basically, it's a waste of time. Every morning I leave home wondering whether I'll go to school that day. If I run into my friends and they're cutting, that's it, I'm out of there. Sometimes we'll hang out in the mall or we go to a friend's house. We either smoke cigarettes, get high, or just veg out. To tell you the truth, even that gets stale after a while.

"My grades are mostly D's and F's. Sure, my parents bitch about it often, but I really could care less. It's really the missed homework assignments and unexcused absences that do me in. I used to try and keep up, but it's too late in the year to salvage it, so I'll just coast.

"I don't mind the other kids in my grade, and sometimes I'll even go to football games with them. Several people have asked me if I want to change schools, but I tell them no thanks. I guess I just don't know what I want anymore."

This composite profile echoes the sentiments of many of the troubled and alienated youth populating our high schools. Frick and colleagues (1991) discuss the association of academic underachievement with conduct disorders. Poor grades and specific skill deficiencies have been repeatedly noted. This population is notorious for truancy, disruptive behavior in the classroom, and poor motivation. They have great difficulty with authority and seem impervious to discipline. Their school histories are often filled with successive failures and difficulty accepting structure and limits. In effect, they have turned off to learning. These youth devote much of their energy to seeking ways to avert boredom and shirk responsibility for their shortcomings. Although many express the desire to do better in school, their efforts rarely back up their words. Both oppositional and conduct-disordered youth pose major problems to teachers, counselors, and administrators. No one is quite sure what to do with them.

## THE SEEDS OF DISCONTENT

School problems are generally multidetermined. Despite some embarrassment about their academic deficiencies, many adolescents feign indifference. Their self-esteem has been eroded by continued failures and frequent criticism about their lack of effort. If learning disabilities exist, the situation is worse. The unfortunate result is typically lowered self-expectations and heightened compensatory actions to mask their inadequacies. Many feel intellectually inferior to their peers and devote more of their energy to beating the system than participating in it. The results are discouraging. Assignments are avoided, there is cheating on tests, and classes are cut indiscriminately. The youngsters develop an apathetic image that serves to justify their poor performance.

The school setting demands conformity to specific regulations. These may include dress codes, rigorous adherence to schedules, and predetermined consequences for misbehavior. Antisocial youth resist the imposition of rules and structure, insisting that this is yet another instance of adults telling them what to do. They often do not feel connected with the school and operate on the fringe. Their relationships with teachers are markedly superficial and distant. They are frequently caught smoking or intimidating others on the periphery of the school grounds. When confronted about these actions, they deny responsibility, project blame, and refuse to accept the consequences.

Clearly these youth do not feel they fit in with the majority of their peers. They insist that their few friends are the only ones who understand them and consequently isolate themselves from the mainstream. This perceived alienation may be an extension of their feelings of rejection in their own family, as well as a result of chronic failures to conform and navigate societal expectations successfully.

The deviant peer group fuels their disenchantment. This is where they gain acceptance and are rewarded for their avoidance of responsibility. Ironically, they conform rigorously to the group's norms and are quite dependent on their peers, despite their protests to the contrary.

Substance abuse often perpetuates the problem. They lack the motivation and self-confidence to face their responsibilities and seek out those who feel likewise. Getting high or drunk regularly can lull them into complacency. In addition, depression may underlie the school problems and perpetuate the inertia.

At times sheer exhaustion, inadequate nutrition, and lack of sleep can interfere with school performance. Although seemingly obvious, these must be considered. Parental neglect crosses socioeconomic barriers and often contributes to difficulties in school. A careful assessment of the home situation should be made to determine the parents' availability and daily involvement with their children. Both school personnel and mental health workers must identify those in need of intervention and make appropriate referrals to a social service agency. If necessary, legal action can be taken to protect the rights of these minors.

Parents give their youngsters powerful messages about school. At one extreme they exhort them about the importance of good grades and berate them for their lack of effort. The more the parents value school to the exclusion of everything else, the more likely the youngster is to rebel. At the other extreme are parents who are indifferent to education, telling their child directly or indirectly, "It's your life, do what you want with it." School effort is not encouraged and the youngster may be saddled with more pressing responsibilities. In neither case is the youngster taught to value school for the sake of learning.

## FACILITATING SCHOOL ATTENDANCE

Subtle learning problems may go undetected in school-avoidant youth. The more conspicuous problems (aggression, violence, and theft) usually demand immediate attention. Antisocial adolescents view truancy and cutting class as a challenge since they can go undetected. They often commiserate about ways to beat the system and mutually reinforce any noncompliance to rules.

Both parents and children must be held accountable if change is to occur. A joint meeting should be conducted to review the situation, analyze the problem, and plan an intervention. Exactly what is the youngster avoiding and why? How long has the pattern persisted? What if anything has been tried to date?

Under certain circumstances school attendance can be a mandate with consequences attached to any violations. The problem can be referred to the courts for disposition. Those already on probation are carefully monitored to ensure compliance. Detention centers and other aversive placements may be considered if needed— as a last resort. Simply compelling a youngster to attend school without regard to the motivational factors will not reduce underlying resistance and feelings of estrangement.

Environmental supports must be sought and cultivated. The parents need help to develop incentives and reduce their reliance on restrictive measures. In effect, the message should be: "Tomorrow is a new day; start attending school regularly and we'll work from there." When possible, positive peer support should be mobilized. Someone in the youngster's circle of acquaintances who values school can perhaps be recruited to serve as an escort in the morning and a spot-checker during the day.

This type of problem necessitates a team approach. The coach can be a parent, teacher, or therapist. A young man is told that his life is serious and warrants close attention. The team's role is to help him do what is in his best interests. Arranging for rides to school, companions in classes, and troubleshooters for difficult situations— all help to give a powerful message of caring: "We want you here, we think you can do it." This is not to suggest that negative peer influences are easily overcome. The intervention simply focuses on getting youth to school in the hope that they will experience some acceptance, success, and intrinsic value from the exposure. Continued follow-up is needed to be certain that this occurs on an ongoing basis.

## KEEPING TEENAGERS IN SCHOOL

Getting kids to school is one thing; keeping them there is another. Schools must be user friendly; that is, a place where youth feel welcome and encouraged to utilize the available resources. Assuming that the desire to learn has not evolved spontaneously, the student's curiosity must be stimulated by creative teaching techniques.

In an extensive study of school programs for disruptive adolescents Safer (1982) found that the motivation to learn was appreciably influenced by the school curriculum. Individualized instruction yielded better results than group teaching with this population. The importance of matching students with competent teachers was stressed. In general, acting out was more likely to occur during dead time and could be reduced through increased structure and student involvement. Ideally, these youth are more likely to learn when they feel there is something in it for them.

The social aspect of school should also be taken into account. Many adolescents have told me that it is the only thing that really keeps them there. A sense of belonging can be fostered by inviting them to join in clubs, organizations, and extracurricular activities. Despite initial reluctance, many will participate if they are strongly encouraged by a prosocial peer group. When the experience is rewarding, they are more likely to extend their involvement to other ventures.

Garner (1982) describes a school program to create a positive peer culture. Teachers were initially asked to identify high-functioning leaders in the overall student population. Those chosen were given credit for attending leadership skill-development classes. They then formed groups designed to help troubled youngsters identify any problems that they experienced in school and formulate constructive solutions with the help of their peers. The targeted adolescents found these groups both supportive and useful in addressing their issues.

Mentors can also be helpful in keeping at-risk youth in school. A recent article in the *American Psychological Association Monitor* (Murray 1995) described several programs that provided supportive adults who developed ongoing relationships with their assigned students. These mentors monitored youth regularly for signs of truancy, acting out, or academic failure. When problems arose, they solicited help from teachers, parents, and community outreach workers. Those students who reported a successful mentoring experience were more likely to stay in school and develop positive attitudes. Community involvement seemed to provide youngsters with an incentive to get an education and take their lives more seriously.

Estimates of the national high school dropout rate range from 15 to 30 percent (National Association of School Psychologists 1992). Prevention programs often stress the importance of individualized instruction, flexible curriculum, and a small class size. Stoner and colleagues (1991) recommend that increased time be spent on academic tasks with corrective feedback given regularly. There seems to be general agreement on the importance of identifying the current level of achievement and building from there. According to McIntire (1985), students should be rewarded at their lower level of performance to instill hope. The assignments must be short, meaningful, and doable if attention is to be maintained.

Rutter and colleagues (1979) reviewed the specific school characteristics that contributed to a favorable outcome with a behavior-disordered population. In addition to an emphasis on academic instruction and remediation, they cite the amount of teacher time spent on lessons and the importance of individual responsibility. Continued praise and appreciation are needed to maintain sustained effort. The working conditions, of course, must be conducive to learning. Distractions should be minimized and the classroom atmosphere made friendly and accepting. The more smoothly the class runs, the less the likelihood that a single student will have the power to interrupt the ongoing activity.

I believe that antisocial youth respond more effectively to a hands-on learning approach. Their high need for stimulation is more readily satisfied when they have the opportunity to interact with both the educational materials and the natural environment. Thus history might be studied at a Civil War battlefield, or science in a research laboratory or nature center. The academic materials should be highly interesting and well adapted to the youngster's achievement level. Involving students in program planning should increase their compliance with the curriculum.

Felner and Adan (1988) established a program to reduce difficult transitions from middle to high school while simultaneously increasing coping skills. The school structure was reorganized so that students at risk could be involved in a stable peer group. They attended classes with a familiar group of peers who spent considerable time together. The role of the homeroom teacher was expanded to include administrative and counseling responsibilities. This grounding of students at the beginning of the day and having the homeroom teacher available for trouble-shooting seemed especially important. The School Transitional Environment Program reported lower rates of dropouts and placements in alternative programs (Felner and Adan 1988).

I have observed similar programs in public school systems where targeted subgroups are clustered together to form a school within a school. The increased familiarity with fewer teachers, a positive peer culture, and specific curriculum adaptations foster positive results.

Good teachers have much to offer through their unique approaches to the learning process. I have spoken with many youngsters who have identified the common denominators of the teachers who seem to reach them. These characteristics include a sense of humor, passion about their subject, and a straightforward approach toward their students. Their interactive levels are high and the teachers are more prone to democratic rather than authoritarian leadership styles. The instructional methods are varied, but the consensus is that these teachers always keep class interesting. They rely heavily on explanation and demonstration, eschewing the pure lecture format. Youth often report that these cool teachers make them feel their thoughts and ideas are important. In general, test grades are less emphasized than independent and creative thinking.

## RECURRENT SCHOOL PROBLEMS

Despite our best efforts, behavior problems will invariably occur in the school setting. Adolescents' difficulty with authority fuels noncompliance and leads many youth into conflict with their classroom teachers. The regrettable outcome of these unresolved skirmishes is diffuse aggression. Managing this behavior is especially difficult because of the youngsters' inability to verbalize feelings, their tendency to act without thinking, and their problems with accepting limits. For their part, teachers must respond quickly and judiciously when faced with a challenge to their authority.

### Case Example

> George was engaged in an altercation when his teacher entered the classroom. Rather than tell them both to go to the principal's office, the teacher wisely intervened. "Listen, guys, I can't have this going on in my classroom. We've got work to do."

George responded abruptly. "Well, we've got something to settle here."

"I'm sure you do," replied the teacher, "but this isn't the time or place. Just get back to your seats and we'll call it a wash. If you can't do that, then you'll have to decide whether you want me to take any action. It's your call. Do you guys take charge or do I?"

George looked at his adversary, smiled, and returned to his seat. The crisis had been averted.

Cheating, missed assignments, and forged excuses also pose significant problems for teachers. My advice is to avoid any bickering here. The obvious should not be debated. A teacher might say, "You owe me for this infraction; here are your choices." The alternatives should involve makeup work rather than unrelated punitive consequences. Overcorrection can be useful in such a situation. For example, a student who has cheated on a test can be asked to write a paper on the examination topic. Missed assignments and classes should be dealt with in a similar fashion. The burden of restitution should be placed on the youngster.

Although detention is still widely used, I do not see it as a learning experience. Sitting around and doing nothing only worsens the problem. If the youngster is to serve time, we should make certain that it is used constructively, either by doing schoolwork or in an alternative activity.

The case against suspension and expulsion is even more compelling. An article in the *American Psychological Association Monitor* (Edwards 1995) emphasized that expulsion from school often backfires. Removing the aggressive student from school only avoids the problem and dumps it into the community. Those who are expelled are more likely to drop out of school, or at least repeat their offenses. While on suspension most kids either remain at home unsupervised and unproductive or hang out in the streets with other like-minded youth. This, unfortunately, reinforces the antisocial behavior that led to the suspension in the first place.

When possible, alternatives to suspension or expulsion should be arranged. For example, someone suspended for drug use might be required to lecture to younger children about the perils of drugs. Such experiences often sensitize adolescents to the ramifications of their behavior. I have had patients tell me that they felt embarrassed about their experiences and protective of their innocent audience. Those with aggressive problems might be asked to conduct a short course on how to deal with bullies. One youngster who was expelled for pulling a fire alarm was not allowed to return to school until he had visited several elementary school classes. His job was to describe what might happen if there was a real fire and no firefighters were available.

School is not for everyone. Despite adequate intelligence, some youngsters are just not suited for traditional academic learning. While a certain foundation in basic skills is necessary, pushing beyond that may further sour the youngster to any educational process. Those who possess mechanical skills or other talents may do better in a vocational or alternative setting where gratification is more immediate. This is hard for some parents to tolerate, yet it must be faced.

## IMPACT OF SCHOOL AT HOME

While some youth have given up on school completely, others use it to remain locked in combat with their parents. Homework is the frequent battleground. Students procrastinate, sit at their books looking around while they should be working, or refuse outright to complete assignments. Many blast their stereos or televisions, insisting that they need the noise to study. The parents grow increasingly frustrated and angry, yet their arguing and threatening is rarely effective. How much monitoring should parents do? My feeling is that homework is the students' responsibility, not the parents'. When the parents are overly invested in the process, their attempts to help invariably fail (Green 1989).

Families should be kept informed about a youngster's assignments and progress in school. When no work is being completed, they should ask the student what he or she intends to do about it. It is useful to focus positively on times past when assignments were completed. Current interferences need to be identified and addressed. The ensuing discussions should focus on concrete problem-solving strategies. If help is needed, tutoring by someone outside the family is often the best bet. It is less humiliating and creates a situation in which the youngster can work with someone fresh and objective. Many teachers are willing to see students after school and peer tutors may also be available.

Most antisocial youth insist they don't need help with their schoolwork. When this is the case, positive natural consequences must be arranged to motivate the desired behavior. Curfews, driving privileges, allowance, television, and the telephone, can all be used for this purpose. Parents usually have much more control and leverage than they realize. A contract should be established to structure expectations from the outset. The tasks should be relatively brief and manageable to ensure a successful experience for both the frustrated student and the parents.

## THERAPIST INVOLVEMENT WITH THE SCHOOL

An effective treatment program necessitates involvement with school personnel. The therapist should initiate contact and maintain an ongoing dialogue. Since teachers often feel overwhelmed, underpaid, and unappreciated, they must be approached with respect and understanding. We need to know what goes on in their classrooms and respond willingly to requests for advice. There are limits on teachers' time and availability to participate in individualized programs. Nevertheless, their support is essential.

A guidance counselor will frequently serve as the intermediary between the therapist and teachers. In larger schools this is a necessity. If possible, a meeting should be arranged with the counselor, teachers, therapist, parents, and student. The message for the student is loud and clear: "You are important. We are all concerned about you and won't let you go down the tubes. The reason we're here is to come up with a program to get you out of this rut. We really need your cooperation to succeed." An alternative is to schedule a separate meeting with the student, an advocate, and the student's identified problem teacher. This provides an opportunity to deal with any personality conflicts and to propose alternatives to acting out and nonparticipation.

I feel strongly about the need to create opportunities for a fresh start. Adolescents often begin treatment at midyear or later, when the pattern of failure is well established. Their teachers continue to insist that they attend class and make an effort, despite the likelihood of failure. Students are well aware of this and see little reason to try; consequently, they continue to cut class and fail to turn in assignments.

Without hope of redeeming oneself or obtaining some positive rewards, there is no incentive to make an effort. My position is simple. If catching up is no longer possible, the youngsters' time should be spent more productively. They can be assigned to a supervised study hall to focus on their salvageable classes or be required to participate in a more constructive and gratifying activity. For some, work–study programs can provide the needed relief.

## CHALLENGING POOR SCHOOL PERFORMANCE

Those who repeatedly experience school difficulties usually avoid any meaningful discussion of their checkered past. They have been asked the eternal question many times: "So how come you're doing so poorly in school?" If they truly knew the answer, it is unlikely that they would still be so stuck. Therapists must explore academic problems from a curious rather than a critical perspective. Failure is humiliating enough; to be lectured about it borders on the intolerable.

Adolescents should be encouraged to ventilate their

complaints in a safe atmosphere. They may feel that there is something wrong with the school. Sometimes they place the blame on the teachers, lamenting that they are boring, bossy, or otherwise out of touch. How might they survive in such a seemingly untenable situation? What options are open to them? Other gripes may involve their school peer group. They describe their classmates as too stuck up, plastic, preppy, or wannabes. Obviously, they don't fit in with them. Are their antisocial friends really any better off? What can they do to get by in this uncomfortable atmosphere?

School underachievement, failure, and truancy are all powerful statements. What are these youngsters trying to tell us? Possibly they are protesting the conventional standards for education and success. They don't see any intrinsic value in school; in fact, it is viewed as of no use to them. Additionally, they may feel a strong allegiance to their deviant subgroup and fear peer ridicule and rejection if they were to try in school.

Some youth will insist that excessive parental pressure has led them to rebel against familial and societal expectations and values. Perhaps, they argue, if their parents cared less about school performance, they might care more.

## Case Example

Dan was a 16-year-old boy with multiple behavior problems. He was failing the tenth grade and his school attendance was worsening. During the course of a discussion, he grew quite sad and angry when describing the emphasis his parents placed on a good education. "The only thing they care about is my school grades," he said tearfully. "They just want to be able to tell their friends that I'm heading for a good college. I don't even think they know anything about me, like my guitar playing or my girlfriend. The whole thing makes me sick."

Inquiries should be made about what youth say to themselves about school. As previously discussed, negative self-talk exerts considerable influence on behavior. Those who believe that they have messed up and have little chance to redeem themselves are likely to make no effort. Such prophecies of doom must be challenged. Can they try and imagine what it would be like to do better? What do they have against praise and success? What could they do differently to make their lives easier? Behavior-disordered youth spend considerable time scheming about how to get the things they want without having to work for them. If they truly want control over their lives, they must come to see that an education is a means to an end. Their fear of failure must be overcome so they can devote their efforts to achievable, prosocial goals.

Paradoxical interventions can be extremely useful in working with achievement issues. Adolescents who are failing school can be encouraged to quit! They can be asked why they stay in such a miserable place if they are truly dissatisfied. They could drop out of school, enlist, drive across the country, or just live in a communal setting. In certain situations I actually offer my assistance to those who feel that such attempts would be blocked. Their reactions are often intriguing. "Do you think I'm stupid? You really can't get anywhere today without a high school education. There's no way I could ever make good money." When we try to tell them that, they're unlikely to listen. Conversely, if we convey that we are not particularly invested in the outcome, they may be more likely to take themselves seriously. In addition, some youngsters actually do better when they have a job by day and attend school voluntarily at night. It helps them feel more connected with the real world and in control of their own lives.

O'Connor and LaSala (1988) employ a similar intervention in the family therapy context. The therapist poses the idea that the family and youngster should think about his or her quitting school. This action is explored along with its potential consequences. The effect is to shift the focus away from the cycle of failure and the parent–child conflicts in the family. Members are asked to unite to try and solve the problem. The authors report that youth find this proposed solution scary and somewhat premature. Again, this intervention helps them to reconsider their options and weakens the power struggle.

The future seems a lifetime away to those who are impulsive, shortsighted, and frequently in trouble. Somehow they must be made to see the connection between their present actions and the most likely outcomes. Lecturing them about how they're throwing their life away does not work. They have heard this many times before and remain in a state of denial. I find it helpful to use an example from their own life to bring home the point. The following reflects a conversation I have had with many young people over the years.

> *Dr. B*: Tell me something. I know you hang out with a fairly large group of kids. Of all those you spend time with, who is the oldest?

*Patient*: I guess that would be John; he's 22.

*Dr. B*: So, John's 22 and he hangs out with 16 and 17-year-olds.

*Patient*: Yep.

*Dr. B*: Well, where does he live?

*Patient*: In a grungy basement apartment he rents by himself. I hate it. It's got roaches and it smells bad.

*Dr. B*: What kind of car does he drive?

*Patient*: A beat-up old Chevy. It's always breaking down and he's trying to grub gas money off everyone.

*Dr. B*: And where does he work?

*Patient*: McDonald's kitchen.

*Dr. B*: What does he tell you about his job?

*Patient*: He says it sucks.

*Dr. B*: Tell me something. If you could push a button and trade places with John, would you do it?

*Patient*: No way!

*Dr. B*: Well, you know something, in a sense John is similar to you. He was in a lot of trouble and eventually dropped out of high school at your age. If you keep going at the same rate, you'll wind up pretty much like John. Is that what you want?

*Patient*: Hell no!

*Dr. B*: Well, if that's the case, we've got to figure out what to do. Can we talk about some other possibilities then?

Certain streetwise youth react differently to this line of questioning. They may point to a drug dealer or pimp who dropped out of school and is now making a great deal of money and driving an expensive car. When I hear this, I usually ask if anyone has been shot in their neighborhood recently. The answer is invariably yes. From that point we proceed to discuss the serious risks involved with illicit activities. Are they prepared to endanger their lives just to have some extra money to throw around? Sadly, for some the answer is yes. Meeting and hearing the life stories of former dealers and criminals is often a useful eye-opener. Local police can usually help to identify such people who are willing to counsel at-risk youth.

## OTHER FAILURES TO THRIVE

The pattern of failure often extends to areas of these young people's lives beyond the school setting. Many have difficulty finding and holding down jobs. They come in frequent conflict with their employers because of erratic attendance and a negative attitude. Despite insisting that they want to work, there is always something wrong with their current job. These inconsistencies must be challenged. What do they really want for themselves? Are they tough enough to go after it? If they enjoy the independence that an income offers, they must learn to bite the bullet and conform to others' expectations. Interpersonal skills training is particularly useful to those who are in frequent conflict with authority.

Many antisocial youth also do not seem to fit in with their peers. Although they deny any strong desire for acceptance, their histories are filled with failures in a variety of group activities. Scouting, team sports, and after-school activities are among the sources of frustration for them. Many lack healthy adult support for their involvement. Any rehabilitative effort should create opportunities for the youngster to reengage in constructive pursuits in a face-saving manner. Role-plays are helpful in getting adolescents to develop some degree of comfort with anticipated interactions. A system should be established to monitor and support any proactive efforts. As their comfort with mainstream activities increases, dependence on the deviant peer group weakens. The cycle of failure must be addressed from every possible angle.

As previously discussed, self-esteem is the product of diverse experiences in the school, family, peer group, and community. Each of these aspects of their lives must be addressed separately and concurrently. Both oppositional and conduct-disordered behavior is often a statement of the youngsters' dissatisfaction with themselves and the world around them. Only as youth acquire prosocial behaviors, learn to cope with school, and experience gratifying alternatives to acting out can they begin to change their antisocial patterns.

# 12

# Working with Families

The family's role in developing and maintaining anti-social behavior has been well documented (Fishman 1988, Gurman et al. 1986, Minuchin 1981, Patterson 1982). High levels of conflict, poor communication skills, lack of positive attention, and inappropriate boundaries are often present in these family structures. Both behavioral and systemic models are useful in formulating treatment strategies. The coercive family process leads to a repetitive cycle of child misbehavior and unsuccessful parental attempts at control (Patterson 1982). As youth enter adolescence, the cycle intensifies and results in further unresolved conflicts.

Fishman (1988) takes a structural perspective, describing two characteristic patterns of delinquent families. In the enmeshed system members are overly involved with one another. Family boundaries are obscured by intrusive behavior and emotional overreactivity. This is illustrated by a mother who excessively monitors her son's activities because she is unable to tolerate age-appropriate independence. The other extreme is a disengaged family with little contact between members and striking emotional distance. Their indifference and lack of ongoing interactions are readily observable.

Antisocial youth feel they do not have to conform to social expectations. The influence of their peer group is far more powerful than that of their family. Comprehensive intervention strategies are necessary to strengthen the family system and precipitate behavior change. Parent management training, functional family therapy, and multisystemic therapy have been the three most extensively studied family approaches (Kazdin 1995). Each makes a unique contribution toward a total family treatment approach with this population.

Parent management training has evolved from Patterson's (1982) work at the Oregon Social Learning Institute. The emphasis is heavily behavioral: identifying and observing target behaviors, establishing reinforcement contingencies, and helping the parents to implement the procedures at home. In practice, the therapist has little direct contact with the child and works directly through the parents. Dishion and Patterson (1992) have found this treatment approach more effective with younger children than adolescents. Many adolescents will become angry and noncompliant when their parents attempt to employ these techniques without involving them in the treatment process. Contingency contracting and negotiating conflicts have proved to be more effective with this population (Robin and Foster 1989). Adolescents enjoy striking bargains and are willing to use therapists as mediators provided that some trust has been established.

Functional family therapy (Alexander and Parsons 1982) integrates techniques from systems, behavioral, and cognitive approaches. It has been widely employed with a delinquent population and the results have been encouraging (Alexander et al. 1994). The approach focuses on understanding the function that problems serve in the family. It presupposes that antisocial behavior helps to meet the family's need for distance or closeness. Behavioral techniques are employed to identify and reinforce appropriate responses. Cognitive approaches are integrated to modify negative attributions and distorted emotional perspectives. The family communication process is viewed from a systems perspective and addressed accordingly.

The broadest based of the family interventions is multisystemic therapy (Henggeler and Borduin 1990). This approach makes the assumption that the adolescent is integrally involved with several systems, which include the family, peer group, school, and community. The treatment is multifaceted in order to address the interrelationship of these systems. It includes individual work, community outreach, and parental guidance. In effect, the treatment choice is governed by the needs of the particular individual and family.

Family therapy techniques are not mutually exclusive. A total treatment program should involve careful selection of diverse procedures systematically directed at both individual and family dysfunction. Strict adherence to a particular model runs the risk of neglecting comorbidity and the complexity of the behavior disorders. The flexible therapist chooses interventions suited to the family's sophistication, motivation, and presenting problems. He or she works rapidly to establish credibility, trust, and an optimism about the possibility of change.

## THE ENGAGEMENT PROCESS

It would be naive to assume that most families have an accurate conception of family treatment or the mental health field in general. The following vignette is a case in point.

Several years ago I was watching the television show *Family Feud*. As you may be aware, this show pits two families against each other in a quizlike competition. Their task is to answer questions that have been responded to in a random sampling across the nation. The correct answer is the one given by a majority of the respondents. A sample question might be: "What do Americans least prefer to get for Christmas?" Fruitcakes, of course, was the most often cited answer. The percentage of respondents for each answer is tabulated and the contestants are awarded points for a match to the sample.

During one show, to my astonishment, the following question was posed. "What would you do if you were experiencing marital problems?" One man responded quickly, "I'd start drinking!" The lights, bells, and whistles chimed. Sure enough, close to 50 percent of the respondents answered similarly. Then a woman hit the buzzer. "I'd have an affair," she stated sardonically. Again the excitement of a correct answer. Some 20 percent had responded in like fashion. Finally, another woman thoughtfully answered, "I'd seek some type of professional counseling." Alas, the buzzer was sounded to indicate an incorrect response. Of the hundreds of people polled, not one had offered that sensible answer! This humorous but sad commentary reflects the mentality of middle America. When problems set in, you grit your teeth, avoid them, and simply accept your fate.

It is best to assume that the family lacks any awareness of the potential benefits of treatment and must be acclimated. The task is to find a way to ally with both the parents and the adolescent. Simultaneously empathizing with two parties at odds requires a delicate balancing act.

As previously discussed, there are distinct advantages to seeing the parents and the adolescent alone before putting them together in the same room. It's easier to get a helping message across when the focus is on the individual's needs and offers a concrete approach to the problem. If the youngster refuses to participate in family meetings, but will attend individual sessions, this should be respected. The patient's discomfort and resistance can then be addressed with assurance that there will be some protection from attack.

A familiar pattern is often seen in the initial family session. The parents are determined to convince the therapist how difficult their youngster is. They are frustrated, angry, and at the end of their rope. They begin by reciting a long list of grievances. The adolescent grows progressively angrier as they proceed. This sequence must be interrupted. The therapist might comment, "I can see that you have many examples of how terrible your daughter is. I understand how strongly you feel, but if you continue, I'm afraid we'll lose any chance for cooperation. I suggest we move on to something else and discuss this further another time."

The adolescent's initial position is also quite predictable. "My parents are always on my case. I think they're both control freaks. They bug me about everything. If they'd just leave me alone I wouldn't get into so much trouble." The parents, of course, react defensively. Altercations often erupt early in the first meeting. Here too the potshots must be stopped. The therapist might comment loudly, "Look, I can see we're not going to get anywhere continuing this way. Let's just change the topic and come back to this when we get better at talking together. I can see we've got a lot of work to do."

Liddle (1995) suggests defining a basic task to help each family member find a personal reason for attending sessions. The adolescent's wish for independence is readily apparent as is the parents' desire for compliance. With some coaxing, the family can usually agree to set these as initial goals.

The parents will express concerns about the youngster's snowing the therapist. The teenager on the other hand suspects that the therapist will be the parents' henchman. These issues must be addressed from the outset. The search for mutual understanding, agreed-upon goals, and a commitment to the treatment process takes precedence. Problems must be viewed as solvable. The challenge is to find the approach that will work for the specific needs of each family.

The therapist takes an active role from the start. Rather than waiting for something to happen, he initiates action. Generally speaking, the more disturbed the family, the greater the need for control. If they begin by expressing their pain and desire to change, be thankful. If not, help them formulate their thoughts and express feelings. Share stories about other families, encourage disclosures, and propose a format for interacting. Each family member should come to feel that the therapist truly wants to get to know them.

Taking a history lends considerable structure to a session but risks increasing the family's impatience to straighten things out. I prefer to view assessment as an ongoing process and initially isolate a problem that can be immediately addressed (curfew violation, truancy, or excessive coercive measures). Families must agree to make the initial task a priority. The therapist attempts to remain evenhanded as the problems are presented, although this is not always possible.

Parent and child must share responsibility for ongoing difficulties. Often the antisocial behavior interferes with the mastery of developmental tasks. A young girl on court probation can hardly view herself as independent. Although the desire for autonomy is great, she has chosen unacceptable ways to accomplish her goal.

Henggeler and Borduin (1990) define the problem in terms of the adolescent's susceptibility to peer influence. The more estranged the family relationships, the greater the adolescent's desire to avoid interacting with them. The family must find a way to reintegrate the troubled adolescent and create opportunities for positive interaction. To accomplish this, they are taught to see one another's behavior as understandable and goal directed rather than hostile and retaliative.

Reframing plays a prominent role in the early work. When family members describe one another in antagonistic terms, alternative explanations are offered. The meaning of negative behavior is changed to convey a more positive explanation (Alexander et al. 1988). For example, a youngster who always gets into trouble is seen as expressing concern for the family by calling attention to their problems. Runaway behavior can be reframed as a need for independence; substance abuse, as a statement of isolation and a desire for closeness. Excessive parental involvement, control, and worry can be interpreted as an expression of caring. Pressure about academic achievement might be relabeled as the parents' desire to see their child be successful and financially secure in the future.

Family members need to see one another in a more positive light. They should be encouraged to speculate about other, more constructive, motives for behavior. Angry feelings are often based on misinterpretation of another's intent and this should be corrected at the first opportunity. The therapist identifies the likable qualities of each family member and helps all of them to further value each other. Their cumulative negative feelings sometimes cloud their objectivity and need to be challenged.

## Case Example

The Davis family came reluctantly to their initial family session. Their 16-year-old son Stephen had been charged with theft after getting caught shoplifting in a department store. The terms of his probation stipulated that he attend regular family therapy sessions. Although he insisted that it was his first offense, there had been several suspicious incidents during the past year. Stephen was often on the edge of trouble. He was impulsive and aggressive and defied authority. The family argued often and blamed him for the tension in their home.

Mr. and Mrs. Davis worked full time to support the family. They resented having to attend sessions and commented on the inconvenience and expense to them. Stephen felt that treatment was a waste of time since he really didn't have any problems in the first place. Their only common ground seemed to be their anger about having to participate in family therapy.

Stephen, his parents, and his 14-year-old sister were seen in the initial meeting.

*Mr. Davis*: Well, I guess we all know why we're here.
*Mrs. Davis*: Yeah, Stephen got in trouble one time too often. We're really getting tired of having to go to all those conferences.
*Stephen*: So don't go! I don't want you to anyway.
*Therapist*: Wait a minute. You're all in this together. The court ordered family treatment for six months, didn't they?
*Mr. Davis*: Yes, it serves us right.
*Therapist*: What does that mean?
*Mrs. Davis*: We should have done something about this a long time ago. It really upsets me that Stephen just doesn't try anymore. Nothing seems to be going right for us.
*Therapist*: You mean not just Stephen, then.
*Mrs. Davis*: Yes, I guess.
*Therapist*: Mr. Davis, do you agree?

*Mr. Davis*: Yeah.

*Therapist*: So, the whole family is under a lot of stress. Jane [daughter], can you tell me something about that?

*Jane*: Well, Mom and Dad always talk about financial pressures and . . . Grandma died a while ago.

*Therapist*: It's been a tough year, hasn't it? *(Both parents nod)* But you're here because of Stephen's problems, aren't you?

*Mrs. Davis*: I guess so.

*Therapist*: You know, I have a feeling all these things are related. Stephen has been getting in more trouble lately. Both of you feel pretty overwhelmed. Maybe he's been sending out a distress signal for the family. What do you think, Stephen?

*Stephen*: I don't know. Maybe.

*Therapist*: Mr. and Mrs. Davis, I think Stephen has been concerned with you but hasn't known how to show it. Stephen, why do you think your parents have been on your case so much?

*Stephen*: Well, they've always blamed things on me. I figure they just get their kicks out of bugging me.

*Therapist*: Stephen, you know better than that. They've been under a lot of pressure. I think that their getting on you is a way of showing that they care. Is that possible, Mr. and Mrs. Davis?

*Mr. Davis*: Well, we've never thought of it that way, but we really would like to see him get straightened out. He used to be so much fun to be around.

*Therapist*: You miss the old days, huh?

*Mrs. Davis*: *(Sadly)* Things have just gotten out of hand. I never thought we'd wind up like this— you know, sitting here with someone because we have to.

*Therapist*: I understand that, but I believe you could all help one another if we step back and try to look at things objectively. Could we just agree to talk about each of your roles for a while? I'm interested in hearing what you'd like from each other. I think it would really make a difference. How about it?

*Mr. Davis*: Well, I don't see why not.

*Mrs. Davis*: There certainly is nothing to lose at this point.

*Jane*: Okay, but I'm not sure what I have to do with this.

*Therapist*: Let me worry about that. Stephen, how about it?

*Stephen*: I guess so. This is a little different than I expected.

*Therapist*: Good, I wouldn't want to be that predictable!

## ASSESSING FAMILY FUNCTIONS

Effective treatment evolves from an accurate assessment of behavioral, interactional, and affective family patterns. The process is ongoing and integrally involved with formulating and implementing intervention strategies.

The initial observations should focus on understanding any potential road blocks to treatment. Anderson and Stewart (1983) define resistance as the interactive behaviors in a family system that prevent it from achieving desired goals. Attitudes, behaviors, and expectations all play a part. How does the family feel about being in treatment? Are they resentful of the mandate or aware of their systems' role in the presenting problem? Those who share responsibility for the difficulties are more likely to change. Do they understand and accept the treatment process or take a cynical attitude? What have been their previous experiences with the mental health delivery system? Generally speaking, the more rigid the family's views, the more difficult is the engagement process.

Each family member is asked to offer his or her own explanation of the problem behavior. Issues of blame are addressed directly by challenging the adolescent and parents to be specific about their complaints. If a parent says that they're fed up because their youngster is always in trouble, we insist that they clarify this. Exactly how often does the behavior occur? What do you mean by a "bad attitude"? The message is given that the problem is not insurmountable. By breaking it down into readily addressed smaller difficulties, the therapist reduces the enormity of the predicament. For example, a chronically aggressive youth is angry, has trouble with interpersonal relationships, and is impulsive in school and at home. When the teenager accuses his parents of being out of touch, he too is encouraged to be more specific. Does it mean that they don't let him do what he wants or that their rules are more stringent than those of his peers? Clarification is sought in order to develop an objective yardstick for potential evaluation. Sometimes insistence on corroboration reduces the intensity of the complaints.

Alexander et al. (1988) recommend a functional analysis of behavior. Members of dysfunctional families are frequently unable to connect their own actions to the current difficulties. Deviant behavior serves a specific function in regulating the family homeostasis. The context in which the behavior occurs should be explored and its impact assessed. Youngsters who smoke pot, cut school, and sneak out at night are increasing the distance between themselves and the family. Yet they may be simultaneously seeking limits. In contrast, a self-destructive youth who is hospitalized following a suicide attempt is more likely attempting to bring the family closer together.

Even the extremes of antisocial behavior serve a function in the family. Seemingly hardened, amoral young people who are at odds with society, often subtly give their parents permission to write them off as no good. This enables the parents to further abdicate their responsibilities and proceed with their own agendas. The youngster's negative attributions are then confirmed, lending credence to their belief that they are outcasts. The cycle must be identified and interrupted to facilitate change.

Family interactions are carefully observed to determine the patterns of closeness and distancing. Are the parents overprotective and insulating the youngster from the consequences of his or her behavior? When one parent is harsh, the other often compensates with overindulgence and rationalizations for misbehavior.

Who is the family spokesperson? During the sessions, is the dialogue balanced or does one parent monopolize the conversation? I asked a 16-year-old how he felt about his parents' constant quarreling. His mother interrupted before he could speak. "I'll tell you what he thinks," she snapped, and proceeded to answer for him. The father passively watched his family interaction without responding. When questioned about his role in the family, he admitted that "he had given up on trying to get a word in."

Observing the distribution of power in the family should provide useful information. Parents who are able to share the responsibility and discipline are more effective. Antisocial youth are masters at dividing their parents on daily issues and preying on the weaker link in the chain of command. As the imbalances are identified and brought to the family's attention, the adolescent is forced to participate more directly in the family system. By instructing the parents to make decisions jointly or defer them if they can't, the issue is crystallized.

The role of each family member is often unclear. There should be sufficient differentiation between the parents and the children. The more difficult it is to determine the distribution of responsibility, the more likely it is that the family is dysfunctional. When the adolescent is used as a confidante by, for example, an alienated spouse, the separation and individuation process is impaired. A parent's excessive dependency can easily become a burden in the same way that emotional unavailability fuels distance. Generally, the existing family subsystems must be identified and ultimately weakened. A father–daughter coalition against a mother, grandparents allied with grandchildren, or a sibling conspiring with the parents against the identified patient—all require intervention. These maladaptive alliances must be altered to restore balance in the family relationships.

The pattern of emotional expression influences family cohesiveness. Are the feelings shared spontaneously or with great caution? During initial meetings the therapist looks for any display of warmth or caring. In these families negative affect is verbalized readily, and is characterized by defensiveness in communication. The adolescent instinctively holds onto his anger as justification for his misbehavior. The parents are frequently distant and have invested their energy in a sibling.

Family communication can range from direct to oblique. Some years ago I was sitting in an initial meeting when a mother decisively pronounced that "this family will get itself together when the elephants come in from the backyard." I was simultaneously stunned and puzzled. Looking at her son, I asked, "Do you know what your mother means when she refers to that?" He smiled and told me he had no idea what she was talking about. In fact, she had been saying that for several years! A quick check with the father revealed a similar perspective. Strange, vague, and unusual statements must be challenged immediately. They are often the entree to family dysfunction.

Critical parents spawn defiant teenagers. The interrelationships are quite striking. The youngster's angry and sarcastic remarks increase the parent's condemnation, which in turn maintains the behavior. These families typically talk to the therapist rather than looking at each other. This sequence must be called to their attention and interrupted. Other nuances such as tone of voice, facial expressions, and body language must also be picked up on.

At times one or more family members will disrupt the dialogue to a point where it is impossible to be productive. A father and son standing and screaming at each other makes problem solving impossible. The intervention is immediate and specific. One family member is asked to leave the session so they can compose themselves. It does not have to be the adolescent, but it should be done without blame. The therapist controls the pace of the session by assertively stating, "Wait a minute. What's going on here sounds like what you've described at home. I'd prefer to discuss this without screaming, but it seems that things have gone too far. I'd like you [father or son] to take a break for a few minutes and rejoin us when you feel ready." If one refuses, the other is asked to "be a sport about it" and show some good will.

Sometimes it becomes apparent that the family has a secret that is not being discussed openly. This might be a faltering marriage, physical abuse, adoption, serious illness, financial problems, or substance abuse. Considerable discretion must be exercised in prompting the family to speak the unspoken. To this end I find it useful to meet with them in different combinations (e.g., just the children, the grandmother, or one parent alone) to facilitate disclosure. The subsystem can be encouraged to speak in confidence about something they are fearful of broaching in the group. It then becomes possible to support and empower them to be the catalyst for change. Once they feel their safety is ensured they can raise the concern as a family issue.

## EARLY CRISIS INTERVENTION

Many families enter treatment in crisis. School suspensions, runaways, drug arrests, and other trouble with the law will typically precipitate action. An immediate and decisive response is necessary. The situation must be highly structured with alternatives proposed. If the family has inadequate problem-solving skills, the responsibility falls on the therapist. When the problems are addressed rapidly, the family becomes more open to treatment.

McCown and Johnson (1993) emphasize the importance of adopting a style consistent with the family's level of sophistication. The therapist proposes straightforward, simple, practical solutions. Family members are urged to talk in turn, stick with the present, and speak for themselves. At times it is difficult to discern the accuracy of the parents' and adolescent's reports. Any attempt to prematurely judge right and wrong can short-circuit the process. The therapist tries to describe the difficulties objectively and offer an interim solution. Inquiries are made about previous crises and how the family has handled them in the past.

## Case Example

The Howard family entered treatment because of their son's suspension from school for fighting. Both parents were enraged about having to attend a school meeting during their workday. Their son David was initially indifferent, but quickly grew angry at his parents for getting on his case. The family had been arguing furiously for the past few days, seemingly unable to resolve their dilemma about how to handle the situation. On two occasions David had run out of the house for several hours.

The school had insisted that he couldn't return until the problem had been satisfactorily addressed.

The initial task was getting the family to agree on a course of action. The therapist asked David and his parents what each hoped would happen. The parents wanted him back in school with no further problems, of course. David claimed that he didn't care about anything and was "sick and tired of this shit." He was encouraged to ventilate his grievances and come up with some ideas he could live with.

David complained about all the school rules but was unable to offer viable alternatives. The therapist proposed that he transfer to another school or commit to making a new start in his current school with the family's help. As he was 15, dropping out was not an alternative. Also, he liked the kids he hung out with in school. After some discussion the family agreed to try a probationary return to his current school. David was to work on managing his anger and agreed to contact school personnel when he felt he was being provoked. The family in turn would attempt to become his allies. This meant they would support him by refraining from nagging and offer their assistance only when asked. The agreement, of course, was temporary, and would be reviewed weekly. It enabled the parents and child to save face and enter the treatment process. Much work had to be done, but the crisis had been averted.

Fishman (1988) suggests that the therapist precipitate a crisis in the session by insisting that the family deal with an identifiable area of dysfunction. For example, if an adolescent was cutting school and shoplifting, the parents would be challenged to turn him in. Protecting antisocial youth from the consequences of their actions serves only to maintain the behavior. A weak parental coalition must be strengthened so that both parents will ensure that the youngster stand alone after violating social norms. Interestingly, youth often remain quiet while this type of discussion is held in their presence. They are not quite sure what to make of it.

## ENHANCING COMMUNICATION

The family dialogue is rarely balanced and free-flowing. Interactions are based primarily on criticism and accusations, with both parents and teenager typically denying fault. Alexander and Parsons (1982) emphasize that the way people talk determines the quality of their relationships. Effective treatment must alter both the tone and the content of the messages exchanged. Sarcasm, hostility, and blaming interfere with the presentation of clear and consistent messages. By the time families enter treatment, they are often avoiding one another and feeling considerable anger and hurt.

The intervention begins as soon as the destructive patterns are identified. In essence, we call it as we see it. Family members are likely to react to one another in the same way in session as they do at home.

### Case Example

Mr. Hill spoke to his son in a condescending tone during the first family meeting. After a few minutes, the therapist commented that she could tell how frustrated and angry he was by the tone of his voice. She simultaneously observed his son's discomfort and emotional withdrawal. "Mr. Hill," she said, "it seems that your son is reacting negatively to your comments about him. What I'd like to do is try and find a way for each of you to talk so that the other will listen. Could you try and rephrase what you said in a more neutral way? Afterwards, we'll ask the family if it seemed less provocative. Sometimes the little things help, you know!"

Families should be encouraged to talk to one another with respect. Alternatives to threats and commands are presented and then practiced. Taking potshot at one another is not tolerated. This may result in a need for frequent interruptions early on, but the tone must be set for some degree of mutual respect. The therapist encourages discussion of present conflicts and discourages recitation of past grievances. Parents and teenagers are taught to reduce blaming by using "I" rather than "you" messages. The goal is to get each family member to take responsibility for his or her own feelings and behavior. While this is awkward at first, families quickly get the hang of speaking for themselves.

Quiet families pose a unique problem. It is extremely uncomfortable for five or six people to sit in a room without saying anything. There have been times when I have felt that I've been with a family for half an hour only to look at my watch and learn that ten minutes have elapsed!

The function of the silence should be determined as soon as possible. Does it stem from resistance, a lack of understanding of what to do in therapy, or a skill deficit? At first the therapist must do the talking. Information about each individual member is sought. Some universal feelings of other families can be shared. A therapist might comment, for example, that many families resent being pushed to attend therapy sessions. If they agree, they are encouraged to elaborate on their feelings. On occasion an entire family will lack the ability to converse comfortably on any topic. In these instances social skills training can be conducted right in the session.

Rambling family members pose the opposite sort of problem. When one person does most of the talking for the family, an imbalance results. The therapist should comment on how hard it is to get a word in, thus interrupting the process. The therapist checks to be certain he or she understands the excessively verbal member's message; it usually can be summed up rather succinctly. Another family member is then asked for an opinion on the topic. This intervention is repeated until some balance is restored in the communication process (Brock and Barnard 1988). The family may be shocked by this ploy, but seems to appreciate it. Another approach is to tell the other family members to thank the verbose member for doing all the work for them. The spokesperson is then asked to take a break and turn over the job to another member.

Proactive efforts are strongly encouraged. I find it useful to ask adolescents about a friend's house where they like to hang out. This creates an opportunity for a safe expression of needs and preferences. Youngsters usually describe a home atmosphere in which the family talks to each other, openly has fun, and helps one another. The parents are then asked how they would feel about such a climate in their home. Naturally they would welcome it. This can serve as a basis for further discussion of their mutual needs, leading to implementation of a new plan. Family commitment can be promoted by discussing possible ideas for pleasurable activities. This is sometimes difficult because of the different tastes of parents and teenagers. In this case each should be asked to try the other's suggestion in exchange for following their own.

## IMPROVING PARENTING SKILLS

Parent management training and behavioral family therapy have been effectively employed to modify the behavior of antisocial children and adolescents (Bank et al. 1991, Kazdin 1995, Patterson et al. 1982, Wells 1995). The parents are seen without the children present and are taught to apply specific behavioral principles at home. While the techniques are extremely useful in conjunction with other approaches, exclusive reliance on them with an adolescent population has met with limited success (Kazdin 1995).

Aggressive and noncompliant behaviors are usually targeted for intervention. Parents learn to identify and monitor the behaviors of concern and then systematically employ reinforcement principles. The importance of praise and naturally occurring reinforcers is stressed although that is not always sufficient. Today's adolescents prefer money, clothing, driving privileges, and curfew extensions.

During the sessions the parents are helped to be

more consistent in enforcing rules and expectations. Their frequent criticisms of the adolescent must be reduced and replaced by positive comments. The desired behaviors are broken down into small steps that can be readily followed and rewarded. The goal is to create a situation in which both child and parents work in tandem.

Punishing inappropriate behavior is a complex task. Conduct-disordered adolescents often defy parental restrictions and persist in their antisocial patterns. Increasing the severity of a punishment is usually not effective. Rather, parents must be taught to identify meaningful age-appropriate consequences that are easily enforceable. Allowance and car privileges are among the few potentially effective punishments. When possible, constructive punishment should be used to deter future offenses.

For example, if a youngster comes home drunk and disorderly, rather than restrict him indefinitely, he could be required to pay back his family by painting a room, doing yardwork, or helping a younger brother with schoolwork. This opens the door to more positive interactions. A harsher, humiliating punishment might lead to further acting out. In all instances the effectiveness of a punishment must be evaluated afterward. If the behavior of concern has decreased, the punishment was successful; if it persists, then other options should be considered.

When employing behavioral family therapy techniques, several caveats are in order. First and foremost, teenagers hate being watched closely. This makes observation difficult and potentially contentious. In addition, it is hard for parents to find and control reinforcers with an adolescent population. The angry and defiant youngsters often insist that they don't care when their parents impose consequences. The parents in turn often give up easily and insist that they have tried all of these approaches before. Finally, there is always the risk of the adolescent manipulating any system simply to get what he wants.

## NEGOTIATING AND CONFLICT RESOLUTION

Contingency contracting is an aspect of behavioral family therapy that is especially useful with a recalcitrant population. Adolescents generally enjoy the negotiating process and readily participate in mediated sessions. Although they are often demanding and insist on immediate answers to their requests, they can be taught to deliberate and work toward amicable compromises.

Robin and Foster (1989) delineate the steps in negotiating parent–adolescent conflicts. To start, the problem is defined and family members are encouraged to exchange views. Disagreements are to be expected and should be viewed as a natural part of raising teenagers. If unrealistic demands are made by either parent or the child, the therapist intercedes as the expert and voice of reason.

For example, a 15-year-old boy's demand to be allowed to go on an unchaperoned overnight beach trip would be challenged. He is simply too young for that degree of freedom. Parents who insist that their 16-year-old daughter be home by 9:00 P.M. every Saturday night present an opposite case. They would be challenged on their overprotectiveness and lack of trust. Age-appropriate expectations must be discussed within the context of the community where the family resides. Negotiations can then take place within a reasonable framework.

The next step in the process is to ask the parents and the child to list several possible solutions to their conflict. Creativity is encouraged and the family is instructed to listen to all ideas nonjudgmentally. After the list has been generated, everyone evaluates the alternatives. Both sides may need to compromise to reach an acceptable agreement. The parents must accept the adolescent's need for independence and autonomy; the adolescent must acknowledge the parents' appropriate concern and need for some regulation. All family members are helped to save face by the therapist's emphasis on their willingness to cooperate and improve family relations. In effect, there are no winners, no losers, and no power struggles.

Once a potential solution has been negotiated, the family is asked to anticipate its effect. Any possible difficulties are discussed along with the criteria for compliance. If the task seems too large for the adolescent, more modest goals are negotiated. The final agreement must be clear, specific, and enforceable. When the family succeeds in negotiating the conflict and carrying out the agreement, the process becomes a model for future problem solving. Should difficulties arise, the contract breakdown is explored, and steps are taken to renegotiate the terms. Some possible explanations for failure include a misunderstanding of the terms of the contract, resentment over being pushed into an agreement, or the difficulty of the chosen task.

## Case Example

Jim felt strongly that he should be allowed to go to a Saturday night party following a football game. It was expected to run from ten o'clock at night until two o'clock in the morning. His parents expressed serious reservations based on his previous troubles with drinking, curfew violations, and the group of youngsters who would be at the party. Jim insisted his parents had nothing to worry about and were making too big a deal of it. The family agreed that they needed to work on the issue of trust.

The beginning discussions focused on Jim's poor track record and difficulty in keeping promises. He pointed out that his parents were too restrictive and never gave him the benefit of the doubt. The therapist shared the parents' legitimate concern but emphasized that they couldn't reach agreement about realistic expectations or the consequences for potential violations. It was suggested that they temporarily forget past experience and try to negotiate their differences openly.

Jim stated that if they allowed him to go, he would come home on time and be sober. He offered no information about the specifics of the party. This made his parents rather uneasy so the therapist asked if there was anything Jim could do to assuage their worries. They grew silent but were quickly interrupted by Jim. "What if I leave you the phone number?" he queried. "That might help a little," his mother said. "But not enough," the therapist interjected. "We really need to have more to go on. Can any of you suggest other possible actions that would help you to feel more comfortable?" The father proposed that he stop by their room when he got home to prove that he wasn't drunk. Jim added that he would call them once from the party to check in. "It sounds like you have the basis for an agreement here," the therapist commented. "One thing is missing though. Jim, what would happen if you broke your word and came home late or drunk?" "I'd give up my car for a few weeks; is that fair?" The therapist felt that they now had a reasonable contract and looked toward the parents. "We'll try it," his father said. They all agreed to review the outcome in the following session.

Once a family has learned to communicate and negotiate, they can apply these skills to most aspects of their lives. Family vacations, use of the car, allowance, and privileges can be discussed in a productive atmosphere. Any unreasonable demands must still be challenged. The adolescent who insists on complete freedom from parental interference is often in need of additional limits. Conversely, the parent who feels that too much freedom will lead to drug use and the deterioration of school grades must be convinced that responsible youth do not abuse privileges that are based on mutual trust and respect.

The negotiation process has a down side, however. Certain antisocial youth are so manipulative that bargaining only exacerbates their difficulties. They must learn to take no for an answer. It is extremely difficult to hold the line with youngsters who are determined to have their own way. The parents need considerable leverage and support to establish guidelines they can enforce. Ultimately it is the consistency of their actions rather than their words that will lead to compliance. If all efforts fail, more restrictive alternatives must be considered.

## RECURRENT THEMES

Authoritarian parents pose specific challenges to family therapists. Often they are rigid, inflexible, and punitive. Their excessive emphasis on control fosters rebelliousness in their adolescent and they tend to be cynical and self-righteous in their explanations of the problem behavior. Intervention must be used to open their eyes to other approaches to discipline.

I find it useful to ask these parents how they were raised. They usually comment that they had it much tougher than their child does. They recall episodes of being beaten with a strap, locked in their rooms, and punished excessively to make them tow the line. When asked how they felt back then, they expressed rage and humiliation. One father commented that he "hated the bastard" who raised him. Others have expressed more forgiving attitudes and stated that it was for their own good. The parallels should be drawn between their own childhood experiences and their current impasses with their teenagers. The point is usually made that they are repeating some of the behaviors that they once detested. The sadness and futility of this can be discussed and other approaches to parenting considered.

Certain parents insist that they turned out just fine

despite their harsh upbringing. When this kind of statement is made, I often look at the adolescent and ask if he or she feels that their parent has it together. Ray's response was illustrative.

"You've got to be kidding," he said. "My father drinks every day after work. He has these huge arguments with Mom and blames everything on her. I've heard him lie to his boss on the phone. He didn't even pay his taxes last year!" Children often can help us challenge a parent's denial. A job well done, Ray.

The other extreme of parenting is a laissez-faire attitude coupled with excessive permissiveness. This pattern is observed in both ultraliberal and weak parents. It too can lead to serious problems.

Several years ago a family provided a graphic illustration in their first session with me. They had decided to begin treatment because their 17-year-old son came home drunk the previous Friday night at 1:30 A.M. He stumbled upstairs noisily, kicked open the door of their bedroom, and told them to "get the hell out of bed" so that he could watch television in their room. To my amazement, they had complied with his request and gone downstairs to another room. This vignette described an extreme violation of boundaries, flagrant disrespect, and a lack of any self or parental control.

These parents lacked the ability to set limits for their defiant son. The situation had worsened to the point where they were hostages in their own home. The appropriate intervention required that the therapist immediately ally himself with the parents. They had to be told that they had a right to their privacy and must establish rules for their own home. This process of empowerment is difficult with families such as these. The boundaries between the subsystems must be delineated and maintained. To accomplish this, the therapist had to emphasize strongly that the situation was intolerable. Once the parents agreed, the adolescent was informed that he would have to adhere to the specific guidelines established in the session. If he was unable to comply, it would be necessary to make other, less appealing, living arrangements for him. The youngster immediately shifted his anger to the therapist, whom he cursed and threatened. This represented the end of his reign of terror, however, and future sessions began to focus on communication and contracting for privileges. The parents were initially apprehensive, but over time were able to move into a more appropriate parental role.

Inevitably we come across parents who are simply unfit. They lack any genuine emotional involvement with their children, are absorbed with their own pathology (substance abuse, schizophrenia, or antisocial behavior); and display little willingness to cooperate or change in any way. In some instances they are abusive and pose a danger to their children.

When family interventions are unsuccessful and the parents have a destructive influence, more extreme measures must be considered. The adolescent must be told forthrightly that their situation is untenable. They have a right to a reasonably stable home with a parent who shows at least some concern. The local social service agency should be contacted so that a thorough investigation can be conducted. If necessary, the youngster is removed from the home and placed in a safer, more supportive setting.

## SINGLE PARENTS AND BLENDED FAMILIES

While no specific statistics are available, it seems that a disproportionately large number of the disruptive behavior disorders do not reside with both natural parents. In single-parent families the adolescent's problems are often magnified by the demands placed upon the custodial parent. These include financial pressures, work stresses, and the burden of running a household alone. The parent's social network may be limited by time constraints and the youngster is often less supervised.

Keshet and Mirkin (1985) stress that a divorce involves adjustment to a new kind of parenting. Adolescents typically gain power when their parent's energy is devoted to diverse concerns. The single parent may look to the adolescent for support at a time the child is grappling with his or her own developmental issues. Acting out sometimes represents an avoidance of the parent's increased need for closeness. As the parent begins to date and establish a new life, it can become harder to set limits and monitor the child's behavior.

These alterations in the family structure must be discussed. If the youngster is going back and forth between two homes, it will be harder for a parent to monitor their behavior adequately. This places increased emphasis on communication between the involved parents. The therapist must foster involvement of both the father and mother while addressing the concerns of each subsystem.

Adolescents frequently challenge their parents on any observed hypocrisy. Drinking, overnights with dates, and value systems become the topics of discussion. Despite the parent's activities, youth must still be held accountable for their own behavior. The emphasis is placed on open communication and clearly defined roles.

Blended families must address the issues of stepparenting. Many adolescents complain that they don't like the idea of another adult telling them what to do. Their increased rebelliousness may be a test of the natural parent's ability to set limits and contain their behavior. In this situation the family work focuses on defining the parents' new roles and strengthening the blended family structure. The adolescent will continue to increase his or her attempts at manipulation until the parents can demonstrate their cohesiveness, consistency, and ability to resolve conflicts.


## PRACTICAL PROBLEMS OF FAMILY WORK

Certain issues are likely to recur in the treatment of conduct-disordered youth. Perhaps the most challenging is the negative influence of the peer group. Parents complain loudly about their children's choice of friends. The youngsters repeatedly get in trouble when hanging out with them, yet insist that the friends are not the problem. This poses a therapeutic dilemma. Adolescents not connected with the family seek a sense of belongingness elsewhere, in a group with potentially destructive influence that offers them their only real source of acceptance.

Antisocial youth must develop areas of competence outside their troubled peer group. This requires that the family encourage and support any prosocial activity with nondeviant peers. Through behavioral contracting, an agreement can be established to reward any participation in extracurricular activities. The goal is to help youth develop any potential strengths or interests they might have.

Somehow the adolescent must be convinced that harmful consequences are associated with continued affiliation with the subgroup (Henggeler and Borduin 1990). The parents must be helped to find a way to reintegrate him or her into the family. This could mean including friends in family activities or allowing the youngster to take an active role in planning. When efforts to redirect the youngster's energies fail, the parents may have to remove the adolescent from the peer group. Simply forbidding children to see their friends usually does not work. Most parents do not have sufficient control over their youngsters' environment to enforce such an edict. This could mean that a school change, move, or placement in a treatment facility needs to be considered. Some adolescents are able to mobilize their resources at this point, realizing that their parents are serious. Others disregard the warnings and persist in their behavior until the issue is forced. In either event the therapist supports the parents in setting the limit, while reminding the youngsters that they still have a choice, but will have to accept the consequences of their actions.

At times the pressure of family sessions is such that a parent or teenager refuses to attend. Under these circumstances the therapist reaches out to the estranged member, helping him or her to save face and find a way to reenter the process. Withdrawal is often prompted by feelings of not being taken seriously. The opportunity to ventilate in a private session can help reestablish a working alliance.

There will be times when adolescents lie to their

parents during a session, well knowing that the therapist is aware of this. Challenging the deceitful behavior when it occurs would violate the confidentiality of the relationship, but overlooking it can fuel the pathology. This bind is best addressed by letting youngsters know that you'd like to speak to them alone at the first available opportunity. This might necessitate an interruption during the meeting or a brief conference following it. Patient and therapist must collaborate to find a face-saving way to broach the truth. If the youngster refuses to deal with it, the potential consequences of forced disclosure must be weighed against those of secrecy. In either event the implications for the therapeutic relationship must be discussed.

## EXTENDING THE TREATMENT GAINS

As the family learns to interact appropriately and to resolve conflicts, its members are encouraged to do the family work outside the session. Issues involving curfew, rule infractions, privileges, and schoolwork are discussed at home and reviewed in follow-up sessions. The emphasis is placed upon the increased respect and mutuality between family members. While the presenting symptoms may abate in several months, the family will need continued work on the stresses and imbalances that fueled the dysfunction.

The newly acquired skills must be practiced and reinforced. The family must continue to take note of positive behavior changes and remain sensitive to the destructive power of criticism. As the adolescent begins to accomplish the developmental tasks of independence, separation, and mastery, the family is freed up to use its energy more productively. Other concomitant treatment modalities and environmental interventions help the adolescent develop more gratifying relationships and an improved self-image. Thus the propensity to seek trouble is reduced.

# 13

# Special Considerations for Group Treatment

The peer group is the single most powerful influence in adolescence. Any effective treatment regime must mobilize the peer group to respond proactively to one another. An understanding of how antisocial youth act in groups, why they do so, and what to do about it is essential to the process of change. Whether the group format is structured and behavioral or free-flowing, the therapist must be equipped to intervene in difficult, recurrent situations.

The face of group therapy has been changing in recent years. Increased emphasis on short-term work has led to a need for specific, focused goals and strategies for matching patients. The challenge is intensified by the propensity of this population to resist treatment and act out in the group setting.

Yalom's (1975) recognized healing elements of universality, cohesiveness, and interpersonal learning are particularly relevant to group work with behavior-disordered adolescents. The therapist must mobilize these forces to develop a productive group atmosphere.

Group work affords the opportunity to utilize peer pressure, challenge the adolescent's egocentricity, and facilitate self-disclosure. Youngsters will bring the same issues to group that they display in extratherapeutic situations. The group setting provides the opportunity to learn and practice skills in a relatively safe atmosphere. In addition, it is socially acceptable to those who might otherwise refuse assistance. Spending time with like-minded peers provides a measure of security and a face-saving opportunity that other approaches do not offer.

Corder (1994) surveyed adolescents in therapy groups to identify the treatment factors they found most helpful. Respondents cited the opportunity to express feelings directly, get feedback from others, and learn to take responsibility for their lives. Interestingly, the majority of adolescents felt that insight was the least helpful variable. As my groups near termination, I sometimes ask them what they will remember most afterwards. The comments I have heard most frequently include, "We had fun," "I could be myself," and "We talked about interesting stuff." Unless specifically directed, they seemed more focused on the experiential aspects rather than the treatment variables.

Certain therapist characteristics appear to enhance effective group functioning. High verbal activity, personal disclosure, and reduced expectation for self-analysis have been substantiated (Corder 1994). The leader must be active, consistent, directive, and able to maintain control during the sessions (Raubolt 1983). Excessive permissiveness with antisocial youth encourages acting out.

Some years ago I was supervising a trainee who was running an early-adolescent boys' group composed primarily of those with behavior disorders. While observing him through a one-way mirror, I noted that the youngsters would mess up his hair, knock off his glasses, and spin him in his swivel chair. His attempts at interpretation and limit setting were futile. The sessions seemed to grow more chaotic with each week. As the group was clearly unproductive, it became necessary to terminate it. Once a therapist has missed the early opportunities to impose structure and set limits, it is often too late to regain control.

Whenever possible, these groups should be conducted with a cotherapist. The youngsters feel safer with two adults in the room and are less likely to test the limits. When difficulties do arise, one therapist can work with the disruptive member outside the session until he or she is ready to return.

## PREPARATION FOR GROUP TREATMENT

Oppositional and conduct-disordered youth expect to have trouble in groups. Their experience with peers, family, and school has been laden with conflict. As the group begins, they are likely to assume the roles that are most familiar to them. Challenges to authority, bravado, and disruptive behavior are commonplace. The less structured the group, the greater the likelihood of occurrence. To our chagrin, antisocial adolescents will seek the approval of their peers rather than of their therapist. This leads to denial of the seriousness of their problems and initial resistance to address them. The peer group becomes the potential agent of change. This requires that the leaders take steps to ensure that the group will coalesce and grow to be mutually supportive.

Antisocial youth should be evaluated for their capacity to benefit from the group experience. They must show some willingness to listen, display self-control, and participate. The leaders must try to anticipate any potential for acting out. Pregroup meetings conducted to orient youngsters about what to expect can reduce undue anxiety.

Generally, the more cohesive the group, the greater its capacity to integrate any disruptive or difficult members. Newly formed groups, on the other hand, should remain highly structured until they can function with some degree of autonomy. This is particularly true when treatment has been mandated for the majority of the group's members.

Early-adolescent groups do best with peers and therapists of the same sex (Carrell 1993). This reduces the social anxiety and enables the introduction of structured activities and games. Their high energy level necessitates a fast-paced, interesting, and stimulating group format.

Groups composed of older adolescents should be coed when possible. The presence of girls often reduces the boys' hostility and promotes useful interactions (Scheidlinger and Aronson 1991). Ideally, a group would be evenly balanced between boys and girls as well as internalizing and externalizing disorders. The heterogeneity lends itself to the exploration of a variety of pertinent issues that might not otherwise arise. For example, a depressed girl who openly shares her negative thinking might encourage the participation of other members who deny their own sadness.

In practice, groups are often formed out of necessity rather than ideal considerations. The behavior-disordered males will usually outnumber the females and their ages and developmental levels will not match perfectly. At the least, early and late adolescents should not be grouped together so that scapegoating and conflicting agendas can be avoided. Less than ideal groupings can prove effective when properly managed. The adolescents are told that they are all experts in different areas and can help one another be "more together."

The group meets at the time least likely to invite resistance. Weekend and late-night appointments are convenient for the parents, but resented by the adolescents. Holding groups in the youngsters' schools is useful, but often not possible. Late afternoon is chosen most frequently as to minimize potential conflicts.

Residential and inpatient settings often have the flexibility to schedule groups according to the youngsters' needs. I recommend morning sessions since the adolescents tend to be more focused and less restless. Sixty minutes is usually long enough for a beginning group. Any longer period (e.g., ninety minutes) may be harder to tolerate and thus invite acting out. In addition, it is always safer to increase the length of a group as it grows more functional and cohesive. A group size of six to eight youngsters seems to work best. Larger numbers are difficult to manage and appreciably smaller groups increase self-consciousness and reduce spontaneity.

## GROUP GOALS AND TASKS

Highly structured groups have specific formats and goals. Anger control, social skills, and empathy training are time limited and psychoeducationally oriented. Open-ended, less structured groups have broader-based goals that are accomplished through reliance on the interactive process. Members are encouraged to reveal themselves in order to feel better understood, accepted, and amenable to change. This evolving feeling of security and belongingness serves to decrease their defensiveness and reduce intragroup conflict. As their communication skills improve, their anger decreases along with their aggressive behavior. This in turn helps build self-esteem and prepares them to negotiate day-to-day conflicts. It is assumed that the relevant issues will emerge spontaneously at some point in the treatment.

The course of group therapy rarely follows such a systematic progression, nor does it occur without turbulence along the way. Effective handling of group conflicts, behavior problems, and spontaneous issues makes the process flow more smoothly. Group leaders must create a climate in which behavior-disordered youth learn to internalize controls and relate effectively to peers and adults. At its best it is a model for life outside the treatment setting. Group work can be done in conjunction with, or separate from, individual work; however, family involvement is a necessity.

## BEGINNING GROUPS

Regardless of the nature of the group, certain rules, limits, and boundaries are established to ensure a safe and productive atmosphere. In the absence of structure, conduct-disordered adolescents quickly become bored, uneasy, and disruptive. Corder (1994) elaborates on the ground rules that must be specified from the start. Youngsters are expected to attend group regularly and arrive on time. While adolescent jargon is acceptable, the frequent use of profanity is strongly discouraged. When conflicts escalate, they will be interrupted and the offenders will be escorted out of the group until they can regain control. Antisocial youth are always curious to learn what will happen if they break the rules. If they are not told in advance, they will test the system to gauge the therapist's response. While excessive emphasis on limits could raise authority conflicts and lead to disruptive behavior, an explanation of the basics should ensure a manageable group.

The format for talking in group should be clear. Members should be encouraged to take turns and wait until the other person is finished. In general, the lower functioning the group, the more important it is to establish guidelines for expressing feelings and exchanging views. Having youngsters raise their hand before speaking is clearly the most structured arrangement. It should be used only when the majority of group members lack internal controls. Spontaneous dialogue is appropriate for most situations, but restrictions can be imposed when necessary.

Adolescents are encouraged to speak for themselves rather than another member. Statements beginning with "I" are more direct and less accusatory, and are likely to evoke an empathic response. As adolescents acclimate to the group process, their conversations will flow more freely. Members should be cautioned in advance that the discussions will occasionally make them uncomfortable. When this happens, the therapist can alert the group so that it can change the topic or permit the youngster to excuse him- or herself from the discussion (Corder 1994).

As the first session unfolds, members will display considerable discomfort. They are likely to be sarcastic, silly, or tough—and to jockey for position. Most will minimize the seriousness of their problems and insist they don't need to be there. Their indifference and bravado are intended to insulate them from rejection. Although they feign independence, they continue to look to their peers for direction.

Resistance is addressed by the leader's brief introductory remarks to the group. I prefer to say something like this: "Look, I know that most of you would rather not be here. It's a pain to have to do something you don't want to do, but many kids have been through this experience before. Most of them didn't seem to mind it. Some even grew to like it after a while. You get to talk about things on your mind and you don't have to worry about getting in trouble for what you say. How bad can that be?

"Since we're going to be working together, we might as well try and make the most of it. To tell you the truth, you guys really have it easier than I do. All you have to do is try and be yourself. Talk if you have something to say, listen if you don't. At first it may take some guts to say what's on your mind, but you'll quickly learn that others may feel the same way. I'll be the one to worry about what happens in here."

Following the introductions, the therapist expedites the process of getting acquainted. The conventional practice of asking a patient to "tell the group about why you're here" doesn't always go over well with this population. Their anger and denial are likely to be high, while their insight is limited. If the group does not begin talking spontaneously, the therapist immediately structures the situation by proposing an activity. Corder (1994) suggests breaking the group up into pairs and asking them to spend a few minutes getting to know one another. They are encouraged to ask questions about school, friends, musical interests, and home. When the time has elapsed, each member introduces and tells the group something about their partner. Members can get involved by asking questions and giving feedback. Most adolescents enjoy being the center of attention and are comfortable with the informational exchange, which rarely challenges their defensive structure. The leaders quickly join in the process and expand the scope of the conversation.

One variation I have used resembles a talk show format. The group decides who the first guest will be and proceeds to conduct a "celebrity" interview. They try to raise questions that will be of interest to the audience. The leaders stress the interactive aspects and ask the members to share related experiences that will further the discussion. When conducted in a spirit of good will, this exercise reduces the initial anxiety and sets the stage for further disclosure.

Issues of confidentiality are raised before the close of the first meeting. While the group must be a safe place to talk, when you put eight adolescents together, the possibility of a security leak is paramount. Members should discuss what they would consider to be private matters. Romantic crushes, family issues, substance use, and confessions of malfeasance are usually mentioned. Some consensus should be reached by the end of the discussion.

Another potential difficulty is relationships developing between members outside the group. Adolescents often congregate before the session and linger afterwards. They are prone to call one another to chat and plan get-togethers over the weekend. The possibilities of new relationships are enticing to those who are socially ostracized. While extremely difficult to enforce, the group must be strongly discouraged from extragroup contacts. When and if they occur, the situation should be discussed with the group as a problem to be solved. Those who learn of other members getting together should feel a responsibility to disclose such an illicit alliance. The destructive potential of such relationships should be raised. The reasons to refrain include inhibition of self-disclosure, isolation from other members, and indirect acting out against the group at large.

Ideally, the opening session addresses the existing resistance to treatment and provides a framework to keep the group on task. They should feel some sense of camaraderie and begin to see the leader as a benevolent authority who lends structure and models forthrightness. The value of the group interactions should be readily apparent as the kids learn about each other and swap stories. This process rarely occurs without pitfalls.

## PRACTICAL PROBLEMS

Challenges to the therapist may arise as soon as the youngsters enter the group room. The choice of seat can quickly become a contest. When couches and chairs are available, they will immediately bicker over who gets the couch. This must be handled quickly and equitably. I recommend either first come, first serve, or seating on a rotating basis. When possible, it is easier to keep all the chairs in the room similar. The less stimulation, the better. Nonetheless, even straight-backed chairs can pose some difficulty. Adolescents may lean backwards until the chair tilts over. They find this quite amusing and sometimes press it to test the therapist's resolve. If someone falls, I'll go along with it, but quickly remind them that they've had their chance. Next time they're out of the group.

It's always better to anticipate disruptions early in the group. Sarcastic comments, teasing one another, and occasional good humor are the most common. If the actions are funny, I'll certainly laugh, and might say something humorous myself. When the group persists, however, the disruptive effects must be pointed out and discussed. Excessive interruptions interfere with the group's smooth flow and suggest an underlying discomfort. Intervention thus becomes necessary. Members are always asked if they have any suggestions for dealing with the offender.

Inappropriate behavior often reflects the youngster's social discomfort and need for attention. I find it useful to give the group clown the opportunity to entertain us for a minute or two. This usually gets it out of their system and enables us to return to work. Another ploy I use involves holding up a humorous sign behind the head of the disruptive youth. It might say, "Thinks he's really cool," or "Everybody pay attention to me." This usually generates laughter in the group and sidetracks the disruptive youngster, who gets either embarrassed or angry. Holmes and colleagues (1991) suggest complimenting the negative group leader before he has a chance to act out. This can sometimes diffuse the propensity to action.

When disruptive behavior becomes unmanageable, the youngster must be removed. The incident should always be discussed afterwards to diffuse the possibility of any further occurrence. A worst-case scenario would be an entire group acting out and refusing to comply with any directives. If this occurs, the therapist must act quickly. If setting a limit does not curb the behavior, something more dramatic is needed to sidetrack them. On occasion I have run to the window and screamed, "Oh, God! Look what's going on outside!" The members momentarily stop what they're doing and run to the window. The brief interval is frequently sufficient to break the disruptive cycle. Over the years I have thrown down chairs, blown a whistle, and blasted the volume of a boom box to interrupt the chaos. While such actions are far from classic therapeutic interventions, good teachers have practiced them for years.

When all else fails, the leader must be prepared to end the session. This can be done by walking out of the room, calling for assistance, or simply announcing that you're giving up. I have found it useful to offer youngsters an option in this situation. I might say, "Look, I can see that you really don't want to be here today. You all really have two choices. We can end the group now and have a make-up session Saturday morning at 8:00 A.M. or we can settle down and finish the group today." Often the youngesters get angry at this prospect, but do comply. When they don't, I have held several early-morning makeup groups over the years to demonstrate my resolve.

On the other end of the spectrum is group indifference. In this situation youngsters volunteer little spontaneously, and may sit in silence. The apathy can represent either resistance or passivity. The leaders must act quickly by addressing the group's need for stimulation and dependence on others to entertain them (Carrell 1993). Other explanations should be sought as well. Perhaps they are cynical about the treatment process and reluctant to give it a chance.

The group is also challenged on their lack of concern for one another. "How can you just sit there when John tells you he wound up in the emergency room last week?" "Ann just shared her physical abuse and no one even reacted. What's the story here?"

Sometimes adolescents will fall asleep during a session. This should be posed as a problem for everyone. What do they feel should be done? Throw her out, wake her up, leave her alone, or challenge her?

Incentives can help to mobilize a lethargic group. Adolescents enjoy snacking, listening to music, and celebrating special occasions. This can be used to our advantage. Group contingencies can be established to reward active participation. I have gone so far as to dismiss group members a little early when they have worked hard during a session. Vouchers can be issued for a future early exit of their choice. While nonconventional, this seems to motivate youngsters since there is a certain status in being granted an exception. The goal, of course, is to get the group to the point where they welcome participation and get direct benefits from the experience.

Over the years I have had my share of embarrassing moments that I have been forced to deal with. Someone placed a whoopee cushion under my seat several years ago. You can imagine the loud, explicit sound as I sat down. The group was hysterical. On another occasion a youngster patted me on the back as he entered the group room. Unbeknownst to me, I now sported a sticker on my back that read, "I'm a real schmuck." When I stood up at the end of the group, the kids cracked up. In both instances I was able to laugh along with them and acknowledge that they got me. There was no need for a limit as we had some basis for respect. Were situations such as these to recur, it would become necessary to make them a major issue; the group could not proceed until they were adequately addressed.

## GROUP PROCESS

As the group unfolds, the focus is on the youngsters' interactions with one another. They are encouraged to talk freely, give feedback, and challenge inappropriate behavior whenever possible. The task is to get them to run their own group. Increased comfort with self-disclosure usually leads to a well-integrated group.

Corder (1994) uses role assignments to help the group begin to flow smoothly. The "policeman" is responsible for maintaining order. He calls misbehavior to their attention and raises possible consequences for noncompliance. The "facilitator's" role is to ask questions and encourage disclosure. He is responsible for helping the youth get to know one another. An "arbitrator" is appointed to mediate conflicts and keep the group on task. The roles are interchanged so that each youngster has a chance to get constructively involved.

The importance of a cohesive group is stressed. I tell youngsters that when seven or eight of them are unified, they are more powerful than any individual. To illustrate this, we do the following exercise. The "toughest" member of the group is asked to lie face down in the center of the room. The therapist and the group members make a circle around him and proceed to hold down his limbs. Several might take his arms and legs while others secure his back and shoulders. When everyone feels that their grip is secure, the youngster who is pinned down is told to count to three and throw everyone off him. At the end of the countdown he lets out a grunt; absolutely nothing happens! The youngster is totally immobilized by the nine people holding him down. He is just not strong enough to break loose. Nervous laughter follows as the kids realize their own power. A valuable lesson has been learned.

Carrell (1993) describes several group exercises that facilitate interactions, trust, and disclosure. In the "trust walk" group members pair up and take turns being blindfolded. The sighted youngster leads the other to an area with various objects to be explored by touch. As the blindfolded partner feels his way around, the guide introduces him to objects (machines, chairs, desks, and so on) and keeps the journey safe. When he has successfully identified everything, the roles are switched.

Following completion of this exercise, the group discusses trust. Antisocial youth are naturally cynical and suspicious of others. They must explore what trust means and how it felt to be dependent on another for direction. One youngster conceded that he feared his partner would "walk him into a wall or something." Another expressed the fantasy that her partner would abandon her with the blindfold stuck to her. The discussions are readily expanded to experiences in their own lives.

The "hit parade" is an exercise used to help youth express themselves freely. Group members are asked to bring in a tape or CD of a favorite song that tells something about them. After playing it, the group discusses the message of the song and its relevance to the youngster's life. Since music is such an integral part of adolescence, the exercise usually generates enthusiasm. As some of today's lyrics (particularly heavy metal and rap music) can be quite graphic, rebellious, and provocative, the leaders must be certain to moderate the youngsters' reactions and carefully make the connection to their issues.

I have found Carrell's (1993) "T-shirt Worksheet" to be quite useful with this subgroup. The members are asked to illustrate the front and back of a picture of a blank T-shirt. The front (which is visible to everyone) represents their public image, while the back is their private self. Group members are asked to draw pictures, use symbols, or write words on the shirts. Adolescents enjoy this exercise as T-shirts are staples of their wardrobes and pose little threat. When their drawings are complete, the group takes turns sharing their significance and exchanging feedback. Tom illustrated the front of his with a "hip-looking kid smoking a joint." On the back he drew a little boy sitting in a corner crying. The discrepancy was quite striking and intrigued the group members who were simultaneously threatened by his disclosure. After admiring his honesty, the leaders were able to direct the discussion to issues of sadness, neglect, and vulnerability.

## CHALLENGING SELF-DESTRUCTIVE BEHAVIOR PATTERNS

Conduct-disordered adolescents readily share their exploits in the group setting. They seek peer approval by showcasing their toughness and lack of concern about the consequences of their behavior. In heterogeneous groups several members will question such attitudes, while others will condone their actions. The leaders must make certain that the discussions are focused and emphasize good judgment.

The following group segment illustrates this process.

*Jeff*: You know, last weekend was pretty wild. My friends and I got bored after hanging out at the mall for a few hours. We decided to rip off some clothing from one of the department stores. There were four of us. Bob and Dave were standing watch while Buddy and I put on a shirt and sweater under our coats. We were heading toward the exit when all of a sudden this guy [plainclothesman] shouts, Hey, boys, wait a minute, I need to talk to you. We know it's trouble so we haul ass for the exit. He comes after us. We get out of the store but he's pretty fast and catches Buddy. We just kept on running.

*Don*: So what happened to Buddy?

*Jeff*: Well, they took him to security. He had to give back the clothing and they called his parents to come get him. Buddy's cool though, he didn't nark on us. I don't know what'll happen. The store told his parents that their lawyer will contact them in the next few weeks. I have a feeling they'll press charges and it'll wind up in court. Buddy was there once before for something else. I don't know if they'll cut him any slack this time.

*Kevin*: Something like that happened to us last year, but we never got caught. It was pretty awesome.

*Eddy*: Yeah, I like that feeling when you get away with something.

*Therapist*: Wait a minute here. Jeff just told us that his friend got caught shoplifting. He's likely to wind up in court. Don't you care about what happens to Buddy?

*Jeff*: Yeah, sure, he's a good friend.

*Tina*: But you're letting him take the rap for you.

*Jeff*: Well, I would have done the same for him.

*Bill*: Yeah, me too.

*Therapist*: You know, you're all thinking about loyalty. I can understand that, but the fact is that shoplifting is a crime. Does anyone care about that?

*Eddy*: (*Laughing*) Here comes the morality lecture.

*Therapist*: No, that's not my point. Buddy could have been any one of you. I just don't want to see that happen . . .

*Bill*: Well, you know, they've got these store cameras that tape everything and it's hard to tell who the plainclothesmen are.

*Therapist*: So it's really pretty risky.

*Tina*: I think it's a guy thing. It's just cool to get away with something. You're always talking about that stuff, Jeff. You don't even care if you get caught.

*Jeff*: Yes, I do. My parents would freak out.

*Kevin*: Mine too.

*Therapist*: Jeff, you've been really lucky. You've gotten away with a lot of stuff but sooner or later . . .

*Bill*: (*Interrupting*) We know, everyone gets caught.

*Therapist*: That's about it. You've got to decide if the risk is worth it. Every time you get away with something, it makes you want to do it again.

*Kevin*: I guess Jeff needs to get caught if he's going to stop doing this.

*Therapist*: Hey, why don't you all look at it this way. Buddy got caught and he's probably worrying about what's going to happen to him. Would you really want to be in his shoes right now?

*Kevin*: No, not really.

*Don*: No thanks.

*Tina*: Jeff figures he'd never get caught, don't you, Jeff?

*Jeff*: Well, I'm pretty slick. I can run fast, and I can sniff out cops.

*Therapist*: And you're certain you'd never get caught.

*Jeff*: Well, not really.

*Therapist*: Jeff, what advice do you think Buddy would give you now?

*Jeff*: (*Smiling*) He'd probably tell me not to do it again. It's not worth it.

*Eddy*: That's probably true.

*Don:* It's pretty risky.

*Therapist*: Well, just think about it, that's all. You all seem to agree that it's taking a pretty big chance.

> *Kevin*: Especially if you don't really need the clothing. I guess we didn't when we shoplifted last year.

## FAMILY CONFLICT

Adolescents readily complain about their parents in group. The themes often involve freedom, trust, and control issues. On a more basic level, they are struggling with feelings of rejection and the independence–dependence conflict. Following is a segment from a group dealing with these issues.

> *David*: I'm getting really tired of my parents bossing me around all the time. Everything has been an argument with them lately. Last weekend I just wanted to go to a party at my friend's house and my father said no. I got really pissed off and ran out of the house.
>
> *John*: How come they wouldn't let you go?
>
> *David*: Well, they made a big deal about his parents being out of town. I told them there wouldn't be any trouble.
>
> *Therapist*: So you think they shouldn't hassle you about that stuff.
>
> *David*: Yeah.
>
> *Mike*: You told us you were grounded last month for staying out all night.,
>
> *David*: I know, but that's history. I've already been punished for that.
>
> *Sara*: I don't know what the big deal is. My parents

just let me go out whenever I want. They've given up hassling me.

*Tanya*: You're lucky. My mother worries about everything. It drives me crazy.

*Therapist*: Boy, Tanya and Sara's parents sound like they are opposites. I think we're all talking about the same thing though. How much do your parents trust you and what can you do about it?

*Tanya*: Well, anybody got any ideas for me?

*David*: Your mom sounds worse than my parents. Can't you talk to her?

*Tanya*: I try to but she just says that she loves me and that's why she worries so damn much. We talk a lot about other things though. You know, what's going on at school and with my friends.

*Sara*: I don't even think my parents care anymore. They're real fed up.

*Therapist*: How do you feel about them giving up on you, Sara?

*Sara*: I don't know. Sometimes it's just easier, but I do get lonely sometimes. No one talks much in my house.

*David*: Mine too. The only time we say anything is when there's something to argue about.

*Therapist*: Now we've got three things on the table. Freedom, trust, and communication at home.

*Fred*: *(Speaks for the first time)* I think they're all related.

*Therapist*: Tell us more about that, Fred.

*Fred*: Well, my parents and I used to fight all the time too. Since we started family therapy, things have eased up. We talk to each other again and now they seem to give me more slack about going places. I guess when you communicate better, they start to trust you.

*Tanya*: But I talk to my mother all the time and she still won't let me do stuff.

*David*: Your mother's got a real worry problem, Tanya. She needs work. *(Group laughs.)*

*Therapist*: You know, that's really not a bad idea, David. Some of your parents give you freedom, some don't. Some of your parents talk to you and some don't. I think we can put all this stuff to use. Why don't we invite Tanya, David, and Sara's parents to a session. We can all talk together. I'll bet our group could help each of them with their problems.

*Tanya*: That sounds cool. I'll try anything.

*Sara*: Why not? I've got nothing to lose.

*David*: Whatever!

*Therapist*: Let's do it. I'll call your parents this week and see if we can set something up.

## MOVEMENT TOWARD CHANGE

During the course of group treatment, various issues relating to antisocial behavior are explored. These include school, drugs, family conflicts, and difficulties with authority. None are more significant than the impact of peer pressure. As the group solidifies, the members become increasingly receptive to feedback from one another. The leaders can capitalize on this to motivate them to seek more adaptive solutions to conflicts. The deviant behavior has been maintained by powerful group contingencies and changes slowly.

If the group therapy process succeeds in increasing trust, sharing, empathy, and belongingness, the youngster leaves with a richer understanding of interpersonal relationships. This in turn reduces the desirability of the deviant peer group. The superficiality, discontent, and wrongdoing no longer gratify the youngster's needs. An adolescent will seek more mature relationships as he comes to feel increasingly competent. Opportunities must be provided for the youngster to move away from his old friends and develop new relationships.

# 14

# Putting It All Together

Throughout this book I have advocated the use of a wide range of therapeutic interventions. While I have attempted to present them in a readily applicable format, the complexities of antisocial behavior often require considerable flexibility in treatment implementation. Ideally, a thorough initial assessment leads to an individualized treatment plan executed according to the recommended format. Unfortunately, this is often not the case.

Practical considerations weigh heavily on the implementation of any treatment regimen. The availability of resources is often limited by geographic, financial, and temporal considerations. Therapist training varies widely and the nature of treatment is influenced strongly by the theoretical orientation of programs and individual practitioners. Consequently, I advocate close interdisciplinary communication between those involved with behavior-disordered adolescents. Broad-based knowledge of potential interventions increases the likelihood of positive responses to treatment.

Although comprehensive psychiatric facilities and established research programs sometimes offer a more thorough treatment approach, their flexibility may be limited by the program design. While I do not recommend watering down any particular intervention, circumstances may limit the depth of involvement and the method of presentation. The same holds true for the extent of environmental intervention. The family and school are not always cooperative to the extent we would wish. Some have abandoned hope and written off the most difficult youth, preferring to devote their energies to those who are more amenable to interventions. (This issue is addressed in greater detail in the final chapter.)

Notwithstanding the constraints on an ideally suited exhaustive program, I would like to present a reasonably successful case in some detail. This is intended to illustrate an application of the techniques presented throughout this book, employed under less than ideal circumstances.

## CASE EXAMPLE

Billy Harrison, a 15-year-old ninth grader, was referred for treatment by his school guidance counselor. The presenting problems included truancy, frequent conflicts with teachers and students, and failing grades. He had been suspended the previous week for vandalizing school property. The parents reported that he defied their rules at home, drank frequently, stayed out all night, and violated any punishments they imposed. They suspected that he was taking money from them, but had never caught him. Billy lied frequently and manipulated other people to get what he wanted. He was contemptuous of laws and social conventions. The pattern had worsened over the past year. Billy was seen briefly for individual therapy in the fourth grade, but the parents felt that it was not helpful.

The parents were seen alone for the initial meeting. They appeared angry, frustrated, and burnt out. Mrs. Harrison did most of the talking while Mr. Harrison affirmed her comments passively. He responded readily to direct questioning but appeared somewhat depressed. Billy's developmental milestones were normal. Although the parents felt he was active in his early years, his behavior had been manageable and both seemed to enjoy him.

The difficulties began around the time Billy entered kindergarten. He was reportedly aggressive and disruptive in the classroom. The teacher felt that he was too demanding of her attention but was a bright and precocious child. As he progressed through elementary school, the problems got worse. Billy was irritated easily and tended to overreact to his teacher's comments. There were repeated incidents of fighting with other students and his grades declined. On several occasions he was caught with other students' belongings in his possession. By the time he reached junior high school he had an established reputation as a troublemaker. He was frequently sent to detention but was unaffected by the punishment and isolation.

Billy's peer relationships were rather superficial. He complained about the youngsters in his grade who seemed to ignore him, and spent most of his time with a small group of deviant peers. They would skip school together and entertain one another by provoking and intimidating others. On several occasions they had sold drugs and extorted protection money. Billy had been caught shoplifting on two occasions, but was only banned from the mall as a result. Despite his repeated violation of social norms, he had not been to court.

On the weekends his group would often drink, look for parties to crash, and stay out most of the night. They depended on one another for validation and stimulation. Billy referred to them as a gang, but in reality they were loosely organized and without purpose. He had a girlfriend for a brief period, but her parents had forbidden her to see him.

Mr. and Mrs. Harrison had great difficulty setting limits with Billy. They felt he was defiant, argumentative, and dishonest. They believed they had tried everything and found that nothing was effective with him; in fact, things seemed to get worse after each argument. He would leave the house and stay away until he felt ready to return.

Mr. Harrison's sales job demanded that he travel frequently, thus leaving much of the responsibility for discipline to his wife. She was resentful of his unavailability and complained that he drank too much when he was at home. While neither acknowledged any marital problems, it was obvious that their communication was poor and little intimacy existed. Their only source of pride was their older daughter, Elizabeth, who was a senior in high school and was currently applying to good colleges. Mrs. Harrison wondered how they could have raised two children who were so different.

Billy agreed to attend a therapy session if, in exchange, his parents would give him the money to buy tickets for a rock concert. He was seen alone for the initial meeting. While he displayed some bravado and a flippant attitude, he spoke freely about his life. Billy was very much aware of why he was referred for treatment and went out of his way to boast about his exploits. At one point in the session he looked at me and queried, "You're not allowed to repeat this, right?" That was my first clue. Billy was testing me by inquiring about the limits of confidentiality. I told him that he was putting me in a difficult position but I would not tell anyone except under the specific conditions I had already reviewed with him. "That doesn't mean that I'm not concerned," I added. "We're still going to have to figure out what to do about all this."

The remainder of our discussion focused on his anger at his parents and teachers. Billy genuinely believed that others were too hard on him. As I had heard many times before, he insisted that his life would be fine if adults would just leave him alone. I pointed out that this was highly unlikely, considering the mess he was in. We joked about his notoriety in school and the neighborhood where he lived.

As the session drew to a close, I told him that he seemed like an interesting guy. He had some good stories to tell and I enjoyed the mutual banter. I imagined that no one really knew him very well and I was certainly no exception. "Billy," I said, "I'm not certain if I can really be of help here. You seem determined to continue what you're doing, but there must be times when you wish things were easier. I don't know what will happen if you don't come back to see me, but I can sure think of worse things than spending time here. If you'll agree to try a few meetings, I will certainly do what I can to be of help to you. Can I schedule you for another appointment?" Billy reluctantly agreed and treatment was launched.

During the next few meetings, we grew better acquainted. Although he was sarcastic and occasionally provocative, he described his present life in some detail. In reality, Billy was often bored and lonely. He acknowledged that he felt very jumpy when he was alone with nothing to do. These feelings propelled him toward his deviant social group. It was there that he felt some acceptance and could forget about his hassles. Unfortunately, their time together was spent seeking excitement and violating social norms. I asked Billy if he felt any remorse over some of the things he had done. After some thought, he denied the seriousness of his actions. In effect, he believed that the stores in the mall could afford to lose a few things and the kids he beat up deserved what they got.

Billy was curious about whether I had ever stolen anything when I was a kid. His inquiry seemed sincere so I answered him honestly. "When I was 9 years old my friends dared me to steal a piece of Bazooka bubble gum from the candy store on my street corner. I went in there alone, took the gum, and slowly walked toward the door. Suddenly I felt a hand on my shoulder. It was the store owner. He turned me around, slapped me in the face, and took the gum back. To make things worse, he called my parents from the store and made them come and get me!" Billy was amused and intrigued by this story. He wondered whether my parents had punished me for the incident and if I had ever stolen anything again. I answered both questions while trying to relate this to his experiences.

Billy began to share some of his vulnerabilities at this point. He acknowledged that he did fear getting caught when he was engaged in wrongdoing, but didn't allow himself to think about it. I challenged him on the effect that his behavior had on other people. The discussion then led to our first real exploration of his family history. Beneath his anger and indifference were strong feelings of hurt and rejection. He recalled vividly his father's drinking and his use of corporal punishment for the things that Billy did wrong. "I wouldn't take that from him now," he added quickly.

Billy had been detached from his family for several years. While his mother had been protective of him, she was now absorbed with the current family pressures. He also expressed resentment about all the positive attention his sister had received. Interestingly, he seemed to get along well with her. Considering how angry Billy was at his family, I asked what he thought they might feel about him. With some sadness, he replied, "I guess they would just like to get rid of me." This confession led to a useful exploration of his negative self-statements, which were gradually challenged with cognitive-behavioral interventions. Clearly we had established some trust and a working alliance could begin.

## Family Work

Four sessions had elapsed at this point. Billy had previously refused to attend family meetings but reluctantly agreed to try. We would continue to meet individually and discuss what had transpired in the family sessions. Billy expressed considerable concern about what would transpire in these family meetings. He feared that the family would have the same old arguments and it would be a waste of time. I asked that he leave that worry to me and assured him that I had been through this many times before.

As expected, the first family session was tense and filled with accusations. The parents expressed their anger at Billy and focused almost exclusively on his difficulties. Billy responded with hostility and counteraccusations. I interrupted forcefully. "Look, this really isn't going to get us anywhere. If this is what it is like at home, I don't see how you can live this way." They were startled by my reaction and agreed that the situation had become intolerable. Despite this, no one was prepared to assume any responsibility. I urged the family members to try and talk about themselves rather than one another.

Since Billy and I had discussed the issue previously, I asked him to try and describe his role in the family conflicts. He responded with some discomfort. "Well, I just don't listen to them anymore. I've sort of got this attitude now. You know, just do what you feel like because it isn't worth it. Besides, they're both so damn uptight, they never let up."

I interjected again: "Billy, you were doing fine until you got sidetracked and started criticizing your parents. How about it, Mr. and Mrs. Harrison, what are your roles in these family conflicts?"

Mrs. Harrison answered first. "I guess that I just yell and scream most of the time. Almost everything seems to be a battle these days. Sometimes I don't even bother to argue with him. I don't feel like I know Billy anymore. He has developed this mean streak and just thinks he's entitled to everything. We're just sick and tired of . . ."

I interrupted again. "Wait a minute, you were talking at first about yourself and then you did the same thing Billy did. I know that it is really hard to stay with it, but you'll all have to learn to do this if things are ever to change. . . . Mr. Harrison, you haven't spoken yet. What is your part in this mess?"

"I don't know," he replied. "I've sort of tuned out of things. I've tried to avoid these battles, but then something happens to push my buttons. Billy and I really go at it sometimes; then I feel bad afterwards."

The family session concluded with the basic understanding that everyone must do their part. Billy and his parents agreed to attend regular meetings at this point. They had moved away from blaming one another but remained considerably angry. Billy's sense of entitlement and defiance continued and his parents were not yet able to manage his daily behavior.

The sessions over the next few months focused heavily on the process of communication and negotiation. The family was strongly encouraged to talk directly to one another. This was extremely difficult, largely because of Billy's anger, impulsivity, and defensiveness. I noted that his father displayed some similar reactivity when he became involved in the family arguments. Although the mother was more composed, she appeared to circumvent the family conflicts by allowing Billy to have his way. This infuriated Mr. Harrison, who would then withdraw and turn to drinking.

I suggested that we have a session with Billy and his father to address some of the antisocial behavior and

06 THE UNMANAGEABLE ADOLESCENT

devise some basic behavioral contracts. His mother would be informed of the outcome afterwards.

In this session father and son were extremely uncomfortable at first. Eventually they managed to air their grievances and generate a minimal agreement connecting allowance to school attendance. This seemed insignificant, given the extent of Billy's problems, but it was a start. Billy's distance from the family was discussed along with other behaviors of concern. Many of the behavior problems were reframed as his attempt to reinvolve his father in his life. He listened quietly and smiled as this was discussed. Both recalled the enjoyable times spent together when Billy was younger. Ultimately they agreed to plan one activity together on the weekend.

During another session the parents reiterated their concern about Billy's alcohol use. He, of course, minimized the problem and lashed out at his father for being a "damn alcoholic." Something significant happened at this point. Elizabeth, who had been relatively quiet during most of the meetings, grew quite emotional and yelled at her parents. "You're both such hypocrites. You always get on Billy for his problems, but you never admit your own. Dad drinks way too much and he's out of it half the time. You're both always fighting and complaining about each other. Why don't you just get divorced!"

The parents were shocked by Elizabeth's tirade. They grew sad and quiet, seemingly at a loss for what to say. I suggested that maybe they were not practicing what they preached. The parents were focusing on Billy's problems to the exclusion of their own. Would they now be willing to seek assistance for themselves as well? I proposed marital therapy and asked that Mr. Harrison attend an AA meeting. Billy seemed genuinely pleased as the focus shifted away from him. His father brought him right back into the discussion. "I'll tell you what, Billy. I'll go to AA meetings if you will. How about it?"

The parents were seen without their son for several sessions. Regarding Billy's persistent antisocial behavior, both felt that they had lost control of the situation and were unsure of what to do next. One of the major issues was their inconsistency and inability to enforce limits. Billy had succeeded in splitting his parents. He was well aware of his mother's need to keep the peace and his father's lack of involvement.

With great difficulty the parents began to work toward establishing a unified front. I supported their efforts to devise a reasonable set of rules with enforceable consequences. We role-played several strategies to deal with Billy's threats, demands, and noncompliance. The importance of praising Billy for small accomplishments was stressed to reduce the negative family atmosphere. Parent management training was integrated with the family negotiating sessions with Billy.

## School Situation

Billy's school difficulties posed yet another major hurdle. We had spoken about these in his individual sessions and eventually he confessed that "if I could push a button and get good grades," he would like to do so. School was discussed in a family meeting and we agreed that I would contact his guidance counselor to assess the situation. After examining his record, the counselor felt there were no suggestions of a learning disability and the problems were motivational. We agreed to try a system of regular contact with the counselor, Billy, and his parents that would include weekly progress reports on his schoolwork. Billy also met with each of his teachers to review what he might do to catch up. They offered their assistance and additional tutoring was arranged as well. He negotiated several specific contracts with his family to reward improved school attendance and effort rather than grades per se.

## Group Interventions

After we had a few productive individual sessions, I suggested that Billy join a psychotherapy group I was starting. I told him that he needed the experience with unfamiliar teenagers and would find it useful. The group was time-limited (sixteen weeks) and would focus on the issues of self-control and getting along better with others. Naturally Billy balked at the idea of sacrificing another hour of his precious time.

I chose to go with good old-fashioned reverse psychology. I told him: "Maybe you're right, Billy. This group might be a little uncomfortable for you. Several of the kids are older than you and two of the girls are pretty mature; you know, they've been around." That was all he needed to hear. He agreed to try the group with the stipulation that "I'll quit if I don't like it."

Billy approached the therapy group with an air of bravado. His initial interactions were somewhat superficial and sarcastic. As he gradually realized that several other members were at least as tough as him, he settled down some. Indeed, most of the adolescents were also there for behavior problems. After comparing exploits for a session or two, they got down to business.

Billy found anger control training to be absorbing and challenging. He willingly participated in the exercises and perfected several techniques that were useful to him. He acknowledged his impulsivity and worked on that as well. The reports received from school began to reflect greater efforts to control his temper and comply with teachers' requests.

The social skills component of group treatment did not flow as smoothly. Billy was embarrassed and resentful of the role-plays, especially those that involved the girls in the group. He refused to participate at first, insisting that "this stuff is a waste of time." I imagine he felt socially inadequate and resorted to disruptive behavior to avoid his discomfort. His resistance lasted for two meetings, until, fortunately, one of the older girls in the group challenged him to participate. "Come on, Billy, I want you to be my boyfriend David in group today. I need to practice how to tell him when he makes me angry." Billy protested slightly, but she wouldn't hear of it. At this point he became reengaged as an active group participant.

Several later group sessions were devoted to addressing the antisocial behavior of three of the members, including Billy. Each had violated the rights of others without remorse. The goal was to broaden their social perspective-taking ability and help them develop some empathy. Billy was an interesting example of a young man who could identify what a victim felt, yet not be influenced by it. He participated readily in the sociomoral reasoning discussions but pointed out repeatedly that "it was just a story."

I spent some time encouraging the group members to share any personal experience of victimization. One girl whom Billy liked tearfully recalled a painful memory of sexual abuse by her stepfather. This was a turning point for Billy. He shared her sense of outrage and went on to relate it to the beatings he had received from his father as a child. Billy could now grasp the victim's perspective both intellectually and emotionally.

## Summary

Through the combination of individual, group, and family work, Billy began to develop more adaptive pursuits. After some coaxing he joined the wrestling club at school and went on two weekend trips with the local teen club. While he still spent some time with his old friends, he began to develop more meaningful friendships with mainstream kids.

Billy's family strongly supported his new activities. The conflicts at home were reduced to the more expected adolescent battles over privileges and trust. His mother and father had learned to coparent more effectively which freed the mother from her angry but indulgent role and the father from his angry but distant role. Billy and his father had reestablished their relationship, based in part on a shared interest in basketball. The father was attending AA and appeared less depressed. His sister was leaving for college in the fall and his mother had taken a part-time job.

Billy continued to have some difficulty with authority figures but no longer engaged in antisocial behavior.

He attended school regularly and achieved passing grades, although his effort was still limited. Billy was uncertain about his future but was attempting to get a part-time job to earn money toward a car. The marked improvement in his self-esteem was reflected in his new peer relationships and increased family interactions. He remained sensitive to criticism, however, and would occasionally grow angry in response to pressure. His reactions were somewhat tempered though, and he could usually talk about the incident afterwards.

Treatment was terminated after about seven months. He had completed his self-control group and was seen intermittently for individual and family sessions during the last month. Ultimately Billy conceded he had been heading in the wrong direction when he began treatment. He now felt he didn't have to get in trouble anymore, but still wouldn't "take crap from people." Our relationship had grown increasingly positive and we were both saddened about the prospect of termination. Billy commented, "I don't need to come anymore, but maybe my parents should continue."

Life was less than perfect at the time of termination. I called the parents several months later to follow up on our work and learned that Billy had been involved in a minor incident in school again. He was suspended for one day for his role in a fight, although it was unclear whether he had started it. The parents felt that it blew over fairly quickly and things had returned to normal again. For his part Billy seemed happier and better integrated into his school overall.

This case reflects an application of various therapeutic techniques and multisystemic interventions. In retrospect I would classify the severity of Billy's disturbance as moderate. He also had support systems available, including an intact family and a cooperative school system. Naturally, the work is far more difficult when the youngster is entrenched in a pattern of severe behavior problems with fewer resources available. We then do the best we can under the circumstances.

# 15

# Hard-Core Youth: Learning from Treatment Failures

## Case Example

John was a 16-year-old urban youth from a working class family. He was referred to treatment because of failing school grades, alcohol abuse, escalating aggressive behavior, and family conflict. On two occasions he had been picked up by the police, first for shoplifting and then for driving his parents' car without a license. No doubt he had been getting away with far more than this before being apprehended. His parents were beside themselves. They were unable to manage his behavior and felt they had tried everything to no avail.

In fact they had tried nearly everything. John had been in individual treatment previously but showed little improvement. His behavior problems culminated in a physical altercation with his father. Following this, he was placed in an inpatient psychiatric facility for thirty days. No intervention was successful in interrupting the progression of antisocial behavior. John insisted that "everything would be fine if people would just leave me alone," yet he was unable to conduct himself in a responsible and trustworthy fashion. He abused alcohol frequently and came home at all hours of the night.

John was contemptuous of authority and justified his offenses by insisting that the other parties were at fault. He displayed little insight into his own behavior and steadfastly refused to cooperate with any treatment process. Although he did have legal charges pending, the court did not order any type of psychotherapy in the interim. Perhaps the judge felt that it would not be useful.

Family and group treatments had been attempted as well. Family work had met with similar resistance. John refused to speak during the sessions other than occasionally express his anger at being controlled before withdrawing again. The parents had inordinate difficulty setting limits on his behavior. John had been defiant since third grade and was described as a real risk taker.

In group he was rather verbal but often disruptive. The cotherapists reported that he was unmotivated and determined to draw attention to himself. His mood was generally irritable and his activity level high. John and his family withdrew from treatment as a result of numerous scheduling problems and the parents' growing frustration and hopelessness. A follow-up conversation six months later revealed that his difficulties had continued and he was currently serving thirty days in a detention center for assault and possession of a deadly weapon.

Cases such as John's are not unusual. While I have not provided many details of his history, the parents were beset with problems of their own. Their communication was poor and they were unable to resolve any conflicts. In effect, the family was dysfunctional. Their inability to become involved actively with treatment, John's negative peer group associations, and the school's failure to engage him from early on all combined to perpetuate a cycle of failure. Treatment was not successful in altering the family's functioning or John's ongoing pattern of deviant behavior.

## WHY TREATMENT FAILS

Treatment failures can be instructive when properly analyzed. Those who fail to respond to interventions, reject any need to change, and persist in viewing themselves as innocent victims pose major challenges to the mental health field. Unsuccessful treatment is multidetermined. Antisocial youth often proceed through a sequence of increasingly restrictive alternatives, which in effect groups the most treatment-resistant youth together.

Unfortunately, a lengthy history of difficulties punctuated by a series of unsuccessful treatment attempts makes for a very poor prognosis. Hard-core youth, that is, those who are entrenched in their ways, can emerge from any socioeconomic subgroup. There does appear to be a higher proportion who present with histories of adverse economic circumstances, broken homes, and inadequate role models (Hawkins et al. 1992). While ineffective parenting practices are commonplace in the development of conduct disorders, many of these youth have been extremely difficult to manage from early on.

Treatment failures often result from an inability to alter the adolescent's basic attitude toward life. Those who feel that their way is the only way leave little opportunity for the consideration of other options. They are convinced that it is easier to take shortcuts in life and play by their own sets of rules. People are viewed as objects to be manipulated and relationships are simply a means to an end. Their day-to-day lives are a battle against boredom and isolation, with thrill seeking the preferred antidote. Antisocial youth are frequently detached from their feelings and adhere rigidly to their own inflexible beliefs regarding their violations of social norms. Hostile attributions, rationalization, and indifference permeate their thinking.

Treatment must somehow alter their emotional and cognitive rigidity and provide face-saving opportunities to let down their guard and seek connections with others. To truly need other people, we must allow ourselves to be sufficiently vulnerable to tolerate the risk of rejection. Many of these conduct-disordered youth lack a solid foundation to anchor them. They feel compelled to display contempt for social convention and the achievement of success through traditional channels. It is not that they don't want the good things in life. They harbor the fundamental belief that the right way will not work for them. They are prisoners of their own egocentricity, impulsivity, poor self-esteem, and lack of compassion for others. The future seems light years away, impossible to influence, and largely irrelevant to their daily lives.

Those who fail to engage in the treatment process often look back on these experiences in very negative terms. They recall it as boring, stupid, and unnecessary. Over the years I have worked with many adolescents who seemed impossible to please. Whether the interventions were intended to be supportive or confrontational, or were simply to ally with their pathology, they invariably found fault. In retrospect, the relationship itself was probably too threatening to tolerate. These youth had similar difficulties in group settings. Structured cognitive-behavioral approaches did not capture their interest and served instead as an opportunity for further acting out. Obviously, regardless of modality, treatment must eventually progress beyond the resistance stage if progress is to occur.

Goldstein (1993) emphasizes the importance of "prescriptive programming" in planning interventions. The match of youth, therapist, and choice of treatment technique must be considered carefully to maximize the likelihood of a positive outcome. Cookbook treatment prescriptions applied in a wholesale manner are generally less helpful in diffusing resistance. Worse yet, they may alienate adolescents even further. Agee (1979) reported some success in pairing delinquent youth with helping professionals based on their respective communication styles. "Expressive" adolescents were described as openly vulnerable and dependent. Both their pain and desire for help were readily apparent. "Instrumental" youth were characterized as independent, nontrusting, and strongly guarded. Staff who were more comfortable dealing with their own feelings served as better role models for the expressive youth. Instrumental staff members were more task oriented than process oriented and came across as confident, cool, and distant. No doubt this was less threatening to the instrumental type of patients and enabled them to relate more comfortably.

Another noteworthy dimension of failed treatment efforts relates to the overall appeal of both the technique and its presentation. Frequently youngsters just don't find the therapy process interesting or in any way captivating. A dry clinical and educational approach to treatment falls far short of the mark. We must seek novel and engaging methods to present our interventions. The reality is that the less educational and psychological the approach feels, the more likely the youngster is to participate. Further research is needed to develop dynamic interventions that employ creativity, multimedia, and forms of immediate gratification. I can only imagine the ultimate appeal of a program designed by a Steven Spielberg-type psychotherapist. Though the idea may seem far-fetched, I see it as a wave of the future.

The unrelenting need for excitement and stimulation must be addressed throughout treatment. Failed interventions often represent insufficient attention to the individual needs of the youngster. By identifying deficiencies that prevent the adolescent from getting what he wants for himself (increased freedom, power over others, and to "enjoy life"), we provide greater incentive for participation in the process. I believe that the motivation to change remains the least addressed and understood aspect of the remediation process.

Throughout this book I have presented a variety of techniques intended to address the specific cognitive, affective, and behavioral deficiencies that underlie oppositional defiant and conduct disorders. Needless to say, not every adolescent must be subjected to the entire treatment armamentarium. In fact, the mistake of excessive, randomly applied treatment interventions is comparable to that of insufficient treatment and poor planning. Youngsters drop out of treatment when they feel unconnected, misunderstood, and held captive against their will. Thorough and effective treatment planning attends to the youngster's needs for excitement, autonomy, and self-respect, while holding the line with expectations, limits, and responsibilities.

A delicate balance must be struck between the more traditional individual and group therapy formats and the cognitive-behavioral approaches. I do not believe that an exclusive reliance on either is maximally effective. The therapist's charisma, ingenuity, and flexibility contribute markedly to the adolescent's receptivity, commitment to the process, and ultimate willingness to let go of old patterns. My least successful cases have consistently been those plagued by difficulties in establishing a therapeutic alliance and diffusing the ongoing resistance. I firmly believe that the earliest interventions are often the most pivotal with this population.

Families often sabotage treatment through their failure to attend sessions and to comply with the recommendations. When parents refuse to see themselves as part of the problem, the youngster's anger and resistance are generally heightened. The family's rigid perception of the youth as "all bad" must be altered if they are to begin to assume some responsibility for the difficulties. Likewise, the youth must be able to acknowledge somewhat his part in establishing this bad reputation and in perpetuating family discord.

Families who are overwhelmed by environmental stressors are particularly difficult to help. It is often impossible for them to make treatment a priority when they are struggling with financial hardship, serious illness, substance abuse, or marital dysfunction. They are prone to disengage quickly if immediate gains are not accomplished. Sometimes the best we can do is support the system and shift the spotlight from exclusive focus on the youngster's behavior problems to the broader family issues.

Perhaps the greatest obstacles to success are the environmental variables that are beyond the control of the treatment agents. Youth who reside in neighborhoods where crime and violence are rampant will have great difficulty internalizing another set of standards. While they may successfully acquire prosocial behaviors, they often report that these are not useful in their natural environment. The peer pressures may be such that it is nearly impossible to withstand negative influences. Clearly this raises broader concerns for those involved with these youth as well as for society at large.

If our goal is for adolescents to develop new and adaptive coping skills, we must provide alternatives to deviant behavior as well as opportunities to participate in potentially gratifying activities. Those who feel trapped in their situations are unlikely to see treatment as useful to them. Excessive concerns with survival, peer acceptance, and immediate gratification may preclude any focus on the future. The broader issue is to find ways to offer hope to these youth. They must come to believe that change is possible. This necessitates involvement by the school, community, and related social service agencies.

Adolescents who come from middle- or upper-class

backgrounds struggle in a very different way. They may fail to believe in themselves apart from their family's success. Their family's ability to support them in the separation and individuation process may be limited. Or they may resent the pressure of high parental expectations. Their peer group has typically taken on a life of its own. Treatment failures in this population frequently reflect an inability to hold them accountable for their behavior and to help them embrace any type of conventional standards. Their anger at society may remain unmitigated and they may choose to isolate themselves from those who could offer them a way out. If their family's values are at odds with their own, they will go to great lengths to rationalize their actions and place blame outside themselves. This subgroup especially must be able to save face if change is to occur. Their treatment needs to be seen as socially acceptable and somehow of their own choosing. The stigma of "patient" is particularly difficult for these youngsters who believe that it's their neurotic, status-focused parents who need help rather than them.

## SPONTANEOUS "CURES"

Some oppositional and conduct-disordered youth seem to get themselves together despite unsuccessful treatment experiences or no treatment at all. Consider the lonely and isolated delinquent who finds a girlfriend who is straight, possesses some family values, and has a sense of decency. The experience can be rather powerful. The youngster is suddenly exposed to a different type of relationship, one based on trust rather than the exploitation of others. This creates an unavoidable internal conflict. If he is unable to sell her on his way of life, he must make a difficult choice. Does he prefer the superficial but safe camaraderie of his deviant peer group or the comfort of a more intimate relationship? It is usually difficult to have both. If the new relationship prevails, the youngster is launched into a different emotional and environmental experience. While seemingly simplistic, I have found this to be a turning point of treatment on several occasions.

The same principle holds when a family chooses to make a major move to an entirely different locale. While antisocial youth instinctively seek out like-minded others, they are sometimes confronted with a new situation in which the prosocial peer group is dominant and rather persuasive. In such a case the youth must conform or face complete ostracism. If an alternate, deviant peer group is unavailable, the opportunity for change arises.

I do not mean to suggest that a family move will singlehandedly address the problems of conduct disorder; however, a change of environment can present new options. It is for this reason that families have sent their troubled youth to live with relatives in rural areas or other parts of the country. While this practice is no longer widespread, we still hear of success stories every now and then. Again the unifying theme is the exposure to an environment that is relatively free of compelling negative distractions and demands the youngster's participation and adherence to specific prosocial norms.

A final opportunity for seemingly "spontaneous" improvement can occur when an antisocial youth hooks up with a powerful role model through circumstances or design. This influential person motivates the youngster to raise his aspirations and to emulate more adaptive behavior. This special relationship often takes on the characteristics of the good, stern parent that the child never had or could not bond with. The caring, firmness, and consistency directly challenge the youth's conditioned hostile attributions. As the bond strengthens, the mentor's values and integrity are inculcated. While this is the stuff of which good movies are made, it occasionally occurs in real life.

## Case Example

I ran into Michael a few years after he had dropped out of treatment with me. He was a salesman in a computer store at the time. I noticed him out of the corner of my eye but debated about whether to approach him. Apparently he saw me also, but did not share my ambivalence. He came right over and started chatting. I asked him how the past few years had been and he proudly told me, "I've got my shit together now."

As it turned out, he had met the manager of his store fortuitously and was offered a job in the stockroom. His love for computers was readily apparent and it wasn't long before he was allowed to play around with the machines. Gradually he developed a solid relationship with his mentor (only seven years his senior). Ultimately he was able to break away from his deviant peer group. His involvement with his job fulfilled his unmet needs for affiliation, stimulation, and positive self-regard. Although he had dropped out of high school, he went back for his G.E.D. and was currently attending a community college.

## RESILIENCE, PREVENTION, AND RELATED VARIABLES

Those who develop competence despite adversity offer important insights about preventive measures. Resilience is the outgrowth of specific positive experiences during the formative years. Youth seemingly at high risk but who turned out okay offer a framework for understanding this process. Nettles and Pleck (1994) have identified specific resources that foster insulation from trouble. These include the availability of a positive role model, accessible educational resources, and a perceived sense of community belonginess, either through neighborhood or religious institutions.

Werner and Smith (1992) conducted a longitudinal study of youth at risk for delinquency. Those who did not develop an antisocial pattern by adolescence displayed higher self-esteem and an internal locus of control, had a supportive role model, and were seen as affectionate by their mothers. They seemed to form friendships more readily and demonstrated some competence in their academic functioning. In contrast, studies of the families of delinquents specify the factors that seem to fuel this behavior. An interactive style characterized by low warmth and affection, high degree of conflict and hostility, and marital discord have been observed (Straus 1994).

A better understanding of the relationship between risk and resilience will hopefully lead to intensified efforts at prevention. Early intervention remains the primary deterrent for later behavioral problems. In a review of the current research on prevention, Kazdin (1995) cites several programs that have yielded positive changes in child functioning. They have often been conducted in schools and communities with a broad-based population. Consequently, it is difficult to identify the specific effects on those at risk for conduct disorders.

Prevention studies are arduous because of the large number of extraneous variables, which are difficult to control. These include the training of therapists, consistency of interventions across groups, and difficulty measuring results. Nonetheless, efforts must continue to be directed at providing recreational opportunities, diversion programs, and mentoring relationships for youth at risk. Goldstein (1993) points out the overlap between prevention and rehabilitation. Though it is likely that broad-based prevention programs will continue to proliferate, further efforts are needed to engage those adolescents most in need of specific services. No doubt, antisocial youth will be more receptive to the least stigmatized resources.

## BROADER IMPLICATIONS

National concern about violence in our youth has been growing. Efforts at crime prevention have increased along with media efforts to discourage smoking, drug use, and unsafe sex. Clearly, more dollars are being spent with the outcome not always known. While public awareness has certainly been heightened, the availability of treatment resources has not shown a concomitant increase. Indeed, the face of our health care delivery system is changing dramatically. Managed care has placed increased emphasis on cost effectiveness. Short-term treatment has become the buzzword of the '90s. Concrete behavioral objectives, specific focused treatment strategies, and symptomatic relief are promulgated as answers to the shrinking health care dollar. Some anxiety and mood disorders seem to fit this model nicely. Time-limited psychotherapy has been demonstrably effective in providing relief to those experiencing intense distress (Beck and Emery 1985, Beck et al. 1979).

The disruptive behavior disorders pose more complex treatment issues. To date, no one has demonstrated that a twelve-to sixteen-session course of treatment can markedly alter the behavior patterns and maintain the changes over time. Rather, specific behavioral and cognitive-behavioral approaches target various deficiencies for change. While mildly troubled youth seem to benefit from situation-specific skill building, with the more disturbed and antisocial population the results are far less promising (Kazdin 1995). The Prepare Curriculum (Goldstein 1988) integrates the best features of interpersonal skills training, anger management, and moral reasoning. More comprehensive in scope, it has been employed successfully with aggressive, antisocial, and at-risk youth. The commitment of time and resources required, however, far exceeds that of short-term treatment.

Family interventions must be coordinated with any prosocial skill-building efforts. These too can be costly and time consuming. I believe that future work with these youth will have to transcend the traditional psychiatric boundaries. Agents of change must include paraprofessionals as well as those more extensively trained. While a thorough treatment plan begins with a comprehensive assessment of comorbidity and organic and familial factors, the ensuing prescription for change will need to be multisystemic and implemented by various disciplines.

Psychiatric inpatient treatment is no longer a viable option due largely to insurance constraints. An average stay of one to two weeks is useful only in emergency situations. The costs are prohibitive and the recidivism rates are high. In general, intensive short-term treatment has not been effective in altering longstanding patterns of antisocial behavior. Although the research is scarce, residential schools for conduct-disordered youth are reporting moderate successes. Some are based on wilderness models in which youngsters learn survival skills and must depend on one another to overcome environmental obstacles. These are typically far less expensive and are staffed primarily by teachers and paraprofessionals. The rehabilitative orientation is primarily experiential, confrontational, and behavioral. A youngster typically spends six months to a year in one of these programs. As one such school director put it, "We don't give up on these kids. We make it clear that we're with them for the long haul and expect that they will change. Our most powerful influence is the peer group. They just have to conform if they're going to survive in this atmosphere."

I am not suggesting that programs such as these are the panacea. They simply hold the potential for bringing affordable treatment to larger numbers of youth in need. Further, they often provide sufficient stimulation to rapidly enlist compliance. Cross-disciplinary communication is essential. Further collaborative work is needed to create challenging, highly energizing environments that utilize powerful educational and motivational strategies to effect behavior change. The components of a thorough treatment program have been identified throughout this book. I believe that the challenge ahead lies in making the necessary resources available so that treatment prescriptions are based on an individualized assessment rather than a forced fit to any single model.

Parent education must be provided early in the cycle of evolving behavior problems. The schools need to take a more proactive stance in addressing early difficulties "within house" rather than referring them out.

The adolescent's world revolves around the peer group. This force should be well mobilized to increase the pressure to conform to acceptable social standards. Rather than isolating and grouping antisocial youth together, we must find new ways to weaken their existing ties and provide gratifying alternatives to deviant behavior. Remediation should be integrated in the school curricula where the audience is captive. Powerful incentives to change must be developed to combat the egocentric thinking of these youth.

Although the specific future direction of treatment is unclear, I remain optimistic. Perhaps we cannot alter the destiny of some of the most hardened youth with our current technologies. It may be years before we find consistent, replicable ways to undo the ravages of childhood traumas, embedded distrust of and contempt for others, and longstanding, self-serving antisocial patterns. Broad-based societal changes may be needed to ultimately overcome the environmental barriers to change.

In the short run we should take some comfort in knowing that we have the foundation for some solutions. There have been numerous reports of successful interventions with mild to moderately disturbed youth. It is now possible to interrupt the progression from transient to chronic behavior disorders; however, the prognosis remains guarded for older, entrenched adolescents.

Our understanding of conduct-disordered behavior has increased markedly. It is time to shift from the "why" to "what to do about it." The challenge to parents, educators, mental health professionals, and legislators is formidable. Improved treatment, prevention, and awareness will ultimately reduce the enormity of the problem. Until that time we must direct our resources to those most likely to benefit from them.

# References

Adler, G., and Buie, D. H. (1973). The misuses of confrontation in the psychotherapy of borderline cases. In *Confrontation in Psychotherapy*, ed. G. Adler and P. G. Myerson, pp. 147–162. New York: Science House.

Adler, G., and Myerson, P. G., eds. (1973). *Confrontation in Psychotherapy*. New York: Science House.

Agee, V. L. (1979). *Treatment of the Violent Incorrigible Adolescent*. Lexington, MA: Lexington.

Alexander, J. F., Holtzworth-Munroe, A., and Jameson, P. B. (1994). The process and outcome of marital and family therapy research: review and evaluation. In *Handbook of Psychotherapy and Behavior Change*, ed. A. E. Bergin and S. L. Garfield, 4th ed., pp. 595–630. New York: Wiley.

Alexander, J. F., and Parsons, B. V. (1982). *Functional Family Therapy*. Monterey, CA: Brooks/Cole.

Alexander, J. F., Waldron, H. B., Newberry, A., and Liddle, N. (1988). Family approaches to treating delinquents. In *Mental Illness, Delinquency, Addictions, and Neglect*, ed. E. W. Nunnaly, C. Chilman, and F. Cox, pp. 128–146. Newbury Park, CA: Sage.

Andersen, B., and Andersen, W. (1989). Counselors' reports of self-disclosure with clients. *Journal of Clinical Psychology* 45:302–308.

Anderson, C. M., and Stewart, S. (1983). *Mastering Resistance: A Practical Guide to Family Therapy*. New York: Guilford.

Arbuthnot, J. (1992). Sociomoral reasoning in behavior disordered adolescents. In *Preventing Antisocial Behavior: Interventions from Birth through Adolescence*, ed. J. McCord, pp. 283–310. New York: Guilford.

Bandura, A. (1977). *Social Learning Theory*. Englewood Cliffs, NJ: Prentice-Hall.

Bank, L., Marlowe, J., and Reid, J. B. (1991). A comparative evaluation of parent training interventions for families of chronic delinquents. *Journal of Abnormal Child Psychology* 19:15–33.

Beck, A. T., and Emery, G. (1985). *Anxiety Disorders and Phobias*. New York: Basic Books.

Beck, A. T., Rush, A. J., Shaw, B. F., and Emery, G. (1979). *Cognitive Therapy of Depression*. New York: Guilford.

Belsher, G., and Wilks, T. C. (1994). The middle phase of cognitive therapy: intervention techniques for five steps in the therapeutic process. In *Cognitive Therapy for Depressed Adolescents*, ed. T. C. Wilkes, G. Belsher, A. J. Rush, and E. Frank, pp. 132–243. New York: Guilford.

Berg, B. (1989). *The Anger Control Game*. Dayton, OH: Cognitive Counseling Resources.

Bernstein, N. I. (1989). Treatment of the resistant adolescent. In *Innovations in Clinical Practice: A Source Book*, vol. 8, pp. 175–185. Sarasota, FL: Professional Resource Exchange.

Brock, G. W., and Barnard, C. P. (1988). *Procedures in Family Therapy*. Boston: Allyn and Bacon.

Burns, D. (1980). *Feeling Good: The New Mood Therapy*. New York: Signet.

Campbell, M., Small, A. M., and Green, W. H. (1984). Behavioral efficacy of haloperidol and lithium carbonate: comparison of hospitalized aggressive children with conduct disorder. *Archives of General Psychiatry* 41:650–656.

Carrell, S. (1993). *Group Exercises for Adolescents: A Manual for Therapists*. Newbury Park, CA: Sage.

Carter, R. L., and Motta, R. (1988). Effects of intimacy of therapist's self-disclosure and formality on perceptions of credibility in an initial interview. *Perceptual Motor Skills* 66:167–173.

Comer, J., (1991). The Comer school development program. *Urban Education* 26:56–82.

Corder, B. F. (1994). *Structured Adolescent Psychotherapy Groups*. Sarasota, FL: Professional Resource Press.

Corwin, H. A. (1973). Therapeutic confrontation from routine to heroic. In *Confrontation in Psychotherapy*, ed. G. Adler and P. G. Myerson, pp. 67–96. New York: Science House.

*Diagnostic and Statistical Manual of Mental Disorders* (1994). 4th ed. Washington, DC: American Psychiatric Association.

Dishion, T. J., and Patterson, G. R. (1992). Age effects in parent training outcomes. *Behavior Therapy* 23:719–729.

Dowd, T., and Tierney, J. (1992). *Teaching Social Skills to Youth*. Boys Town, NE: Boys Town.

Duggan, H. A. (1978). *A Second Chance: Empathy in Adolescent Development*. Lexington, MA: Lexington.

Edwards, R. (1995). Expulsion from school often backfires. *American Psychological Association Monitor*, February, p. 41.

Farley, F. (1986). The big T in personality. *Psychology Today*, May, pp. 45–52.

Feindler, E. L., and Ecton, R. B. (1986). *Adolescent Anger Control: Cognitive Behavioral Techniques*. New York: Pergamon.

Felner, R. D., and Adan, A. M. (1988). The school transitional environment project: an ecological intervention and evaluation. In *14 Ounces of Prevention: A Casebook for Practitioners*, ed. R. H. Price, E. L. Cowen, R. D. Lorion, and J. Ramos-McKay, pp. 111–122. Washington, DC: American Psychological Association.

Ferenczi, S. (1955). Confusion of tongues between adults and the child. In *Final Contributions to the Problems and Methods of Psychoanalysis*, vol. 3, ed. M. Balint, pp. 156–167. New York: Basic Books.

Ferguson, T. J., and Rule, B. G. (1988). Children's evaluations of retaliatory aggression. *Child Development* 59:961–968.

Feshbach, N. D., and Feshbach, S. (1982). Empathy training and the relation of aggression: potentialities and limitations. *Academic Psychology Bulletin* 4:399–413.

Fishman, H. C. (1988). *Treating Troubled Adolescents*. New York: Basic Books.

Flaherty, J. F. (1979). Self-disclosure in therapy: marriage of the therapist. *American Journal of Psychotherapy* 33:442–452.

Flanagan, J. S., and Flanagan, R. S. (1995). Psychotherapeutic techniques with treatment resistant adolescents. *Psychotherapy* 32:131–140.

Forman, S. G. (1993). *Coping Skills Interventions for Children and Adolescents*. CA: Jossey Bass.

Freedman, B. J., Rosenthal, L., Donahoe, Jr., C. P., et al. (1978). A social-behavioral analysis of skill deficits in delinquent and non-delinquent adolescent boys. *Journal of Consulting and Clinical Psychology* 46:1448–1462.

Frick, P. J., Kamphaus, R. W., and Lahey, B. B. (1991). Academic underachievement and the disruptive behavior disorders. *Journal of Consulting and Clinical Psychology* 59:289–294.

Friedman, H. (1973). Confrontation in the psychotherapy of adolescent patients. In *Confrontation in Psychotherapy*, ed. G. Adler and P. G. Myerson, pp. 347–368. New York: Science House.

Gardner, R. (1973). *The Talking, Feeling, and Doing Game*. Cresskill, NJ: Creative Therapeutics.

——— (1988). *Psychotherapy with Adolescents*. Cresskill, NJ: Creative Therapeutics.

Garner, H. (1982). Positive peer culture programs in schools. In *School Programs for Disruptive Adolescents*, ed. D. Safer, pp. 317–330. Baltimore: University Park Press.

Gibbs, J. C. (1987). Social processes in delinquency: the

need to facilitate empathy as well as sociomoral reasoning. In *Moral Development through Social Interaction*, ed. W. M. Kurtines and J. L. Gewirtz, pp. 301–321. New York: Wiley.

Gibbs, J. C., Potter, G. B., and Goldstein, A. P. (1995). *The Equip Program: Teaching Youth to Think and Act Responsibly through a Peer-Helping Approach*. Champaign, IL: Research Press.

Goldstein, A. P. (1988). *The Prepare Curriculum: Teaching Prosocial Competencies*. Champaign, IL: Research Press.

———— (1993). Interpersonal skills training interventions. In *The Gang Intervention Handbook*, ed. A. P. Goldstein and C.R. Huff, pp. 87–157. Champaign, IL: Research Press.

Goldstein, A. P., Sprafkin, R. P., Gershaw, N. J., and Klein, P. (1980). *Skillstreaming the Adolescent: A Structured Learning Approach to Teaching Prosocial Skills*. Champaign, IL: Research Press.

Gorkin, M. (1987). *The Uses of Countertransference*. Northvale, NJ: Jason Aronson.

Green, R. J. (1989). Learning to learn and the family system: new perspectives on underachievement and learning disorders. *Journal of Marital and Family Therapy* 15:187–203.

Gurman, A. S., Kniskern, D. P., and Pinsof, W. M. (1986). Research on marital and family therapies. In *Handbook of Psychotherapy and Behavior Change*, ed. S. L. Garfield and A. E. Bergin, pp. 565–624. New York: Wiley.

Harper, J. F., and Marshall, E. (1991). Adolescents' problems and their relationship to self-esteem. *Adolescence* 26:799–807.

Hawkins, J. D., Catalano, R. F., and Miller, J. Y. (1992). Risk and protective factors for alcohol and other drug problems in adolescence and early childhood: implications for substance abuse protection. *Psychological Bulletin* 112:64–105.

Hazel, J. S., Schumaker, J. B., Sherman, J. A., and Sheldon-Wildgen, J. S. (1983). Social skills training with court adjudicated youths. In *Social Skills Training for Children and Youth*, ed. C. LeCroy, pp. 117–137. New York: Haworth.

Henggeler, S., and Borduin, C. (1990). *Family Therapy and Beyond: A Multi-Systemic Approach to Treating the Behavior Problems of Children and Adolescents*. Pacific Grove, CA: Brooks/Cole.

Hipp, E. (1985). *Fighting Invisible Tigers: A Stress Management Guide for Teens*. Minneapolis: Free Spirit.

Hoffman, M. L. (1983). Affective and cognitive processes in moral internalization. In *Social Cognition and Social Development: A Sociocultural Perspective*, ed. E. T. Higgins, D. W. Ruble, and W. W. Hartup, pp. 116–152. Cambridge, England: Cambridge University Press.

Hollin, C. R. (1989). *Cognitive-Behavioral Interventions with Young Offenders*. New York: Pergamon.

Holmes, G. R., Heckel, R. V., and Gordon, L. (1991). *Adolescent Group Therapy: A Social Competency Model*. New York: Praeger.

Huff, C. R. (1993). Gangs in the United States. In *The Gang Intervention Handbook*, ed. A. P. Goldstein and C. R. Huff, pp. 3–20. Champaign, IL: Research Press.

Kazdin, A. E. (1985). *Treatment of Antisocial Behavior in Children and Adolescents*. Homewood, IL: Dorsey.

———— (1995). *Conduct Disorders in Childhood and Adolescence*. 2nd ed. Thousand Oaks, CA: Sage.

Kendall, P. C., Ronan, K. R., and Epps, J. (1990). Aggression in children/adolescents: cognitive-behavioral treatment perspectives. In *Development and Treatment of Childhood Aggression*, ed. D. Pepler and K. Rubin, pp. 341–360. Hillsdale, NJ: Erlbaum.

Kernberg, P. F., and Chazan, S. E. (1991). *Children with Conduct Disorders*. New York: Basic Books.

Keshet, J. K., and Mirkin, M. P. (1985). Troubled adolescents in divorced and re-married families. In *Handbook of Adolescent and Family Therapy*, ed. M. P. Mirkin, pp. 273–294. New York: Gardner.

Kohlberg, L. (1984). *The Psychology of Moral Development: Essays on Moral Development*, vol. 2. San Francisco: Harper and Row.

Kohlberg, L., and Higgins, A. (1987). School democracy and social interaction. In *Moral Development through Social Interaction*, ed. W. M. Kurtines and J. L. Gewirtz, pp. 102–130. New York: Wiley.

Lewis, D. O., Pincus, J. H., Lovely, R., Spitzer, E., et al. (1987). Biopsychosocial characteristics of matched samples of delinquents and non-delinquents. *Journal of the American Academy of Child Psychiatry* 26:744–752.

Lewis, J. (1978). *To Be a Therapist*. New York: Brunner/ Mazel.

Liberman, R. P., DeRisi, W. J., and Mueser, K. T. (1989). *Social Skills Training for Psychiatric Patients*. New York: Pergamon.

Liddle, H. (1995). Conceptual and clinical dimensions of a multidimensional, multisystems engagement strategy in family based adolescent treatment. *Psychotherapy* 32:39–58.

Lindsay, W. R. (1987). Social skills training with adolescents. In *Working with Troubled Adolescents: A Handbook*, ed. J. C. Coleman, pp. 107–122. London: Academic.

Lochman, J. F., White, K. J., and Wayland, K. K. (1991). Cognitive-behavioral assessment and treatment with aggressive children. In *Child and Adolescent Therapy: Cognitive-Behavioral Procedures*, ed. P. C. Kendall, pp. 25–65. New York: Guilford.

McCown, W. G., and Johnson, J. (1993). *Therapy with Treatment Resistant Families*. New York: Haworth.

McHolland, J. (1985). Strategies for dealing with resistant adolescents. *Adolescence* 20:349–367.

McIntire, R. (1985). *Losing Control of Your Teenager*. Amherst, MA: Human Resource Development Press.

McKay, M., and Fanning, P. (1987). *Self-Esteem: The Ultimate Program for Self-Help*. New York: MJF Books.

McManus, M., Alessi, N. E., Grapentine, W. L., and Brickman, A. (1984). Psychiatric disturbance in serious delinquents. *Journal of the American Academy of Child Psychiatry* 23:602–615.

Meeks, J. (1986). *The Fragile Alliance: An Orientation to the Psychiatric Treatment of the Adolescent*. Melbourne, FL: Krieger.

Meier, S. T., and Davis, S. R. (1993). *The Elements of Counseling*. Pacific Grove, CA: Brooks/Cole.

Miller, D. (1986). *Attack on the Self: Adolescent Behavioral Disturbances and their Treatment*. Northvale, NJ: Jason Aronson.

Minuchin, S. (1981). *Families and Family Therapy*. Cambridge, MA: Harvard University Press.

Murray, B. (1995). Good mentoring keeps at-risk youth in school. *American Psychological Association Monitor*, September, p. 49.

National Association of School Psychologists (1992). *Helping Children Grow Up in the 90's: A Resource Book for Parents and Teachers.* Silver Spring, MD: National Association of School Psychologists.

Nettles, S. M., and Pleck, J. H. (1994). Risk, resilience, and development: the multiple ecologies of black adolescents in the United States. In *Stress, Risk, and Resilience in Children and Adolescents*, ed. R. J. Haggerty, N. Garmezy, M. Rutter, and M. Sherrod, pp. 147–191. New York: Cambridge University Press.

Novaco, R. W. (1975). *Anger Control: The Development and Evaluation of an Experimental Treatment.* Lexington, MA: D. C. Heath.

O'Connor, J., and LaSala, M. (1988). An invariant intervention of last resort: treatment of chronic school failure in adolescents. *Journal of Strategic and Systemic Therapies* 7:53–66.

O'Donnell, D. J. (1985). Conduct disorders. In *Diagnosis and Psychopharmacology of Childhood and Adolescent Disorders*, ed. J. M. Weiner, pp. 249–287. New York: Basic Books.

Orlinsky, D. E., and Howard, K. I. (1978). The relationship of process to outcome in psychotherapy. In *Handbook of Psychotherapy and Behavior Change*, ed. A. Bergin and S. Garfield, pp. 283–330. New York: Wiley.

Patterson, G. R. (1982). *Coercive Family Process.* Eugene, OR: Castalia.

Patterson, G. R., Chamberlain, P., and Reid, J. B. (1982). A comparative evaluation of parent training procedures. *Behavior Therapy* 13:638–650.

Patterson, G. R., DeBuryshe, B., and Ramsey, E. (1989). A developmental perspective on antisocial behavior. *American Psychologist* 44:329–335.

Pope, A. W., McHale, S. M., and Craighead, W. E. (1988). *Self-Esteem Enhancement with Children and Adolescents*. New York: Pergamon.

Raubolt, R. R. (1983). The clinical practice of group psychotherapy with delinquents. In *Adolescent Group Psychotherapy*, ed. F. D. Azima and L. H. Richmond, pp. 143–162. Madison, CT: International Universities Press.

Reeves, J. C., Werry, J. S., Elkind, G. S., and Zametkin, A. (1987). Attention deficit, conduct, oppositional, and anxiety disorders in children: clinical characteristics. *Journal of the American Academy of Child and Adolescent Psychiatry* 26:144–155.

Robin, A. L., and Foster, S. L. (1989). *Negotiating Parent Adolescent Conflict: A Behavioral Family Systems Approach*. New York: Guilford.

Robins, L. N. (1981). Epidemiological approaches to natural history research: antisocial disorders in children. *Journal of the American Academy of Child Psychiatry* 20:566–680.

Rosenberg, D. R., Holttum, J., and Gershon, S. (1994). *Textbook of Pharmacotherapy for Child and Adolescent Psychiatric Disorders*. New York: Brunner/Mazel.

Rosenberg, M. (1979). *Conceiving the Self*. New York: Basic Books.

Rutter, M., Maughan, B., Mortimore, P., and Ouston, J. (1979). *Fifteen Thousand Hours: Secondary Schools and their Effects on Children*. Cambridge, MA: Harvard University Press.

Safer, D. (1982). Dimensions and issues of school programs for disruptive youth. In *School Programs for Disruptive Adolescents*, ed. D. Safer, pp. 67–90. Baltimore: University Park Press.

Samenow, S. E. (1984). *Inside the Criminal Mind*. New York: Random House.

——— (1989). *Before It's Too Late*. New York: Random House.

Scheidlinger, S., and Aronson, S. (1991). Group psychotherapy of adolescents. In *Adolescent Psychotherapy*, ed. M. Slomowitz, pp. 101–119. Washington, DC: American Psychiatric Press.

Schiff, H. B., Sabin, T. D., and Geller, A. (1982). Lithium in aggressive behavior. *American Journal of Psychiatry* 139:1346.

Shepherd, I. L. (1970). Limitations and cautions in the gestalt approach. In *Gestalt Therapy Now*, ed. J. Fagan and I. L. Shepherd, pp. 234–239. New York: Harper and Row.

Sifneos, P. (1973). Confrontation in short-term, anxiety-provoking psychotherapy. In *Confrontation in Psychotherapy*, ed. G. Adler and P. G. Myerson, pp. 369–383. New York: Science House.

Stewart, J. T., Myers, W. C., Burket, R. C., and Lyles, W. B. (1990). A review of the psychopharmacology of aggression in children and adolescents. *Journal of the American Academy of Child and Adolescent Psychiatry* 29:269–277.

Stoner, G., Shinn, M., and Walker, H., eds. (1991). *Interventions for Achievement and Behavior Problems*. Kent, OH: National Association of School Psychologists.

Straus, M. (1994). *Violence in the Lives of Adolescents*. New York: Norton.

Tavris, C. (1982). *Anger: The Misunderstood Emotion*. New York: Simon and Schuster.

Tisdelle, D. A., and St. Lawrence, J. S. (1986). Interpersonal problem solving competency: review and critique of the literature. *Clinical Psychology Review* 6:337–356.

Took, K. J., and Weiss, D. S. (1994). The relationship between heavy metal and rap music and adolescent turmoil: real or artifact? *Adolescence* 29:613–621.

Weiner, I. B. (1975). *Principles of Psychotherapy*. New York: Wiley.

Weiner, M. F. (1972). Self-exposure by the therapist as a therapeutic technique. *American Journal of Psychotherapy* 26:42.

Wells, K. C. (1995). Parent management training. In *Conduct Disorders in Children and Adolescents*, ed. G. P. Sholevar, pp. 213–236. Washington, DC: American Psychiatric Press.

Werner, E. E., and Smith, R. S. (1992). *Overcoming the Odds: High Risk Children from Birth to Adulthood*. Ithaca, NY: Cornell University Press.

Wexler, D. B. (1991). *The Adolescent Self: Strategies for Self-Management, Self-Soothing, and Self-Esteem in Adolescents*. New York: Norton.

Wilkes, T. C., Belsher, G., Rush, A. J., and Frank, E., eds. (1994). *Cognitive Therapy for Depressed Adolescents*. New York: Guilford.

Wilson, R. (1984). A review of self-control treatment for aggressive behavior. *Behavioral Disorders* 9:131–140.

Yalom, I. (1975). *The Theory and Practice of Group Psychotherapy*. New York: Basic Books.

York, D., York, P., and Wachtel, T. (1982). *Tough Love*. New York: Bantam.

Zovodnick, J. M. (1995). Pharmacotherapy. In *Conduct Disorders in Children and Adolescents*, ed. G. P. Sholevar, pp. 269–298. Washington, DC: American Psychiatric Press.

# Index